Praise for *Hipster Death Rattle*

"Richie Narvaez has created something that's been missing from recent fiction: a vivid, loving look at city living from the street view."

—Sara Paretsky, award-winning author
of *Shell Game*

"*Hipster Death Rattle* is a smart piece of work featuring the unlikely yet likeable hero Tony 'Chino' Moran. Fierce and funny...with a light touch that masks Narvaez's biting social commentary."

—Reed Farrel Coleman, *New York Times* bestselling
author of *What You Break*

"Narvaez has some brutal points to make about gentrification... that gives the text a crackling fission you don't find in a typical mystery."

—*Mystery Tribune*

HIPSTER DEATH RATTLE

ALSO BY RICHIE NARVAEZ

Roachkiller and Other Stories

HIPSTER DEATH RATTLE

RICHIE NARVAEZ

DOWN & OUT
BOOKS

Down & Out Books
3959 Van Dyke Road, Suite 265
Lutz, FL 33558
DownAndOutBooks.com

The characters and events in this book are fictitious. Any similarity to real persons, living or dead, is coincidental and not intended by the author.

Cover design by JT Lindroos

ISBN: 1-948235-63-3
ISBN-13: 978-1-948235-63-1

For Denise

PROLOGO

The bicyclist stopped and watched a small herd of them emerge from Teddy's. (The stained glass outside read "Peter Doelger's Extra Beer," but absolutely everyone in the neighborhood knew it was Teddy's.) And right away the bicyclist, watching from the shadows under a tree on North 8th, picked out one of them as perfect.

Organic, one hundred percent, artisanal, locally sourced hipster.

Teddy's used to be a great neighborhood bar. But now it was a bistro, one of hundreds, thousands, millions within a few blocks' radius, all crowded and pricey and pretentious. Because of people like this.

The herd parted, walking forward, some carrying on conversations with each other, yet all looking down at their phones. The one absolute perfect hipster separated like a scrawny calf from the fashionable herd.

White. *Check.*

Male. *Check.*

In his twenties. *Check.*

He ambled off alone on Berry Street's narrow stone sidewalk, his man bun a tiny tumbleweed on top of his head bop-bop-bopping to some no doubt obscure tune on those headphones. Huge headphones trapping him in his bubble, cutting him off from the world, cutting him off from the sounds around him. The sounds of the bicyclist in the street, pedaling slowly, achingly,

1

quietly as possible to keep up and still remain in the bike lane.

The hipster wore a big and Brillowy beard that overlapped the keffiyeh wrapped blithely around his neck. It was a chilly spring night in New York City, and cold rain still glowed on the sidewalks, so maybe why the scarf. But there was no excuse whatsoever for the bright red cat-eye shades this late at night—three in the morning, the dark night of the soul—on this dark a street. Cat eye because ironic, obviously. Which made what the bicyclist had to do even more necessary.

No—the orange flip-flops did that. The orange flip-flops slapping the wet sidewalk made this one's death essential.

On North 10th Street, the hipster took a left turn. Perfect. While much of that block had been renovated, turned into unattractive, industrial-looking, overpriced condos, some of the block was still old warehouses, decorated with the colorful honesty of graffiti. It was a quiet block. Desolate.

The bicyclist hopped onto the sidewalk and, focused on the target, failed to notice a fire hydrant. Hitting it on the slick sidewalk, the bicyclist was almost thrown but stopped himself by stepping hard. The bike's rear end lifted in midair at a forty-five-degree angle, back wheel spitting rainwater. It came down with a clang.

The bicyclist froze. But the hipster hadn't noticed a thing. Bubble.

"No one there is who loves a hipster," the bicyclist whispered.

Leaning the bike against the hydrant and taking out the machete, the bicyclist caught up to him halfway down the block. Swung hard. Bang, right in the keffiyeh. It got stuck on the neck bone.

Cat glasses slipping, the hipster mouthed one word: "Fuck." Or it could have been "Fleek."

The bicyclist slashed him again across the face, aching to wipe those glasses from existence.

Back on the bike, the bicyclist pedaled home. It was a chilly night, but tomorrow would be much warmer.

CHAPTER ONE

To Tony "Chino" Moran, the whole thing was ridiculous. First of all, staring at him was a small pod of tourists who had made the trip to Brooklyn from their Manhattan hotel no doubt, a family by the looks of their matching polo shirts and plaid shorts. The mom and dad aimed pad-sized cameras at him from the side of the pétanque court. As if he were an animal in a zoo. An animal! Their matching offspring gawked, while simultaneously texting.

Ridiculous.

Ever since Tony was a kid coming to McCarren Park, there had always been soccer players, softball players, handball players, stray toddlers, stray drunks, stray soccer balls. And always that one breakdancer spinning on a flattened box, practicing for the day backward-worming became cool again. In some distant future. The last twenty years had added bicyclists, skateboarders, hipsters, yuppies, purebred dogs, and baby strollers (of phenomenally increasing dimensions—large enough to rent as studios).

But now: tourists. Hordes of them, sometimes bussed in in large numbers from the city that never sleeps, the capital of the world.

People who came to the park to watch other people come to the park.

Ridiculous.

Second, the latest annoying heat wave had refused to dissipate.

It wasn't even summer yet. If this kept up through August, the streets would run with sweat.

Tony wore loose clothes but still the heat and humidity clung to him like plastic wrap. The pétanque court sat out in the open, in the corner of the park near the track and the soccer field, next to the handball courts and the Italian ice man who—if he kept ringing that bell of his and shouting, "Iceeeee, iceeeeeee here. Come get it!"—would get a solid two-and-a-half-pound pétanque ball thrown at his face.

Third—and truly bizarre—this guy Yogi Johnson, some stoner hanger-on, some guy who had only recently started playing and was strictly mediocre, but had now, somehow, out of nowhere, acquired superhuman accuracy and control. *Bastard.*

"I've got the *qi* working," Yogi had said to no one in particular, karate chopping the air, strutting around the court, his graying blond dreadlocks flopping under a red bandanna. "The *qi* is on!"

With a careless, epileptic toss, Yogi had made his ball land decisively—barely any sand rustled—close to the cochonnet (the small target ball), on the court, closer than anyone else.

Qualem blennum! thought Tony. Idiot.

So it was Tony's turn now. The object of the game was to toss hollow metal balls called boules as close as possible to the cochonnet, displacing if necessary any balls nearby. They were playing triples—two three-person teams. After a brutal back and forth for most of the game, Tony's team had been closest. But now Yogi's ball sat nestled against and in front of the cochonnet, guarding it like a Park Slope helicopter parent. Tony would have to throw what was called a carreau—a difficult shot that would knock away Yogi's ball and place his own on the same spot.

The game was in Tony's hands. *Wonderful.*

Tony crouched low on the packed sand of the court and concentrated on the cochonnet, trying to visualize his play. In the background, pad-sized cameras snapped.

"You can totally do it." Eric was clapping his hands to encourage him. "You can totally carreau." If Eric had used those hands more athletically, Tony wouldn't be in this spot.

"The carreau does not want to be had. Man ain't got the *qi* working," shouted Yogi, while performing something embarrassing to watch, something between a tango and tai chi. "Nope. Not today."

It was just a game. Nothing to worry about. *No pain, no pain.* If only he hadn't bet twenty bucks on it. Twenty bucks he couldn't afford to bet, with his savings currently undernourished and freelance work becoming as frequent as free lunch. Fourth and most ridiculous.

Sweat trickled down Tony's back into his shorts. He made a line of sight down his straightened arm toward the cochonnet. He breathed in and, with an exhale and a flip of his wrist for backspin, tossed. Camera snap.

The heavy ball arced high in the air. It landed on Yogi's ball with a hollow knock, moving it just out of the way and sticking in place. Sand stirred. But Yogi's ball wiggled backward on some anomaly of sand and moved to the side, knocking another of Yogi's team's balls closer to the cochonnet. Camera snap.

"Crap," Tony said. His ball and the other ball hugged the cochonnet. It would be close.

Both teams walked up and hovered over the balls to debate. "Sssoooo close." "No qi, I'm telling you." "I think you did it, Tony. You totally did it." "Merde." "I don't know, man."

The referee, Pepe, a wiry man with a barbwire mustache, took out a hand-carved measuring tape dispenser from his back pocket. He bent down, cigarette in mouth, and measured the distance of Yogi's teammate's ball from the cochonnet. "One and three-quarter inches, baby," Pepe said, puffing. And then he measured Tony's. "One and...one and, uh oh, one and seven-eighths."

"It's ours!" Yogi said. "Yes! Praise the universe!"
Ridiculous.

Tony went to shake Yogi's hand. "Good job."

"The *qi* was on fire, man."

"Something was on fire all right," Tony said, getting a full whiff of the marijuana cloud around Yogi.

"You gotta work on your *qi*."

"I can tell you where to put your *qi*."

"You really need to lighten up, man."

Gary, who had been standing on the sidelines, walked up to Tony. "Pay the piper."

Tony reached into his wallet and got out a twenty. A lonely ten-dollar bill remained. "I hope every beer you order is flat," he said.

"C'mon, it's just a game," Gary said. "Speaking of which, you playing Saturday?"

"Nah. This Saturday I'm at the paper."

"The paper that pays ten dollars a story?"

"Fifteen dollars," said Tony.

"Fifteen! Big money."

"I do it for the glory. Hey, how's the new place, by the way?"

"Ah, we're going to have to move again. You know I had to sell my condo in Manhattan to pay for my co-op here, and now Julie decides it's a nice place to visit, but she doesn't want to live here, you know what I mean? On top of that, the cost of living is killer. You know how much a hamburger costs at the joint down the corner from my house? Forty dollars. It's a decent hamburger, but for forty dollars it should give me a blowjob and make me breakfast."

"That would be quite a hamburger." Tony shook his head. "Man, if you're finding it tough, imagine the rest of us."

Gary smiled good-naturedly. "You coming to Tim Riley's for, you know—" He pantomimed the pouring and drinking of a pint of beer. "I'll buy the rounds."

"Thanks. But not tonight. It's Thursday."

"Oh, that's right. Okay, see you soon then."

"Yeah."

"Hey, watch out for the Slasher Gang."

"Is that what they're calling them now? A few slashings and everyone goes crazy. First of all, statistically, I'm unlikely to be attacked. And second, I've got my shield." Tony handed over his messenger bag. "Feel that."

Gary hefted it and said, "Damn. What the hell do you have in there?"

"Laptop. Notebook. Extra T-shirt. Socks."

"Socks?"

"Clean socks. And of course my pétanque balls. It should block or slow down any machete. If it doesn't break my back first."

"Sure, tough guy." He gave Tony a man-hug and walked off for the bar. "Stay safe."

Tony put his messenger bag over his shoulder. It was as heavy as Catholic guilt, but he needed everything in there, every day.

He stopped to wipe sweat off his face and neck. The pod of tourists still stood there, watching the pétanque court as if they expected a Disney musical to burst into life on it.

As Tony passed them, the Tourist Mom said, "Could you recommend a good authentic local restaurant, something very Brooklyn?"

He smiled. "Of course. You see this street here," he said, pointing to North 12th. "If you go up this street, about eight blocks, you'll find a place called Mack...Donald's. You'll love it."

"Thank you," the whole family seemed to say in unison. "Thank you very much!"

Tony put his earbuds in, moved forward, and left the park smiling. If the pod followed his directions, they'd end up in the East River.

CHAPTER TWO

At the Bedford Avenue subway station, several blocks from McCarren Park, commuters filed non-stop into and out of the entrance like they were on conveyer belts. This was not rush hour. This was three o'clock. On a slow afternoon. Tony merged into the queue and inched down the stairs with the riders. A train was rattling in, but the people in front of him walked at a zombie's pace, as if they weren't in the greatest city in the world where things were supposed to move fastfastfast. Tony zigzagged around the zombies, swiped his MetroCard at the turnstile, and hopped down the stairs to the sweltering underground platform.

An L train was pulling in from Manhattan.

The train disgorged itself of dozens and dozens of commuters, but it remained full. Tony shrugged off his messenger bag and slid sideways into the heavily air-conditioned subway car, which smelled, as New York City subway cars tended to do in warm weather, like hot dog broth, sweet coffee, and dried urine.

Some yutz wearing a backpack almost large enough to hold an average American child leaned against the middle pole, blocking its use by anyone but the yutz. So Tony was forced to squeeze past him and hold onto a bar above the seats. Below him was a hipster couple, holding hands and reading their devices. The woman had arms green with tattoos and hair blue with dye, and she nibbled on a half-eaten scone. Her beloved wore an abundant Smith Brothers beard, covered with stray crumbs.

8

The train lurched into motion.

With a rattle of doors, a subway preacher came in from the next car and, neck veins bulging, exhorted the passengers (a trapped audience) to find salvation in Christ. This was why scientists created earbuds. Tony turned up the volume on Tom Waits.

At the Montrose Avenue stop, he got out and walked four blocks to a brick-faced apartment building. A three-unit row house with shingled siding that looked like pieces of an ugly, fuzzy-but-comfortable green and pink and gray sweater. Two-bedroom, heat and hot water included. Tons of dining and shops, and laundry literally steps away. Tony let himself in with his keys.

"Hey, Ma."

Tony's mother was as solid as a stove and not much taller than one, with a soufflé of gray and copper hair. "*Niño. Entra. Entra,*" she said. "Sit down."

"It's warm in here."

"I just turn on the air condition."

"Just now? You should keep it on all the time in this heat."

"I'm not married to Con Edison," she said.

She put a plate of spaghetti with chicken and a bottle of beer in front of him. She always kept beer in the house for Tony. There was no telling her not to. Although he would've preferred if she spent the money on something else. She sat down and watched him eat.

The kitchen was lined with dark fake-wood paneling that had likely gone up in the '60s. The stucco ceiling was just as ancient.

"You look skinny," she said.

"I'm fat." Tony smacked his soft middle.

"You're skinny."

"You always say that. Anything new?"

Both of her hands shot up in papalesque fury. "They closed my ninety-nine-cent store!"

"The one here on Bushwick Avenue?"

"Right at the corner," she said. "They close. Now I have to walk three more blocks."

"It's important to get those ninety-nine-cent bargains."

Picking up on the sarcasm in his voice, she said, "Smartypants. They cheap. Everything is so expensive at the supermarket."

"You're completely right. It's probably going to turn into another CVS or TD Bank," Tony said. "Just what the world needs."

"You want some more spaghetti?"

His plate was still half full. "Give me time to eat this, Ma. What's up with the landlord, by the way? Anything happen with that?"

"They still going to raise my rent. Nine hundred dollars! That's double."

"Almost double." Tony couldn't help correcting her. "You've been very lucky so far. But that's why you need a lease. Needed. I told you."

"I live here ten years with no lease."

"That was with Norma's mother. But Margarita died, and now Norma can do whatever she wants because you didn't sign a lease."

"Margarita was my friend. She no raise my rent for eight years."

"I know, Ma. When would the new lease start?"

"*No sé.* She said maybe August."

"You know," he said, "you could move in with Jerry." Tony's brother Geraldo—who insisted on being called "Jerry"—was a successful stockbroker who left the neighborhood the first chance he got. He lived in six-bedroom McMansion in Montclair. "You'd have to babysit his four kids."

"They nice kids."

"You called them dirty brats. And you hate his wife."

Tony's mother shrugged. "She's nice."

"First of all, you called her a two-face and a drunk."

"A little."

10

"Second, they have two cats."

"*Ai, gatos!*"

"The brats and the wife are fine," said Tony. "But it's the cats that upset you."

"We see," she said, patting his hand. "I love this apartment. This is my home."

"I know, Ma, but it's not a horrible idea to move to Jerry's. I have no room at my place."

"*Ai,* but you could move back here. You eat good every night. Your room is there ready."

Tony's mother had moved here from the apartment where he had been born (literally, in the kitchen) and raised in Los Sures (the Southside), after the landlord had hiked her rent. Somehow she had kept his old bedroom intact, like a museum exhibit, all those years.

Moving back home made financial sense, but it had taken him years after college to save enough to move out, and there was no way he was coming back, not for all the spaghetti and chicken and beer in the world. "Not happening, Ma."

After dinner, she watched her favorite *novela* while Tony read through the news on his laptop.

First, the *Daily News.* Groping teacher's aide. Shooting at a concert. Owner of hipster BBQ spot stole overtime pay. Nothing on the slasher attacks. The *Post,* same. *Gothamist, New York Times, nada.* He worked on the *Times* crossword.

When Tony got up to leave, his mother said, "Already?"

"Yep."

At the door, she said, "You have to be careful. Somebody cut those people on the news. Two people got stabbed."

"Technically, they were slashed. But, Ma, those happened late at night, way on the other side of the neighborhood. You don't have to worry."

"That girl they got was by the big bank, right over here."

"That's a mile away. And it's not the Williamsburgh Savings Bank anymore. It's a gallery. Or a CVS. Or a TD Bank. Something like that."

"They said it was a guy on a bicycle."

"I also heard it was ten guys on motorcycles. I don't know which one is true. Maybe they used hoverboards."

"You have to be watching. Remember what happened to my friend Rosa."

"That was a year ago and completely unrelated."

"You should find out what happened. You could do it."

"Not my job, Ma. Not anymore. I've got smaller fish to fry."

"You want some ice cream before you leave?"

Without waiting for an answer, Tony's mother served him a bowl of ice cream, and when he finished it he asked her if she was okay for rent. She said she was fine. He kissed her good-night and took his last ten bucks and handed it to her.

"You keep it," his mother said, gently pushing it back to him.

"Ridiculous. Take it."

"I'm not ridiculous. You're ridiculous," she said. "You need it more than me."

She was right, of course. He said, "About your rent—"

"Don't worry," she said. "I find a way."

On his way home from the L, Tony stopped at a corner to change his music. Too much Tom Waits and your brain turns to cigarette tar. The night air was dense with humidity, and Tony pinched and pulled the front of his T-shirt to unstick it from his skin.

The traffic light was against him, and like any New Yorker he would have crossed anyway, but there was a car service car, a couple of *Titanic*-sized SUVs, then a Mini Cooper, and so he waited. He felt the weight of the pétanque balls, the laptop in his bag, the thick sweat on his face.

Directly across the street, some dude, wearing huge head-phones and texting away, walked straight into the traffic. A car screeched around him.

"Just asking to get killed," Tony said to himself. As the oblivious dude walked past, Tony gave the dirtiest look he could muster.

So Tony didn't see the cyclist rocketing down the sidewalk behind him until he zipped by, inches in front of him. The spokes of the bicycle wheels ticked madly away.

"*Sesquiculus*," Tony swore. Asshole and a half!

He remembered then what Gary had said and what his mother had said. Tony liked to think of himself as brutally logical, but he couldn't stop the goosepimples rising along his arms and the hair standing up on the back of his neck. *Ridiculous.*

CHAPTER THREE

On his way to work at the *Williamsburg Sentinel,* Patrick Stoller skateboarded up Bedford Avenue. One of Brooklyn's major arteries, Bedford was usually filled with cars and buses and jaywalkers. All those vehicles, all those people were a total killjoy and turned skateboarding from a pure hum of a ride into ugly, jagged noise.

But that early on a Saturday morning, the streets were empty, except for a truck or car, a few homeless people, and stragglers getting home late or starting the day early.

Patrick skateboarded past South 3rd, South 2nd Street, South 1st, Grand Street. Back in Allentown, PA, he used to glide every day along the smooth and steep blacktop of "Weed" Avenue. (It was really Tweed Avenue, but someone would cross out the "T" every time the street sign was replaced.) That's what Bedford was like this early in the morning, smooth sailing from door to door.

He jumped a curb at North 1st to cut in front of a galumphing B62 bus whose driver, perhaps not wanting to break the sweet tranquility of the morning, gave him a half-hearted honk.

Patrick wore a dirty mint-green Mets baseball cap over his curly red hair. He wore glasses with thick, black frames; navy blue velvet sneakers; and a too-small black T-shirt that read "Does NY ❤ You Back?"

He intentionally stopped at the corner of Bedford and North 7th to check his iPhone. His background pic was of his ex-girlfriend Kirsten (in that lacy pink teddy of hers, *grrrr*). He'd have to change that picture someday. She lived a block from where he was standing, in a walkup above The MeatLoaf Shoppe. But she'd be sleeping off her bartending gig right about then. No chance he'd run into her, although what would be the harm of just riding past her window?

There it was.

There it went *slowllllly*.

At the corner, he stopped again, kicking up his board and heading into a bakery. He ordered a yogurt muffin and a chai latte.

But back on the blacktop, he hit a divot and the bag of latte and muffin flew—crashing and splashing into the street.

"Double fuck," he said. He used the stop as a chance to check his phone again.

Patrick had moved to Brooklyn six years ago, to live in the city where some of his all-time favorite writers use to work and love and dream. *Auster! Wolfe! Eggers! Klosterman!* A friend had had a place in Greenpoint, a two-bedroom with crooked floors and more roaches than Patrick had ever seen in his life. Colonies of them! He crashed on the couch there. Five roommates. No heat in the winter. But at least it wasn't Allentown. At least it was a step closer to his literary dreams.

There was a bodega up the corner from the office, one of those old-fashioned ones with a red corrugated metal awning and yellow panels of lettering announcing "Hot & Cold Sandwiches," "Comida Latina," "Meat & Groceries." He usually avoided bodegas because the first time he had gone into one the cashier didn't speak English, or pretended she didn't, and she totally over-charged him. But he was too hungry now to be picky.

Inside, an old man stood behind a clear plastic wall on the counter. The wall was lined with cubbyholes filled on the lower levels with candy and on the top levels with band-aids, aphrodisiacs, and more candy. Skateboard in hand, Patrick asked for a coffee. The old man behind the counter pointed, and Patrick turned to see a coffeemaker and a column of cups.

"Whoa, styrofoam," Patrick said.

But where was the milk? He turned to the old man, who was already pointing at the refrigerator case.

Patrick looked around the counter for food. He couldn't identify some orange things with rainbow sprinkles in the plastic case, so he grabbed what appeared to be an apple turnover in cellophane.

"I get a bag?" he said, not looking at the cashier but down at his iPhone again.

The *Williamsburg Sentinel* inhabited a storefront on Roebling Street. It lived in two small backrooms of the copy shop/real estate/notary public business of Bobbert Swiatowski, the publisher of the *Sentinel*. Patrick came in almost every day but got the most work done on weekends, when Bobbert was not around and constantly asking about ad sales.

Of the two back rooms, one was all Bobbert's. It was piled high with thirty years of back issues. As managing editor, Patrick had his desk in the other room, a cramped ten-by-twelve space he shared with three old metal desks for the freelancers. An archaic air conditioner loudly kept the room tolerable. But when the freelancers came in, as they liked to do on weekends, it would get crowded and hot in there. Another reason he liked to arrive early.

He thought he might work on his novel before the freelancers showed up. He checked in in the airless, windowless little bathroom they had, then he put his iPhone right on the desk next to his mouse, stuck in his earbuds.

Just after 10 a.m., Tony Moran came in carrying his messenger bag, in shorts and a faded T-shirt. He looked grumpy. But he always looked grumpy.

"Hey, Tony," Patrick said. "Listen, I got some things that need revising, and, uh, I was wondering, would you mind ghostwriting Psally the Psychick's column again? She's still in Budapest, and she says she's not feeling inspired, so..."

"But she's the one with the magical powers. I just used fortune cookies and Oprah quotes."

"Can you please write it? You did so good with it in the last issue."

"As long as I get the same rate she does."

"Of course."

"When do you need this by?"

"Today?"

"Oh boy," Tony said. "I've got four other stories to turn in. I can squeeze this in. After this though, I'm retiring my psychic powers."

"Understood. You're a pal, Tony, you really are."

"Don't get emotional on me."

A half hour later, Gabrielle walked in, in a haze of auto-tuned music that screeched from her earbuds. She wore gray leggings, beach flip-flops, an oversized T-shirt. Her hair was pulled back severely into that smooth head and ponytail that Latinx women seemed to like to do. She mumbled a "Good morning."

Patrick could smell the fast food in her bag. He saw her eat a yogurt. Once. At times, he had smelled the liquor and cigarettes on her from the night before. She plopped herself down at her usual desk by the door.

Tony, popping out his earbuds, said to her, "Did you oversleep again or are you just coming back from a rave?"

"A rave? Shut up. I got a mad headache," she said. "Hey, guess what I saw on the subway this morning?"

"What?"

"A guy with a suit made out of grass. Real grass, I swear!"

Patrick thought this sounded totally cool, but before he could say anything, Tony said, "You're kidding. He was wearing a lawn?"

"Yes! I'm mad serious."

"That's Williamsburg for you," Tony said. "Halloween all year long. I hope he likes his job at the art gallery and/or coffee shop."

17

"Lolz."

In the early afternoon, everyone in the room worked in their own little worlds, earbuds on. Gabrielle worked on ad sales, but on weekends she helped to proofread articles. Although she never found any mistakes.

A loud spaceship alarm went off. Patrick's iPhone. He rushed to pick it up, almost knocking it on the floor. It was a call.

Jackie Tomasello was a real estate queen in charge of Tomasello Management, one of the paper's biggest advertisers. She emailed them all her ads. If she was calling, it was to complain.

"Patrick, how are you?" she said. Without waiting for him to answer, she said, "There's a typo in my ad on page six in the last issue. It's a one-bedroom on Berry Street, not Berry *Stret*. It's a full-page ad, Patrick, with a mistake in it. It cost me a lot of money. I'm not paying for this ad, you understand? I get page six next month again. Free. Tell your boss. Thank you." She hung up.

Bobbert would not be happy about this. But it wasn't unusual. She got a lot of free placement in the paper all the time. They needed to fill the pages anyway.

As he went to put his phone down, it sounded again—a teletype noise. He gripped the phone tightly. That meant a text. *This was it.*

The text read: "Kent + S 3. 1AM 2nite."

"1AM?" Patrick texted back.

"2nite or never."

"It's cool. I'll b there," he texted back. Then he added: "How will I know u?" Which felt like a cliché, amateur question as soon as he sent it.

"I no u."

Patrick didn't know how to respond, so he just typed, "k." Out of habit, he was about to add a smiley face but stopped himself.

He stared at his phone screen. It was actually going to happen.

At his desk, he tried to concentrate. He put back all the contractions he had removed from a profile of a local mayonnaise artisan.

Gabrielle yelled from across the small room. "I read what you gave me. I didn't find any mistakes," she said.

Patrick thanked her.

"So I'm going to go."

When she left, Tony told her to "Get home safe."

She answered, "Yeah, right."

They laughed, but Patrick didn't see what the joke was. These two always had their in-jokes. He had tried to hang out with them a couple of times, to be more of a friend than a co-worker, but they never seemed to click.

Soon afterward, Tony packed up to go. Patrick stopped in the middle of editing and swiveled around.

"Hey, Tony, listen. Uh, you busy tonight? I'm working on something, something for the paper, something long range, and I could use some help."

Tony looked up, eyebrows raised high. "Nope. Sorry. Got plans. What is it? A rewrite? Maybe I can help out tomorrow."

"Um, nah, that's okay. No worries. It's nothing. I can do it."

"All right. See you next week."

Tony stopped at the door. "I was going to ask you—anything happening with Rose Irizarry? You know, the old lady who disappeared."

"Yeah, I know who you're talking about. What do you mean? Why the interest?"

"No, no real interest. Funny thing is my mother asked me about it again. They knew each other from church. Not good friends, but she's always bringing it up to me as an example of rampant crime in the neighborhood. Anyway, it's been a year since this lady's disappearance. Are we going to do a follow-up story on the anniversary, where the investigation is, that kind of nonsense?"

Patrick flipped his hands up, accidentally sending the red

pencil in his hand flying. As he bent to look for it on the floor, he said, "Oh, totally. It's going to be a cover piece. It's important not to let her be forgotten, you know? Why do you ask? Did you—" He found the pencil and held it up like an exclamation point. "Did you want to help on it?"

"Nah," Tony said. "It's not my sort of thing. I was just curious."

"Yeah. Okay."

It was late when Tony left, and Patrick was left alone in the office. He tried to work. The room felt very warm and very quiet.

CHAPTER FOUR

At a quarter to one in the morning, Patrick shut down his computer and locked up the office. He boarded down the streetlamp-lit sidewalk on Metropolitan Avenue. The heat had relaxed, but the humidity was still thick. People were out, walking hand in hand or in shoulder-to-shoulder groups. He had to skateboard through and around and right in front of them.

On the stoops and in front of tenement buildings, Latinx families were gathered together. How family-oriented those people were, how tightly knit. *Totally cool,* Patrick thought, *totally nice.*

He zigzagged across Berry Street, onto South 1st, then Wythe, South 2nd, and finally came to stop at the corner of Kent Avenue and South 3rd. Almost no one was around. There was an empty lot across the street, a closed store on the other side. Behind him, an abandoned factory blocked the glittery and valuable view of Manhattan. Prime real estate. It wouldn't be abandoned for long. Through its fences, past years of discarded cans and weeds cracking through the concrete, he could still see the East River crawling along, black and viscous.

It was quiet on that corner. The usual Billyburg crowds were probably at home being lulled to sleep by their air conditioners.

Sweat flowed down Patrick's back.

He waited.

He checked his iPhone for no good reason, and when he did he realized the light around him was dim, dimmer than it was farther up and down the street. Neither of the two streetlamps on the corner where he stood was lit. He looked up and saw that the remnants of the jagged remnants of their bulbs. Kids playing ball in the streets, probably. He used to be rambunctious once, too.

He waited. It sure was hot.

With his earbuds in, Patrick didn't hear the flutter of bicycle wheels. But as he made a slow circle out of boredom, he saw someone on a bike coming fast down Kent. A man or a woman. Too dark to tell. *This could be it.* He thought about waving *Hi,* but reconsidered it. That wouldn't look cool. Anyway, at the speed this person was moving, he or she must've just been rushing to get home.

Whoever it was *was* coming really fast.

And then Patrick noticed: The biker wore a hoodie tied tightly around his or her face. *Why would anyone do that in this stifling heat? Maybe someone trying to sweat off weight...*

Then he saw that the bicyclist held something in his or her hand, against one of the handlebars.

A knife. A very large knife. A machete.

Patrick stepped hard on his skateboard, but at the wrong angle. It slid out from under him and he tumbled onto the concrete. He dropped his phone and his earbuds popped out.

The biker sped right past him. Patrick relaxed. He felt like such a douche. What a story he would get out of this. Maybe an editorial. Maybe a blog post. Maybe something for the novel.

Then he heard wheels spin on asphalt. The biker, twenty feet away, was turned toward him. The machete raised in the biker's hand.

"Oh shit!" Patrick said. He reached for his iPhone, but his hands were slick with sweat, and he couldn't grip it. The spokes ticked closer.

"Shit!" He decided to go for his skateboard. There were people, crowds of people, only a block or two away.

The first slash came so fast Patrick didn't register it till he felt a line of pain in the back of his leg. "Dammit!"

He backed up against a wall of the abandoned factory. He

steadied himself against the brick wall and pulled up his skateboard like a shield, its wheels spinning.

"Stop it! I'm a reporter!"

The biker halted his bike in the street. In the dimness, his face was hidden. He raised one long leg over the handlebars and let the bike clang on the blacktop. He took a small step to the right, and Patrick moved to the left. Then the biker went left and Patrick wondered if he should go right. Patrick was paralyzed against the wall, waiting for an opening to run. Back and forth the biker feinted, like a little dance, holding the blade up high.

Then, to Patrick's surprise, the biker tackled him, knocking the skateboard away and crushing him into the brick wall. Patrick tried to punch, but the biker knocked his hands way with one hand then forced his elbow into Patrick's neck, knocking his head back and pinning him against the brick.

"You fucker. Just take my stuff," Patrick grunted, staring at the machete. "Fuck! Please! Just take it!"

The biker placed the tip of the blade right under Patrick's sternum, just under the "❤" of his T-shirt, then pulled back and jabbed once, twice.

Patrick sank back against the wall. He tried to block, but the machete bit into his arm. It stuck. The biker put his foot on his chest and pulled out the blade, making a wet sound.

"Oh god, oh god, oh god, oh god." Patrick tried to reach for his iPhone again but it wasn't anywhere near him and his trembling hand was greasy with blood and he felt so weak, so weak.

The biker faked a swing to the left and then to the right. In the hoodie, his laughter was muffled. Then he stepped forward and, using two hands, casually took one more swing and then another.

Patrick slumped onto the concrete. He looked up at the black sky. He thought of his parents, of his mother, of his ex-girlfriend in her lacy pink teddy. He thought about Brooklyn. He thought about his apartment. He loved his apartment. Someone else would snatch it up in no time, and no one would remember he lived there.

CHAPTER FIVE

As Erin Cole and her husband Steven Pak burst through the entrance of the Verge—a thirty-five-story glass tower condominium complex on Kent Avenue, perfectly situated on the waterfront and boasting breathtaking river and city views—she was greeted by the smiling, moon-shaped face of Angel, their tries-too-hard doorman.

"Mr. Steven. Ms. Erin. Are you okay?" he said. In his little, worn-out doorman uniform with dirty white gloves.

Steve blurted, "Oh god, we—" but Erin cut him off. "We're fine," she said. "Just tired."

"You sure?" Angel said.

"Absolutely," she said. "It's just so so so so hot."

She walked as quickly as she could. She was very pregnant and genetically thin as a straw, so now she looked like a straw with a pea stuck to it. She held her baby pea as it bounced, past Angel's little podium and to the elevators. "We're so happy to be home."

"I hear that," Angel said. "But—"

"We're fine. Thank you. *Gracias!*" she said using her best Spanish accent, which she knew was good because some of her best friends back home in Texas were indeed Mexican, and they said her accent was good.

Angel probably thought they'd just had an argument. Whatever. Let him think what he wanted. He was just a doorman. Come tomorrow morning, he'd forget he'd ever seen how scared they must have looked.

That's what they were, right? Scared. Freaked out.

As soon as the mirrored elevator doors closed, Erin backed herself against the wall. Steve looked ill, like he was about to hurl. And she hoped he wouldn't because that would make her hurl. Catching herself in the mirror behind Steve, she realized she didn't look so great herself.

Her hubby was about to talk, but she shushed him. "Be quiet, kumquat," she said, whispering. "I think these things are bugged."

Steven smacked his forehead. It was something he liked to do when he couldn't understand her. It always left a red mark on his head. "But we have to help that man."

"Quiet! Wait till we get upstairs!"

She crossed her arms as well as she could across her belly and stared ahead. Her ears were hot. But with the mirrors, she was stuck seeing her husband's look of complete discombobulation and the red mark on his forehead staring back at her.

They had been walking home from dinner on South 6th Street, a new Burundian place that had been written up in *New York*. It wasn't a short walk, and the night was hot, but Erin had nixed the idea of a cab. She was seven months pregnant and her body temperature was all over the place, so she couldn't stand the idea of being trapped inside a car with the air conditioning going on full blast, feeling like some momsicle.

They had been talking about getting out of town for July 4—before she popped, before their lives changed forever, and because New York became such a ghost town then except for all the very, very slow, very, very fat tourists.

And as she and Steve turned down from South 4th onto Kent, they heard a sound, maybe like the chopping of wood—no, more like the sound of a ceramic knife hitting a bamboo cutting board. They didn't look and kept walking. They weren't native New Yorkers, but they had learned there were too many weirdos and too many strange things that happened in the big city, you just couldn't worry about them all. In this town, you were on your own.

But then she had looked down the street and over, and slumped halfway to the ground was a young guy, and covering his shirt—was that? It was! Yes!—blood. *Blood* blood.

Standing above him was a man with a long machete. That machete was the clearest thing she could see and it shined with that blood. It was surreal, something out of a horror movie, so she and her McSteven just watched it like it was one, frozen in place, holding hands.

That's when Erin realized the guy with the machete had been wearing a hoodie. Only because he had stopped to tug it off. Who could blame him? With the heat.

It was dark, and they weren't that close. Did she really see something of his face, or did she just imagine it? She couldn't be sure.

Then they heard something between a moan and a wheeze from the man on the ground, a sound like her Grandma Betsy made just as she passed.

Steve-o-rini fumbled with his iPhone, aiming it. He was going to take a picture! But her survival instinct made her back away, pulling hubby and his phone with her. They looked at each other and turned and began to walk. Quick, firm steps. When they heard the sound of bicycle wheel spokes—yes, there had been a bicycle on its side behind the man in the hoodie—so they began to walk-run. Erin held her belly and Stevie reached out to hold it, too. They turned back onto South 4th, kept going up to Bedford, where stinky hipsters crowded the streets like a thick-bearded herd of buffalo.

She usually hated them, hated the way they smelled and dressed and talked and everything, but this time she was ecstatic to be around people, oh Lord Jesus, even some stinky hipsters.

Without talking, she and Steve walk-ran through the herd and up to North 5th. Then they turned back toward the riverside park and their building. Here, blazing streetlights cancelled the night. Here, preeminent luxury condominiums jutted into the sky, and adults and children and dogs could mill about safely away from the darkness.

She and Stevely had never looked back, back at the scene on Kent, which was only a few blocks down. But she knew her husband was thinking the same thing she was thinking, although neither said it out loud: *Did the man with the machete see them seeing him?*

Upstairs, before Steven opened the door, Erin heard their dog, Deeogee, whimpering. She knew he was twitching his butt with excitement on the other side.

"Hurry," Erin said to Steve.

She knew if he didn't open the door fast enough, their lovely chocolate cocker spaniel would let his excitement get the best of him.

But Steve's hands were shaking. Erin took the keys from him and opened the door. They were too late. The dog had messed on the floor of the uniquely spacious layout.

"Dammit, Steverino," she said, then to the dog: "Bad Deeogee! Bad, bad Deeogee!"

The shameless dog spun in the thoughtfully designed and appointed vestibule like a dervish, like it was trying to tuck its head into its ass.

Erin stepped over to the chef kitchen and got the mop. She handed it to Steven.

But he stood there, not mopping. "We just saw somebody get killed."

Erin turned the thermostat down to frigid—*now* she wanted to feel like a momsicle. She turned on the OLED TV.

"We don't know that," she said.

"If we see something, we're supposed to say something."

"That's for terrorists, m'dear."

Steve mopped the stunning but pissed-on white oak floor. Then he took out his iPhone and began tapping in his passcode. Erin trotted up to him and slapped it out of his hand. It clunked on the floor.

"My phone!"

"What are you doing?" she said.

He picked up his iPhone, shaking it to see if anything was loose. "Calling the police."

"Stevebug, we're not going to get involved. Let someone else call the police."

"What if he's still alive?"

"Please. Leave it alone. Someone else will find him."

"Erin, I can make an anonymous call."

"That anonymous stuff is bullshit. Nothing is anonymous in this world anymore," she said, massaging her belly. She felt totally gassy. "They'll know who we are."

"I can't believe you're being like this."

She went to the leather couch and sat down, cradling her belly. "Fuzzy Penguin, please," she said. "My stomach. I've got such heartburn. Can you get me a ginger ale?"

He stood there unable to move.

"We still have ginger ale, right?" she said.

Later, in bed, she couldn't sleep. In her mind, she saw the man's blood on the street—redder than she had seen it in reality, color-corrected by her imagination. She kept seeing what had happened, over and again. The guy on the ground—was he young? Not a boy? No. A guy, just a guy.

And the man with the machete. Had he been sitting on the bike? Or was he standing next to it? Of course, he hadn't seen them, right? Or else he would have kept coming after them, right? It's not like they were getting away on horseback.

The killer's—that man's—face had mostly been a blur. But, yes, he had been facing them. From a block away. Was it a long block? She didn't remember.

Enough!

She was about to get out of bed, when Steven suddenly did. He couldn't sleep either. No wonder.

He had run to the bathroom. Even from their bedroom, Erin

could hear him vomiting, which of course made her think about vomiting. Maybe the Burundian bananas and beans dinner didn't agree with him. Or that weird wine, which had tasted off.

A few minutes later, she heard the whir of his electric toothbrush.

She focused on that sound—she knew he would take a while—and rolled off the bed and got on her knees. She scrunched down and got a box from underneath it.

She remembered what her father had said about New York. "Lots of criminals and rapists," Daddy had warned her. "Better safe than sorry," he had told her. "Always be prepared." From the box, she took out the gun that her father had given her, a Taurus PT-111 9mm semi-auto, on her seventeenth birthday— "Not heavy or gritty and easy to conceal," he had told her— and put it in her purse. She added the ammo, sealed in a sandwich baggie, that Daddy had given her the day she left for New York.

Better safe than sorry.

CHAPTER SIX

Just after two a.m., Detective Jimmy Petrosino parked his silver PT Cruiser on Kent Avenue, behind a trio of patrol cars.

Wide, tall, and thin as a front door, Petrosino had a helmet of hair, cotton white, and a thick mustache, stained nicotine yellow. He also happened to be wearing a green polyester tuxedo with a white shirt and red leather bowtie. His shoes were white bucks.

And he didn't want to hear any smartass jokes about it.

When he climbed out of his vehicle, Detective Eddie Hadid marched over. This was Petrosino's new partner, assigned to him just three weeks ago. The kid had so far shown himself to be a quick thinker, good with the paperwork. Boxy and broad, he looked like he'd do good in a scrape. The real problem with Hadid was his mouth, 'cause, boy, did he like to run it.

Hadid started talking before he was even in Petrosino's earshot. "...sorry to get you away from whatever I got you away from, but wait till you see this. You're gonna like it and you're gonna hate it, wait and see—whoa-ho! Wait! What's with the getup, Petro? You look like a Christmas tree. Is Christmas coming even earlier this year?"

Petrosino held up a finger to shush him. There was a crowd beyond the yellow tape, a bunch of oglers with their cell phones out. Williamsburg. They couldn't just rubberneck like normal people. They had to take pictures and share the moment.

Without looking at his partner, Petrosino said, "Get a couple of uniforms go around tell them to stop taking pictures."

"Really? Can we do that?"

"Yeah," Petrosino said. "Why not?"

"Hey, while I'm at it, I can have them ask if they saw anything."

"You're learning, brother. Now go. Then come back and give me the what's what."

Petrosino shook out a cigarette, lit it, and looked over at the crime scene. Hell of a lot of blood. A Mets fan telling by that hat. Deadhead skateboard a few feet away.

Hadid walked back, his mouth again working before he even got in hearing distance. "...I want to know is why Brooklyn smells like shit? I mean, it's like a sewer went to the bathroom out here."

Petrosino blew out smoke. "And I suppose the Bronx is all perfume and roses?"

Hadid coughed and waved the smoke away. "Well, it ain't perfect. But it ain't this bad, Petro. I mean—"

"Run this down for me."

"Vic's still alive, but barely. On his way to Woodhull. White male, twenties. Multiple stab wounds, slashes. But we still got his wallet."

"ID?"

"Patrick Stoller. Got some cards and other numbers in here."

"Cell phone?"

"That's a 'no.'"

"Right-o," Petrosino said. "So, is it what I think it is?" His instinct told him the answer but he had to ask.

"Yeah, that's what I was telling you, was why I interrupted whatever it was you were doing dressed like Christmas puked up on your night off. Looks like the attacker used something long, something sharp. Likely a machete."

"Dammit," Petrosino said, flicking his cigarette all the way to the other side of the street. "Another one."

"That's number three. That means we got a trend. This

neighborhood sure like its trends, am I right? The papers ain't got a good name for these guys, the Slasher Gang. It should be something cool. Like 'The Cutting Crew.' Or 'Brooklyn Rippers.' Or 'Slashr,' you know, without the 'e,' like an app—"

"Hadid!" Petrosino lowered his voice to a hostile whisper. He moved his partner away from the tape. "You ass. If one of these iFucks catches you mouthing off, you'll be all over the fucking Twitter in less than a New York second. Listen to me: This isn't the Boogie Down Bronx where nobody gives a shit what happens. Here we're being watched all the fucking time."

"Shit. Me and my big mouth. My wife is always telling me I have to reel it in. Sometimes I can't help myself. Listen, I didn't—"

"'S'enough."

"Yeah. Sorry, Petro."

"And, dammit, cut it out with the fucking nickname."

Hadid slunk away, and Petrosino fished in his jacket for another cigarette. As he was doing that, he realized one of these hipsters in the crowd was snapping a picture of him.

Before he could sic a uniform on him, the hipster was turning away, waving and yelling, "Merry Christmas, officer!"

Petrosino lit up and inhaled deeply. And the night had started so well.

CHAPTER SEVEN

Not for the first time that night, Tony wondered what the hell he was doing. The jagged Manhattan skyline bounced and bobbled in the distance, or that could just have been his soggy head bouncing and bobbling. He was looking out the back window of the back car of the number 7 train, and he ached to sit down, lie down, knock out. He had been standing for hours. He had been drinking for hours. (The cocktails had been surprisingly cheap and surprisingly strong.) But he couldn't rest because he was crushed against the conductor door in a very crowded car with a very drunk Gabby leaning what seemed to be her entire weight on him.

The train inched its way along an elevated line over Queens.

Gabby had suckered him into going to a poetry reading in a lounge on Hooper Street. She had texted him at the office, from four feet away. He texted back that he hated poetry.

"U h8 evryting :(," she wrote, but then added: "plz dis naybrhood not safe w/ dat machete guy slashing ppl. I don't wn 2 gt slashed. UR a big guy +U cn B my bodyguard."

"Sure," he had texted back, kicking himself as he did.

He met her at the lounge, which was dimly lit, low-ceilinged, and lined on one side with sagging velvet curtains and on the other with inspirational posters ("Failure is temporary. Giving up is permanent"), like some high school version of a literary salon. But the air conditioning was spot on.

While Gabby sat on one of the few stools, Tony did his best

not to roll his eyes at the poets. The first poet recited—or was that singing? Or was that rapping?—a piece about how much he loved and respected his grandmother. The next poet rhymed about how much she loved and respected her mother and grandmother. Grandmothers turned out to be a popular subject. This went on for a while.

Between each reading there was a break, and an irritating sound that stabbed at Tony's ears blared from the speakers.

"What is that?" he asked Gabby. "Is that *bachata*?"

"Duh. *Reggaeton*," she said.

"It's musical waterboarding."

"Not a surprise," she said, touching his chest. She had been touching him a lot. It was probably because of all the rum and cokes she had been downing. "By the way, Tony, thanks again so so *so* much for this. I get all paranoid, you know?"

"Yeah."

"Oh, and can you walk me home later, okay?"

"I guess," he said. "Wait a second. Don't you live in Queens?"

"Let's dance!"

"I do not want to dance."

Undiscouraged, she turned around and found a dance partner immediately, so Tony turned and struggled to get the bartender's attention. The *reggaeton* pecked at Tony's brain, and he felt only alcohol could protect him.

"Chino? I thought that was you."

He turned, spilling beer on his face and neck. Few people still called him "Chino" anymore. It was an old nickname that had withered away when most of his childhood friends had died or moved out. But he knew that voice.

"Magaly."

Magaly Fernandez had grown up a block away from Tony in the Southside of Williamsburg. Her curly hair bounced and swayed, like a separate entity atop her head, and she wore an oversized man's shirt over black leggings. Over her shoulder was an enormous purse that seemed to hold a litter of bulldogs.

Her large brown eyes flared with life, and her lips looked as sensual and inviting as they always had.

"You look good. What's it been? Ten years?" she said.

"About."

"Was that your niece I saw you with?" She waved to the bartender and he came right over to her. She ordered two white wines.

"Co-worker."

"Uh huh."

"Yeah," Tony said. "So, you like poetry?"

"I love poetry. I love all art. My boss wanted to come here, so…long story. But what about you, Chino?" she said.

The bartender came back with two white wines incredibly fast. Tony tried to catch the bartender but he floated away without charging Magaly.

"Don't tell me you developed a love for the arts since I last saw you?" she said. "Or does your co-worker have something to do with it?"

Tony smirked. "I can appreciate art."

The emcee was announcing the last reader of the night. Standing just behind him was a man in his forties with a shaved head, goatee, and a gray suit sharp and shiny enough to qualify as good cutlery. The man looked familiar. Some community guy. The emcee introduced him as Luis De Moscoso, director of El Flamboyan Community Center, and that clicked it for Tony. There was a lot of applause. De Moscoso was in the *Sentinel* very often, but not in Tony's beat.

De Moscoso said his poem was called "*Adios, Bodega de Mi Corazon.*" *Goodbye, Bodega of My Heart.* Half of the lines were in Spanish. The other half were the same lines in English. He read from his smartphone.

Where is Jose? He is gone! Where is Josefina? She is gone!
They got gone, moved over, paved over, left
By the colonizers, the gentrifiers, the sanitizers, the backstabbers

They come creeping onto our shores
Like Cristóbal Colón and his merry merchant ships
They invaded Los Sures. They took our stores.
They took our homes. They took our streets.
And they just want us to disappear, they just want us to
evaporate
But we can't let them pave over us like a steamroller
We have to be more than WOKE! We have to be ready for
WAR!

On and on it went like that for ten minutes. Tony had no appreciation for poetry, but this one got a standing ovation. But that wasn't hard since there were so few seats.

Magaly had been watching De Moscoso intently. Tony was about to ask her a question when suddenly that bald head—and a cloud of cologne—stepped between him and Magaly.

"I'm done here," De Moscoso said. He slid his arm possessively around her waist. "Let's go."

"*Calmate, hombre. Carajo,*" she said, pushing the arm away. She pointed out Tony. "I want you to meet an old friend. Anthony Moran. We used to call him 'Chino.' Chino, this is Luis De Moscoso, my boss."

De Moscoso stuck his hand out but didn't look at him. Then Magaly said, "He's a journalist. You're still a journalist, right? I see your name in the *Sentinel.*"

De Moscoso rotated toward Tony and looked him up and down and did not seem impressed. Then he broke into a brilliant white grin. "Luis De Moscoso," he said, tightening his grip. "Director of El Flamboyan Community Center. *Un placer.* I'm always available to meet with journalists about issues that are important to the community."

Behind and unseen by De Moscoso, Magaly's eyes signaled one word: "Behave." Tony's face broke in a smile as wide and pure as the East River. He said, "Hey, great poem! Really terrific. Shakespearesque."

"You like it? Thank you. It's not usually my thing but I like to dabble. Perhaps you could publish it in the *Sentinel*."

Magaly. Eyes.

Smiling, Tony said, "Terrific idea. But I have to ask my editor about it."

"Of course," De Moscoso said. "Let me give you my card."

Tony took the card and held it like a piece of used tissue.

Then De Moscoso turned to Magaly and said, "We need to run. Nice to meet you, Mr. Chino."

De Moscoso had his hand on Magaly's rear end as they headed for the door. She grabbed it and held it, and when they left the lounge, Tony saw they were holding hands.

Gabby was suddenly at Tony's side with two rum and cokes in her hands. She drank from both of them.

"Can I have one of those?" Tony said.

"But I already drank from them."

"Just give me."

"All right, Cranky Man."

Tony finished the drink in a gulp.

"Wow, somebody's thirsty," Gabby said. "So, who was that? That lady you were talking to. I love love love her hair."

"That was my ex."

"Ex-wife?"

"Funny. Ex-girlfriend. Five years. Right out of college. But we were friends long before that. We grew up in the Southside together."

"I love her hair."

"You said that. Is it time to go yet?"

Gabby chugged the last of her drinks. She said, "Now we can."

They walked out into the night heat to the G train. They waited a long time for it to arrive, standing since all the platform seats were taken by homeless men. After the G, they transferred for the 7 and waited a while for that to show, no seats open again. Now, rumbling along on the 7 train, Tony looked down to see Gabby drooling as she leaned her body against him. He sighed.

When his phone rang, he had just enough room between him and Gabby to dig into the pocket of his shorts. He noted the time. It was two in the morning, and a phone call at 2 a.m. could be very good news (unlikely), very bad news (more likely), or a drunk friend (highest probability).

"Hello, sir. Is this Tony Moran?"

"Yeah."

"This is Officer Thomas of the NYPD—"

Police. *Very* bad then.

CHAPTER EIGHT

Woodhull Hospital was wedged up against the elevated train at Flushing Avenue. The modernist hulk of steel, glass, and rust-colored brick looked less like a hospital and more like a place to serve consecutive life terms. Tony hated Woodhull. He hated hospitals. They smelled of piss and disinfectant.

"How much?" he asked the car service driver.

"*Diez y nueve.*"

"Nineteen!" Rip-off. Tony handed over a twenty-dollar bill. It was the last of his money, and he'd had to borrow it from Gabby, who was suddenly wide awake at her stop. ("Reflex," she'd said.) He found a car service base a block from the train, and the driver had played *reggaeton* the whole ride.

Tony waited. Then he held his hand out. The driver looked at it, then handed over the dollar bill change.

"Thanks," Tony said.

He rushed into the emergency entrance—*piss, disinfectant*—and asked for the officer who called. The security guard at the desk made a call, and a minute later, two men walked over. One was tall with a dirty yellow mustache. He wore a flashy tuxedo with the colors of the Italian flag. The short man next to him wore a knit tie and a plaid shirt. So one or the other had missed the memo. The tall one said he was Detective Petrosino and his partner, Detective Hadid.

The tall one, Petrosino, said, "I'm sorry to inform you that your friend passed not two minutes ago."

39

"Oh fuck." Tony stared at the cops. "Damn."

Patrick had not been a friend, but Tony had worked with him for years. He wasn't sure what to feel, what to say.

Detective Hadid said, "Listen, since you're here already, sir, would you mind terribly identifying the body for us, sir?"

"'Terribly?'" Tony said.

Petrosino said, "And if you can give us any contact information on a family member for Mr. Stoller, we would appreciate that as well. Yours was the only number we found in Mr. Stoller's wallet."

"That's what the officer who called me said. And Patrick's phone was stolen?" Tony said.

"No phone was found near the body, no."

They walked him down the hall under the nauseating lights of the ER. Miserable-looking people sat in the few seats that were available. One man, whose right foot twisted in an unnatural direction, looked bored scrolling through his phone. Next to him, a large woman wrestled with a large child, who was begging his lungs out for Cheez Doodles.

Tony followed the cops through a swinging door. Beds were separated by curtains.

The cop on the phone had been cagey. Patrick had been attacked. Was in very bad shape. "If I were you, I'd get here right away," he'd said.

Tony had seen dead bodies before, once in the street after a car accident—although from twenty feet away—in a couple of funeral homes, and of course online (for a clickbait piece on celebrity autopsies). So he hoped against logic that it would be the same thing, without the bad makeup and mouth sewing. He'd say, "Sure, sure, that's him," and he'd be home in an hour.

They led him to near the back of the room, behind a curtain. On it was a sheet on top of what seemed to be the shape of a person. But in several places, the sheet was wet, red-black.

Petrosino said, "Are you ready?"

"No," Tony said. "Do it anyway."

Petrosino pulled back the sheet. Tony's stomach flipped, his balls tightened, and, to his surprise, tears welled in his eyes. All he saw at first was red—an unnatural-looking jelly-red. It didn't seem like a human. Most of Patrick just didn't seem to be there anymore.

"Take your time," Petrosino said. "I know he's your friend."

Tony tried to compose himself the only way he knew how. "Actually, we were just co-workers," although his throat was so dry and he said it so quietly, he didn't know if anyone heard him, even when Petrosino said, "Right-o."

Tony looked more closely at the red mass, leering open like bloodied lips. Over to its left—part of a nose, a mouth. The left eye closed, the skin pale, almost green, curly ginger hair above.

Tony took a breath and said, "Him." He didn't trust his voice to say more than that.

"Thank you, sir," the plaid-shirt detective, Hadid, said.

Petrosino began to put the sheet back in place, but Tony stopped him, moved his arm. The detective gave him a look. Tony looked back and mumbled, "One second."

Tony was shaken. Patrick had been alive just hours before, had asked him to work on some project, seemed nervous. But what project? And why nervous?

Patrick's upper body, clotted with blood, and his arms—they looked like they'd been savagely attacked, but from the looks of the wound where the blade hit, Tony began to visualize the scene.

"He...he put up a fight, didn't he?" Tony said.

"You can say that again," said Hadid. "Lots of defensive cuts, and a nice cut right in the chest. I'd say the killer was left-handed from the direction of all the cuts." He pantomimed the killer's slashing as he spoke. "See. Like that, probably."

"Actually, that's a misconception," Tony said. "There's really no way to tell. The attacker, or assailant, as you guys say, could have struck from multiple angles, used a right hand, left hand, both hands."

"What's that, now?" Hadid's face scrunched.

"And from some of these wounds," Tony said, "I doubt you guys can tell for sure if the assailant or assailants stood in front of him, behind him, one side or the other..."

"Well, fuck me," Hadid said. "Is he right?"

Hadid looked at his tall partner, who nodded.

"Me and my big mouth."

Petrosino put back the sheet. "Mr. Moran, when was the last time you saw your Mr. Stoller?"

"Um, just today—I mean, yesterday," Tony said. "He was at the office. Can I ask—where did this happen?"

"He was found on the corner of Kent Avenue and South 3rd," Petrosino said. "By the way, did Mr. Stoller ride a skateboard?"

"With a passion. It had a Deadhead sticker on, even though he hated the Grateful Dead."

The short cop was going to say something when Tony interrupted. "Yeah, so, then, he was attacked by someone on a bike or a moped or maybe even somebody else on a skateboard?"

Petrosino tilted his head like a dog's. "What makes you say that?"

"Patrick was skateboarding, so he must have been in motion. Of course, he could have been just standing there on that corner, but why? If my memory is right, there's nothing much over that far, some stores and a lot—unless they put up a hotel or a mall there by now. Which is certainly possible. But Patrick lives over by the BQE, way in the other direction. What was he doing, joyriding at night?"

"These are all good questions for us, Mr.—"

Tony interrupted Hadid again. "Wait, did you find his backpack? He has a backpack. Purple, I think. Lots of buttons."

"No backpack," Hadid said, making a note. "He only had this little plastic wallet on him. The one with your number on a piece of paper in it. And a Metrocard and debit card."

"Any eyewitnesses?"

"No."

"But it's the slashers, right? Or slasher?" Tony said. "That makes the third killing in a month. But before that, two people got slashed and survived. What did they say about whoever slashed them?"

Petrosino rubbed his mustache and spoke through his hands. "Unfortunately, I cannot go into details about this or any other cases."

"That sounds like public relations speak," Tony said. "Listen, be honest with me, I'm a reporter, well, kind of sort of a reporter, and—"

"Jesus, Mary, and Joseph," Petrosino said, palming his face.

"I mean, I work—worked—with Patrick at the *Williamsburg Sentinel*. Only part-time, but—"

"I'm sorry, Mr. Moran. I think we're done here. If you have any official case-related questions, you can contact our press department."

"This is ridiculous," Tony said. "It's only the *Williamsburg Sentinel*. It's not the *Times*. It's not even *Greenline*."

Hadid steered Tony away from the body. "You've identified the body, and we thank you for taking the time and coming down. We and the City of New York are sincerely sorry for the loss of your friend."

Tony stopped in place. He wasn't in favor of being steered. "'The City of New York?' Do they make you say that?"

They didn't exactly throw him out. They just hovered closely and authoritatively until he was near the exit. Petrosino gave him his card and shook his hand, and Tony said he would try to find contact information for Patrick's family. Hadid nodded and Tony nodded back.

As Tony walked outside the hospital, the humidity of the night covered him like slime. A couple walked past him, the man gingerly cupping his own ass, the woman calling him a baby and carrying a half-melted bag of ice.

CHAPTER NINE

Taxis were once rare to see in Williamsburg, but more than a few passed by Tony as he walked home. He would have loved a ride, by taxi or car service or Uber, no matter the amount of *reggaeton* and pungent car deodorizer. But his wallet echoed with emptiness, and there was no train or bus going in that direction. So he walked, slowly and with steady perspiration. It was almost four in the morning.

He thought about checking Facebook for leads on Patrick's family, but he had a feeling he should keep his eyes and ears on the sidewalks and streets in front of him. He headed for home, but when he was halfway there he veered instead toward the *Sentinel* offices. He figured he would find the information he needed there. It wasn't that he had been friends with Patrick, or that he'd ever liked him very much. But no one should sit in a morgue like unclaimed baggage.

The air conditioning was off on Sundays, so the offices were warm enough to serve as a low oven. He went over to Patrick's desk. It felt eerie to sit there, a dead man's desk, as if the touch of death covered everything. *Ridiculous.*

Tony booted up the PC. The *Sentinel's* computers were more than five years old, ancient by computer standards, so they took a while to come to life. When the screen came on, Tony faced a password prompt. *Ridiculous.* Why did Patrick bother to put a password on a computer at the *Sentinel*?

A halo of neatly aligned Post-It notes framed Patrick's monitor. One or two had notes on it that seemed like passwords (such as "Awesomesauce!"), but they didn't work. He tried to guess. "Skateboard." "Patchouli." "Ginger." Nothing. He even tried "PASSWORDSARESTUPID5000" to no avail.

There was nothing helpful on the desk, so Tony looked through the drawers for anything that could be an address book or a password. It was a violation of privacy, but he guessed Patrick didn't have any privacy anymore. *Who did?* His hands were slippery with sweat, and paper stuck to him. Pay stubs and paper clips in the top right-hand drawer. In the middle drawer was a box with what looked like dozens of flash drives, neatly arranged and with a number written on masking tape around each one. He would say Patrick was paranoid about losing work, but the *Sentinel* computers did have a tendency to go comatose.

In the bottom drawer were file folders, *Sentinel* story pitches, clippings. There was one particularly thick folder at the back. At a glance, Tony saw that it contained information about the missing person case of Rosa Irizarry. He pulled that folder out on the desk and kept digging.

In the bottom of the left-side drawer, he struck gold—a Christmas card, paper-clipped to an envelope behind it. Tony picked it up—a snapshot slid out. He picked it up off the dusty linoleum floor. An older burly man in flannel standing next to an older woman in a black and white wool sweater. The card was signed, "Hope to see you sooner than later. Merry Christmas, Love, Mom & Dad."

He turned over the envelope. The Stollers lived in Allentown, Pennsylvania. Tony thought of coal mines and Billy Joel—that's everything he knew about Allentown. But there was the address.

"Optime."

He called information and got their number. He tapped it in but stopped before hitting the call button. He looked at the couple's photo. It was very early in the morning, and he imagined waking them up, breaking the horrible news, tears, wailing, questions upon questions. Not something he was in the mood to go through. Instead, he called Detective Petrosino.

"Thank you," Petrosino said. "But we tracked them down ourselves. We're the police. We do that."

"Well, that's it then, I guess."

"Mr. Moran, just wanted to let you know: I told them the Stoller family were kind enough to come down and ID their son, so they asked for your number. Since you guys were friends, I figured it was okay for me to give it to them. Okay with you?"

Tony looked at his phone and silently cursed the detective.

"So, is that okay?" Petrosino said.

"Sure. Why not?" Tony said. "That's great."

When he got up to leave, he shut off Patrick's computer. He said, "*Requiescat in pace,* Patrick," and then he looked at the Irizarry file. He was going to put it back in the desk. What was he going to do with it, after all? But then he decided *What the hell* and put it in his bag.

Tony finally made it home to his basement apartment on South 4th Street at just past 6 a.m. A bright (if he turned on all the lights) and spacious (if he were a dwarf) studio, close to transportation (under a mile), supermarket (bodega), and restaurants (affordable if he decided not to pay rent). No pets (but rodents seemed okay). He put his bag by his small metal desk and tossed his clothes on top of other ones on the faux parquet floor.

He thought he should take a shower, but he sniffed himself and figured it could wait. He plopped onto his futon, bought off of Craigslist and barely used ("There's a stain, so I knocked off twenty bucks," the ad said), and tried to fade into sleep.

He closed his eyes and saw Patrick's shredded face. He tried to think of other things: the asinine poetry he'd heard at the reading, the look on Magaly's face as she said good night, the weather, upcoming pétanque tournaments, draft beer, puppy dogs. Slowly he began to relax.

Then his phone rang.

"Hello, is this Tony Moran?" said an older man's voice. It sounded beaten, tired.

Tony didn't recognize the voice and hoped it was a dream.

"Hello? Hello?" the voice said. "This is Ken Stoller, Patrick's father."

"Mr. Stoller," Tony mumbled. He knew he should say something, the expected condolences, but he didn't know what to say that would mean anything.

"Yes, Tony. Well, the police, they called us this morning, and, well...I, I wanted to...to thank you for...doing what you did for my son. I'm glad a friend was there."

Tony said, "No problem," and he winced as soon as he said it.

"He mentioned you many times. You were a good friend."

"Sure thing." Tony winced again.

Stoller said, "Tony, I wonder if I could ask a favor of you."

Tony could tell from the thickness in his voice that the old man had been crying. And he knew that whatever the old man was going to say, he was going to want to say "No."

Ken Stoller said, "We're, uh, we're driving up this morning. Hopefully, there won't be too much traffic. We'd love to meet you while we're in town."

"Oh," Tony said, fumbling. "Yeah, I think I'm going to be pretty busy this week actually."

"That's too bad." Stoller sounded disappointed. "It would've been great to meet you. Well, maybe you could help us move Patrick's—his stuff. We have to pack it up, you see."

Before he could stop himself, Tony said, "Sure. Maybe."

Afterward, Tony sank back into the futon, feeling like an ass but not so much that it stopped the train of exhaustion from running him over and dragging him to sleep.

CHAPTER TEN

In the parking lot of the 90th precinct police headquarters, Detective Hadid held his arms out to the sides, hoping to get a breeze to pass under his armpits and cool him off, even just a little. His polyester knit tie felt like a battle rope around his neck, and his socks felt wet. It was only nine in the morning, and the day was already damned hot. Brooklyn felt hotter than the Bronx, for sure. He wondered why that was and made a mental note to google it later, once they got inside.

"It sure is hot, brother," Hadid said. "Hot enough to melt shoe leather. I feel like I'm going to turn to steam."

"Thanks for the weather report," his partner said.

The precinct building sat ugly and blunt on a triangle of land, surrounded by ninety-nine-cent stores, closed storefronts, and one fast food joint after another. Woodhull Hospital was a short distance away, and in less than two weeks in the 90th, they had been back and forth over there so much Hadid thought it should be annexed. Maybe they could build a bridge connecting them. An enclosed, air-conditioned bridge.

In the meantime, he had to stand there because his partner Petrosino was taking his sweet time with a cigarette.

"I can't believe people still smoke," Hadid said.

"Everyone needs a bad habit," Petrosino said, exhaling a cloud of cancer.

"You should really quit."

"Oh, I've quit. At least five times. I felt good and healthy. I could walk up a flight of stairs without wheezing."

"You see."

"I was never so bored in my life."

Hadid was pretty sure his new partner didn't like him so much, and he thought he knew why. But he was a friendly guy, after all, everybody liked him once they got to know him. He said, "Hey, thanks again for that apartment lead, Petr—. Uh, it's tiny and parking is hell, and that blue discount sure helps out."

"Glad to hear it." Petrosino took out a comb and touched up his helmet of white hair.

"Yeah, it's got tin ceilings and crown molding and—"

"Uh huh."

"—the bathroom is cozy, but the plumbing needs work. My wife's going to love it when sh—"

"Yeah, that's great. Come on." Petrosino chucked his spent cigarette onto the sidewalk. "Handsome is waiting for us."

They went into the precinct building—Hadid felt the cool air enveloping him. "Ah. That's the good stuff," he said—and they walked up to the second floor, where Petrosino put a toothpick in his mouth and knocked on the frame of an open door.

A tall African-American man in a pinstriped suit was on his cell phone. He waved them in.

"I looked at a property this morning. Right off the park. Amazing views, amazing," the man said. "Yes, we have the place in Forest Hills, a lovely Tudor, three-bedroom. But the commute can be a drag. Traffic and the like, especially on late nights...this is going to be more than a little pied-à-terre for me. It's also an investment for the future...Of course. Of course... Yes. Exactly. But when this thing gets moving, it's going to move fast, so I want to give you a high sign so we get all our ducks in a row...Absolutely. Absolutely. Oh, I forgot to tell you the best part: garage. I get hard just saying it: garage."

Hadid noted there were lots of pictures of this guy on the wall: one of him trying to look fierce in goggles and a paintball rifle. Hadid sneered inside. A sport for idiots who don't know how to handle a gun. Then there were pictures with the mayor, with the chief of police, with Sylvester Stallone, George W. Bush, and was that Mel Brooks? Beneath that was a small red and blue flag with a white cross in the middle, and a menorah made out of *Star Wars* characters.

The man hung up and said, "So, if it isn't the 'Christmas Cop' and his partner. I caught your picture online. How are you, Petrosino? You look good."

The two shook hands, and Hadid thought that Petro looked at this guy the way Petro looked at him. Like, not in a happy-to-see-you way.

Petrosino turned to him and said, "Detective Hadid, this here's Lieutenant Esteban Tuchman, precinct gang task force leader."

Esteban? Hadid noted. Okay, so not African-American but maybe Spanish, but maybe both and something else? That last name.

"A pleasure," said Tuchman, shaking Hadid's hand. "I'll save you the trouble. I'm a Dominican Jew."

"No, why would I—"

Tuchman grinned widely and cut him off. "You transferred down from Mott Haven, I hear? Vice."

"Yeah, yeah. Wife wanted to be closer to her family and whatnot, so."

"Fantastic," Tuchman said. "Now you might think of this as a rank-pulling exercise, but you can be assured that it is not. It's what the mayor wants, what the commissioner wants, what the chief wants, so it's what we want."

"Right-o." Petrosino chewed hard on the toothpick he had in his mouth. "You show me yours, I'll show you mine."

"Exactly." Tuchman picked up a small statue from his desk. It took Hadid a second to realize it was a well-worn Batman figure. "This meeting is in the spirit of twenty-first-century police work, to ensure that information, leads, hunches, what have you, are all being shared, for complete and utter transparency."

Hadid said, "But if you got the report, we already showed you ours."

"But it's so much better to hear from the horses' mouths," Tuchman said, pointing the Batman at them.

"I guess we'll go first," Petrosino said. "The news has been reporting only about the recent attacks. But we've had reports for at least a year about people on bicycles with a machete. Buzzing people. Cutting bag straps. Defacing property. All relatively juvenile stuff. About two months ago, we saw an escalation.

"On April 13, Maxine Channing, twenty-three, at the corner of Broadway and Berry Street. Slashed, both hands, very deep. Lucky her, she had her phone up to her face, or else she might have lost a nose. She fell back, didn't see the guy. Too fast, she said. But she did say she thought the bike was red.

"On May 3, Elijah Sackler, twenty-seven, South 9th Street, cut deep across the left leg. Lost a lot of blood. He remembers the bike disappearing around a corner. He says the bike was green, by the way.

"On May 10, we get our first fatality. Ty Nelson, twenty-five, on North 10th, walking home from Teddy's. Got it right in the back of the neck. Died on the spot. Our guess is whoever slashed him was not on a bike. The street's pretty narrow, so either he got off his bike or was on foot. Still, it was one blow."

"Then on May 25, Murray Hewitt, one superficial slash across the head and then stabbed in the back, right through the kidney. DOA at Woodhull. We're still waiting to hear confirmation about the size and shape of the blade, but it is looking like the same weapon. Also, one witness, who didn't see the attack but saw someone speeding away from the area of the crime on a Citibike."

"And then just this Saturday, things escalated like a rocket. Patrick Stoller, twenty-six, on North 3rd and Kent. He got slashed to pieces."

Hadid piped in: "Coroner estimates thirty-seven wounds."

"Right-o. Thirty-seven," Petrosino said, not looking at him. "Otherwise, the M.O. looks to be the same. These all took place late at night, in spots where there were few to no other people around. The attacks all took place incredibly fast, so the few people who were around saw very little."

Tuchman twirled with the Batman in his fingers. "And so what's your conclusion, detective?"

"I know we have conflicting reports on the color of the bicycle, but eyewitnesses are notoriously unreliable," Petrosino said. "My gut tells me this is a lone whack job who started out small, testing the waters, and is getting braver and braver."

"And what's this hack j—excuse me—this *whack* job's motive, do you think?"

"I think maybe he's got a bone to pick with these hipsters, for whatever reason. He started with scaring them. That used to be enough. But now he's actively hacking them to death. Look, all the victims are young and white, mostly male. We don't need Langley to get a profile going. This is basic stuff."

"Is it?" Tuchman said. He finally put down the stupid Batman.

"I bet you've got a theory," Petrosino said.

"You know me too well, Jimmy. Detective Hadid, you're from the Bronx."

Hadid sat up. He didn't realize he had been slouching. "Actually I'm from Long Island, but I was stationed in the Bronx. Melville, originally, then we moved to Massapequa."

"Great. You get some heavy-duty gang action up there. In the Bronx, I mean."

"Oh, sure. Let me tell you," Hadid said, "these gangstas and wannabees, I think we should put them all in a stadium and let them fight it out to the death. Clean up the streets one-two-three." He laughed to himself, then he realized no one else was laughing.

Tuchman just nodded. "While gang situations can often seem untenable, we have found what I feel are more effective ways to deal with gangs in this part of the city."

Hadid took out his notepad and made a quick note to look up the word "untenable."

Tuchman smiled broadly and then took a deep breath, like he was getting ready to give a speech. "Just to get you up to speed, Detective Hadid, in the 90th, the primary gang organizations are the Trinitarios, DDP, the Latin Kings, MS-13, and the Southside Quistadoreys, who the largest and most violent. These gangs all have initiation rituals, some involving beatings of the new member by all the other members, and some involving some random act of violence, for no reason but to show if the new member has the guts. What you're describing to me is obviously a series of gang attacks, most likely initiation rites."

Petrosino shook his head. "I was thinking along the same lines, until they started to kill people."

Tuchman placed the toy figure down right in front of himself, facing them. "Okay. I hear you. But the M.O. of these gangs is to terrorize the neighborhood. These gangs want us to think they're in charge. Let me share this with you: Eladio Cortés, one of the prime movers in the local Quistadoreys, was released from Sing Sing eight months ago and we know he found his way right back to the 'hood. Cortés is one vicious motherfucker. He was serving time for aggravated assault with a deadly weapon, but he's suspected of at least fifteen murders on his scorecard."

"Guys like that get out of jail all the time," Petrosino said. "Why connect this to him?"

"Wanting to reassert his power, no doubt," Tuchman said. "But here's the tickler: At Cortés's trial, the lone witness against him was a white dude, in his twenties. Some dude who had just moved into Cortés's apartment building."

Hadid saw where this was going. "Anybody know where this dude is now? Is he one of our vics?"

"He moved to Cali and works for a software company now. But the point is Cortés could be trying to even the score in a general way. You know: 'Kill all the white dudes.'"

Hadid looked at his partner, and he didn't seem to be buying it. "That's a stretch," Petrosino said.

"Look, these slashings are Gang Tactics 101. I'm absolutely, absolutely certain that Cortés and the Quistadoreys are responsible. We know who they are. My people identify these gangstas ASAP, and then we circle them like sharks, all day, every day. Normally, they can't go to the toilet without us being there to watch them wipe their asses."

"Ain't that an image," Petrosino said.

"I say 'normally.' But the thing of it is—"

"You can't find him," said Hadid.

Tuchman knocked over his figurine and picked it up again. "It pains me to say it, but yes, exactly. Of course, I would appreciate you guys keeping your eyes and ears open for him."

"Anything else?" Petrosino said. "If we're gonna have to coordinate, I'd like to know as soon as possible, so I can phone, tell the wife I'll be stuck in meetings all day. No offense."

Hadid turned to look at his partner and realized he wasn't all nicotine and hairspray.

"None taken," said Tuchman, a really obnoxious smirk on his face. He placed his elbows on the desk and clasped his hands together. "Now, keep your investigation low key. We don't want the public to think that this neighborhood is suddenly a gang war zone. For now, we tell the press this is a string of coincidental separate attacks. No need for anyone to panic. Everyone go back to sipping lattes and shopping online. That's our play. You understand?"

"Right-o."

"My task force will do the heavy lifting, but per the chief, you will work with us on this, looking for witnesses, interviewing locals, running leads. And I'd personally like you to help us chat up some gangbangers we think have intel."

"Anything else?"

"And send me a report at the end of each day."

"Why did I ask?"

Tuchman smiled and stood up, making it clear to Hadid that the meeting was over.

"And as always, always keep the lines of communication open," Tuchman said. "And, Jimmy, I'll try not to inundate you with unnecessary meetings."

Hadid followed his partner out of the office and quickly down the stairs. "So, what now, partner?"

"I'm going out for a smoke. Maybe two," Petrosino said. "But you stay here. I don't want you to evaporate."

CHAPTER ELEVEN

To Tony, community board meetings in Williamsburg played out like professional wrestling matches: an uninterrupted series of chest-thumping, sleeper holds, and foregone conclusions. Amid the free-for-alls over affordable rents, new developments, and zoning, and cage matches over club licenses and liquor licenses, everyone understood ahead of time that the tag teams of developers and their political lackeys were going to walk away with the belt. The community organizers and housing advocates knew they would spend most of their time being smacked into a turnbuckle or crushed and twisted on the mat. Still, they showed up to fight. Which was, to Tony's mind, either very stupid or very foolish. All this action took place at the Swinging 60s Senior Center, a squat cinder block building on Ainslie Street.

Community affairs were Patrick's beat for the *Sentinel*, but with him gone, Bobbert Swiatowski, the *Sentinel* publisher, told Tony to cover the next meeting. It meant he would have to pay attention to the issues, but Tony didn't want to pay attention to the issues.

"C'mon, you're a good reporter," Bobbert had said. "And I can't get anybody else."

"I love the vote of confidence. How about triple the rate then?"

"Triple! I could do it myself then."

"But you don't want to. Double then. Do we have a deal?"

"Deal. Thief."

Tony found himself entering the shaky metal doors of the Swinging 60s Senior Center. At least the air conditioning was good. And there was free bottled water.

He put one bottle in his messenger bag and was opening up another to drink when he heard a familiar voice call behind him.

"Chino!"

He turned, spilling water on his shirt.

"Magaly!"

"I don't see you in years, then it's two times in one week," she said. Her thick, curly hair was barely tamed in a ponytail. She wore red plastic-frame glasses, the same design she'd had since she was a teenager. He guessed it wasn't what she used to call a "contacts-worthy day."

"Are you stalking me?" she said.

Tony stammered some meaningless noise.

"You know, I was going to say, you look the same," she said. "You never change."

"It's the Botox," he managed to say.

"Yep. Still the same. Listen, I heard about Patrick. I knew him. He was really a nice guy. It's terrible what happened," she said. "These slashings are crazy. It's why I don't stay out late anymore."

"Yeah, I had to ID his body at the hospital. He's looked better."

"Oh my god, you're horrible," she said.

"You're right. It was actually pretty rough."

"Oh, Chino, I'm sorry," she put a hand on his chest. "Come, the meeting's starting. Sit with me."

Magaly directed them to seats near the front, by the aisle. The room was crowded, and Tony wondered if it was because of the issues or the air-conditioning. There were a bunch of people who looked like they needed to be seen as important seated at the long table at the front of the room.

"I haven't been to one of these in a very long time," he said. "Who are the gasbags?"

"See the man with the goatee almost in front of you, that's

Congressman Pedro Alvarado. More handsy than an octopus and more corrupt than the MTA. Next to him, that's Representative Camila Santiago. I've hated her from day one, and day one was four terms ago. She's tacky—yellow shoes, Chino! Yellow shoes!" Magaly seemed to be trying to whisper, but it was not something she was capable of doing.

"What's on the agenda?"

"Most of the time it's deciding who to give liquor licenses to. There's another high-rise development going up. They give all this lip-service about affordable housing, but you should see what they think affordable is."

"Ridiculous."

"You said it. Hey, are you free for dinner after this?"

Tony thought about the thinness of his wallet. He knew she liked pizza. Maybe they would just get pizza. "Sure," he said.

During the meeting, several liquor licenses were indeed approved, and then there was a fierce debate over a development whose claim of low-income housing seemed extremely specious. A line of attendees queued up to speak to the board, including Magaly's boss, Luis De Moscoso. He wore the same shiny suit he'd had on the night at the poetry reading. He must have snuck in to the meeting late. Tony hadn't seen him come in.

"As all of you know," De Moscoso said, "I represent El Flamboyan, Brooklyn's most comprehensive Latino cultural and community advocacy center. I have spoken at these esteemed gatherings before, but I like to keep coming back and continue speaking truth to power."

"Snooze," Tony whispered.

Magaly pinched his thigh. "Shhh. Don't be a hater."

"Me? I don't hate your boyfriend."

"Yes, I know you too well. He's just a friend."

"I always let friends touch my ass."

"Shhh." She pinched his thigh hard enough to make his eyes water.

De Moscoso went on. "You guys are talking about putting in

more apartment complexes, putting in new bars and new restaurants. But what I'm not hearing about is the people. What
about the people? The people who have been here for over fifty
years. The people who have invested their lives and their culture
and their blood in the very fabric of this neighborhood. They're
disappearing. We have to keep their culture alive. Now it's fading, not just in the Southside, but in all of Williamsburg because
almost everyone has moved out. When you wake up one morning and you see the corner bodega has been replaced by another
fancy new coffee shop or bistro, and you see your neighbors
being pushed out because they can no longer afford the rent,
and all of a sudden your friends have disappeared into thin air,
you begin to wonder 'Am I next?'"

A cluster of people in the back applauded. Tony idly wondered if they'd been paid.

De Moscoso went on. "These developments, the rezonings,
they are nothing but racist weapons of mass displacement used
to push out the poor and all the long-term residents of color."

There was another rush of applause, much louder this time.

Tony said, "Seems like somebody likes to hear himself talk."

"That's for sure," Magaly said, "but he's not wrong."

Despite De Moscoso's plea, and the mood in the room being
decidedly against the new complex, it was approved by the
Community Board anyway.

Before the end of the meeting, Congressman Alvarado ad-
dressed the recent slashings but said he would take no questions. "My friends at the 90th Precinct are doing their best and
working on some very good leads." He then quoted statistics
that made the neighborhood sound as safe and peaceful as an
empty church. Then he said everyone should continue enjoying
their lives and feeling safe. Then he added, "Go, Nets!"

As people were getting up, Magaly said, "Let's go while my
boss is busy working the room."

"Why? Could there be drama? Drama's fun."

"Chino! Let's go."

CHAPTER TWELVE

"I haven't been here in years," Tony said, "but it looks like there's a private party."

Through the windows, a crowd of people were standing and drinking to salsa music. They had walked from the meeting to Gloria's Spanish Food, at the corner of Grand Street and Union Avenue. The place had been there for as long as Tony could remember. The food was excellent, but he remembered they had increased their prices in recent years. It was definitely not a pizzeria. His wallet sighed.

"I don't see a sign," Magaly said. "Do you see a sign? I think we can go in."

Before he could say anything, she had opened to the door.

A short woman in jeans and a T-shirt that read "Gloria's Spanish Food—The Best" came up to them immediately.

"*Hola, Gloria!*" Magaly said. "Is this a private party?"

"*Hola, mi amor.*" The old woman kissed Magaly on the cheek and said, "No, it's a going-out-of-business party. Everything on the menu is half off."

Tony nodded. "So they're going to turn this into some hipster bar?"

"Who knows?" Gloria said. "They're knocking down the building."

"Oh."

"I don't care. I'm moving to Florida."

The place was small, the walls paneled in wood, and the

panels covered with clocks shaped like Puerto Rico, maracas with the Puerto Rican flag on them, a framed poster that read "*Borinquen. Donde he nacido yo*"—Puerto Rico. Where I Was Born—pictures of Luquillo Beach, coquis, and Pedro Albizu Campos. People were crowded into the aisles, some drinking from plastic cups, some dancing to the salsa, some doing both. Tony and Magaly spotted an empty two-seater squeezed into a corner by the kitchen door. Tony plopped into the seat away from the door traffic.

He caught Magaly shaking her head but didn't know why. She sighed and said, "I remember when you used to hold the chair for me when I sat down."

"Yeah, before you yelled at me for being a sexist Neanderthal."

"I was so radical then," she said, laughing. "Remember that white girl you ended up dating after me. What happened to her?"

"She thought I wasn't ready for a relationship."

"Imagine that. Maybe you gave her the 'fat is good' lecture too many times."

"Fat *is* good for you. You can't live without fat. A lot of people don't realize that their bodies need fat. In fact—"

She held up a hand. "Chino! I heard it already. *Ai,* I'm so sad about this place closing. It's like a kick in the gut. There are so few Boricua food places left around here. I don't think people understand how emotionally exhausting it is to constantly see your community being knocked down and replaced!"

Tony said, "The other day I walked by my old barbershop. It's a Thai fusion place now, whatever that is. I used to go there to get my fades. I can't believe I used to get fades."

"The Southside is all bars and restaurants now, everywhere! These white people don't cook!"

"Or they're foodies or, worse, vegans."

"Exactly. So I can't get my cheap lettuce anymore at the supermarket."

"But you can get kale now."

"Who the hell likes kale?" she said. "No one! Not really. Anyone who says they like kale is a liar."

"There's no point in getting upset about it. The people with the money have the power and the privilege and always win. *Semper idem.*"

"So just lay back and enjoy it while your community gets erased, you mean? No thank you, Mr. Sunshine."

Tony rolled his eyes. "I'm just being realistic. By the way, I think my thigh is going to be black and blue where you pinched it."

Magaly laughed. "Good!"

The owner came over and gave them two cocktails.

"We didn't order this," Magaly said.

"On the house! Rum and coke. *Disfrúta!*"

Tony brought the plastic cup to his lips. "My god, I'm getting a buzz just from smelling it."

"I love it," Magaly said, taking a good sip. "So, what do you do? You still playing bocce almost every day in the park?"

"It's pétanque."

"It's the same thing, Chino."

"It's not the same thing."

"It looks the same."

"The strategy is completely different. You should see us play."

"If I want to take a nap in the park, sure."

"What have you been up to? How's the family?" he said, changing the subject and mentally preparing for the long monologue he knew would follow.

Magaly told him about how her parents still lived on the same old apartment building, still together after many years on-again, off-again, and all his abusive behavior, they didn't want to leave a place they'd known for so many years, and her half-brother's wife might have AIDS, might not, they were drug users for over twenty years, met in a shelter, fell in love, her sister looked like a man trying to look like a woman but hated being called "transgender." "I don't get it," Magaly said. Her other sister was happily married to a man she was sure was gay, divorced him, and it turned out he had a wife and a whole other family in the Bronx. "Why can't we ever get happily ever after? Does anyone?"

"You're asking me?"

Magaly ordered *bifstec* but changed her mind when she heard Tony ordering *chicharrónes*.

"I haven't had *chicharrónes* in forever," she said. "And I love the way they make them here."

"Then you should have them."

"So, how is the reporting business? I hate to say it, but I lost track. I remember you were at the *Daily News*."

"Yeah, I was a stringer for the *Daily News* for a while, but then I branched out to some other locals, and I did that for as long as I could stand it."

"What happened?"

"Well, number one, editors were telling me, 'Hey, I love your story. But I'll only print it if I can share the byline.' Blackmail! Number two, I wrote at least four stories about our former businessman mayor—you remember him?—and they all got nixed for no reason. One editor told me later that the mayor was too popular, they didn't want to lose readers. Number three, the pay started getting smaller and smaller. I was doing all these interviews, all this research and getting paid less than a barista. After a while, I realized I could make just as much money doing articles I could write in my sleep. In fact, I think I did write a few in my sleep. Now I write for the *Sentinel,* as well as an online content aggregator, and I even edit resumes on the side. Which is probably the most lucrative thing I do. I have a bunch waiting for me at home, but if you want me to look at yours, I'll rush it to the top of the pile at no extra cost. I live check to check, week to week. I just scrape by, but I don't have to answer to anyone, which is exactly how I like it."

Magaly nodded, sucking one of the ice cubes out of her cup and crunching on it. "Listen," she said. "I have to ask: Is your paper going to do anything about Rosa Irizarry? It's almost a full year since her disappearance."

"Funny you should ask. I had been talking to Patrick about her, and he said he was going to do something. My mother knew her, too, not well, but they came to the neighborhood about the same time."

"You should do the story then."

"Yeah, right. First of all, I don't know very much about it."

"Don't you read the articles in your own paper?"

Tony shrugged. "It wasn't in my section."

"¡Carajo!"

"Come on, tell me about it."

"Well, she was a really sweet old lady—okay, not always so sweet. She could get mean. She threw a spoon at me once when I went to counsel her. She was being harassed by her landlord to move out."

"She had a rent-controlled apartment?"

"Yes, they are as rare as a unicorn or an honest politician," she said.

"Or a unicorn riding an honest politician."

"Exactly, and that's $250 a month when some hipster or yuppie would be willing to pay five, six, seven times that for the same space. They could do a basic 'upgrade'—new fridge, paint job—and then shoot the price up to market value. That's why they wanted her out."

"Urban renewal."

"First, it was the usual tactics. They turned off her heat. They turned off her hot water and then all her water. But that lady toughed it out. She grew up in the mountains, so that was nothing for her. And then they had the nerve to start putting roaches and then rats in her house! And this was a lady who prided herself on being *immaculate* immaculate. Not a crumb in the house. But she would wake up and there'd be roaches all over her floor, on the walls."

"All very illegal. So what did she do?"

"She complained and complained, and they did nothing. So she came to us, and we were able to get the heat and water turned back on, and to get them to call an exterminator."

"But that wasn't the end of it."

"No," Magaly said, obviously just warming. "Wait till you hear this. This was the worst thing. There was a fire in her apartment—a very suspicious fire—and she had to leave for a year and live with her sister till they repaired the damage."

"Did they repair it?"

"Ha! No. But she went back anyway. The kitchen ceiling and cabinets were burned, and it stank like smoke. But this lady was like a tiger. She went in there and cleaned it up as best she could. That was her home, dammit."

"And that's when she vanished?"

"A few weeks after moving back in, she was going to a party to celebrate her birthday. But she never showed up. Can you believe it? Disappeared on her birthday. No one ever heard from her again."

"And Patrick did some stories on her. That I know."

"Well, she lived in his building. He took it upon himself to try to find out what happened."

Tony rolled his eyes. "Trying for a Pulitzer."

"Well, at least he tried. But I think after a while he gave up too. The police never found anything, but if you ask me it was the building owners who got rid of her. But there was never any proof. Now the place has been renovated—barely—and it's being rented at $2,100."

"Who owns that building?"

"It's co-owned. Tomasello Management is one owner. They manage or own half the buildings in the neighborhood and Greenpoint. Italian. That's Mafia. You know that has to be Mafia."

"That's ridiculous. Maybe some of these guys have watched

The Godfather too much, but that's it."

"And the other owner of the building is Elias Litvinchouk."

"That name is familiar," Tony said, flipping through his memory. "But it couldn't be the same person."

"Are you going to follow up on the story?"

"Sure. A little anniversary story. I'll get a couple new quotes. Easy money."

"No, no, I mean you have to find out what happened to her?"

"Why would I do that? How would I do that?"

"You used to want to do this stuff. Without Patrick around, who is going to bother? The *Daily News* doesn't care. The *New York Times* doesn't care. The *New York Post* certainly doesn't care."

"Listen, Magaly, I'm a hack. I write about high school softball games and gallery openings—oh, and I do horoscopes—for a neighborhood rag that exists more to run local real estate ads than anything else."

"And you waste your time playing in the park every day."

"What more could anyone want out of life?"

"What the hell, Chino? This is important. This is your community." Her voice was rising. This was very familiar to Tony.

"I'm my community," he said.

"What happened to you? All you want to do is play with your balls now."

"Funny."

"I expected to see your byline in the *New York Times*. I look for it all the time."

"Nothing happened. I've always been this way."

"No, you weren't. You wanted to make a difference and write about real issues. What happened?"

"I grew up. Have you not been paying attention to the state of the world? There are no journalists you can trust. There are no causes to champion. There's no way to win."

"So you don't believe in anything?"

"I believe that this beer is flat. And I would like another not-flat beer. That's what I believe." Tony tried to get the waitress's attention, but she couldn't see him behind all the dangling artwork.

"You're just cynical."

"'*Mordacitas modus iniucundus veritatis dicendae est.*' 'Cynicism is an unpleasant way of saying the truth.'"

She shook her head. "Who is that? Aristotle?"

"Aristotle? No, Lillian Hellman," Tony said.

"Poor baby. Can't change the world in a day."

"The world never changes."

"Somebody has to do something," she said.

"That somebody is not me."

Tony was grateful that the food arrived then.

After they ate, Magaly paid for the meal. "I invited, so I pay," she said.

"If there's a gene for pride, and there probably is, I don't have it. I won't argue."

Before they left, Tony took pictures with his phone of the people still crowding the aisles.

"Pictures?" Magaly said.

"I'm sentimental."

Outside, Magaly pointed out the additional street sign under the Grand Street sign. "Borinquen Plaza," she said, sighing dramatically. "How long before they change that?"

They walked slowly to Magaly's building on Driggs Avenue, a former theater renovated long ago into a tenement—the sole reminder of its history was a baroque sign ("Novelty Court") carved in stone above the entryway. Twenty-nine units, no washer/dryers allowed.

Magaly was quiet on the way, so Tony knew she was upset. But he didn't have the magic words to make her feel better. He had never had them.

Tony said, "You know this is the same building where Serpico was shot? Right in the kisser."

"I told you that years ago."

"Yeah, actually you did, didn't you? Thank you for dinner, by the way."

"My pleasure. Well, have a good night, Chino. It was nice to see you again." She kissed him on the cheek and went in through the gated door of the building.

Tony watched her walk through the second gated door and down the marble hallway, her hair bouncing in the dim light. She looked twenty-two all over again, and he felt twenty-two all over again. *Id est*. Clumsy and foolish, that is. It made him want to kick himself in the balls.

He walked home, hoping there was beer waiting in the fridge. To forget about Magaly. And because he'd been having trouble sleeping. He'd found that lately every time he closed his eyes, he saw Patrick's shredded face.

CHAPTER THIRTEEN

Yogi Johnson sat on a plastic milk crate and exhaled slow plumes of wispy ganja smoke out of the back window. Blowing cannabis clouds outside was a habit he'd picked up while living with his second wife, who said she didn't want their apartment to smell like roadkilled skunk or a seventeen-year-old's basement cave. Or was that his first wife who'd said that? One was Elaine and the other was Ellen, so he got them confused all the time.

It was something o'clock in the morning—he was vaguely sure it was still morning—and he was thinking he would head over to McCarren Park in a bit, see if anyone was around for a few games of pétanque.

The window faced north to the low, flat horizon of Queens. Yogi lived in a one-bedroom railroad apartment in a three-story, pre-war row house covered in chocolate-milk-brown vinyl siding. Large windows! Bright and quiet! Great closet space! And down outside, in the building's backyard and in the velvety summer heat, was Mr. McShane, the landlord and super, tending to his wilting garden.

"One can't grow flowers from a stone, Mr. McShane," Yogi said to himself, then giggled. "There's no way you're going to harvest the joy. Better to let it rot and hope for something better with the next crop."

At that moment, the old man turned to look up, and Yogi leaped off the crate and onto the floor.

"Fuck. Fuck!" he said and then he laughed, looking up at the ceiling, a long series of half-stifled giggles.

When it passed, Yogi got up and relit his doobie. He ninja-snuck up on his window, crouched and sliding along the wall. He peeked out. The old man was at it again, ripping weeds out with his hands and shoving them into a giant black garbage bag.

Mr. McShane had to be in his late seventies or early eighties, Yogi figured. The building had been in McShane's family for at least three or four or five generations, Yogi wasn't sure, going back to the early 1900s. Yogi was proud of the old man for not going to Florida to die with all the rest of the retirees. *Good for you. Hang in there.* McShane's grandpa had been a cop, Yogi remembered, so he came from tough-as-leather stock. *That's right, hold on, Mr. McShane, it's your neighborhood. Hang on till it bleeds.*

Yogi was wondering if he had already finished all the cheese in the house and was going to go check when he noticed the old man gripping his chest and stomach.

"Oh no!" Yogi said. "No no no no no. Heart attack? Could it be a heart attack? It has to be a heart attack."

The old man didn't look so good. Not good at all. The sun was blazing, and there was no shade. He fell to his knees.

"Get inside. Get inside already," Yogi said, sucking up the last of the joint and getting up wobbly. When he looked back, Mr. McShane was on the ground, clutching his stomach.

"Oh shit!" Yogi took a few strides toward his door, his legs feeling puffy and boneless, then he stopped with his hand on the knob. "Wait. Wait, wait, wait." The old man's front door downstairs would be locked. Only one way to get to him.

Fire escape! Down the fire escape!

Yogi wobbled back to the window and pulled it open all the way and lifted up the screen behind it. He moved his one rubbery leg, then the other onto the fire escape. It was hot under his bare feet, reminding him momentarily of that one time he went firewalking but got badly burned because the two people firewalking in front of him had stopped to take pictures. He was so upset he was ready to—and then he remembered Mr. McShane.

"Hold on! Oh shit. Oh shit. Oh shit." He wobbled down one flight, then he lifted himself up and around to the ladder. It didn't occur to him to unhook it from the top so he could lower it to the ground, so he just started climbing.

"Don't die, old man. Don't die," he said. But he had run out of ladder and dangled ten feet from the ground. "Fortune favors the foolhardy!" he said and let go, landing hard on his naked feet but then tumbling into an old barbecue grill and knocking it over. "Oh shit. Oh shit. Oh shit."

He got up and ran to Mr. McShane, who was lying on his back with his eyes open.

"Oh god, don't be dead, Mr. McShane. Are you dead?"

"My stomach," the old man said.

"Your stomach? Then it's not a heart attack. Is it indigestion then?"

"Hurts all over."

Yogi took his old flip phone—the cheap, pay-as-you-go kind, the only kind he could afford—out of his back pocket. The front of it had a new crack in it from the fall. "Shit!" he said, but it still worked and he dialed 9-1-1.

As he cradled Mr. McShane's head in his lap, Yogi wondered if the old man would stop nagging him about late rent. Yogi didn't live a normal, capitalist-consumerist lifestyle, so money was always a little hard to get together. Or maybe, just maybe, if whatever was happening to Mr. McShane was really, really bad and not just some bad calamari that he ate, the old man would even knock off a month or two of Yogi's rent, just for saving his life.

CHAPTER FOURTEEN

Steven Pak got off the L train at the Bedford Avenue stop and walked slowly up the steps to the exit. He had worked late and afterward had gone out for a few drinks with the guys. His wife Erin let him go out one night per week, and it was a good arrangement. Good for him, good for their marriage. Still, it was only another six weeks to go before the baby arrived, and he felt guilty about having a good time.

How many beers had he had? Three? Four? Six? He was supposed to stick to his usual limit of two pints of Guinness. Creamy Guinness. Beyond that, according to Erin, he became what she called an "atomic tomato face."

Steven paused at the top of the stairs and blinked. People kept bumping into him to get past, so he moved, swaying on the sidewalk.

He didn't want to leave his pregnant wife home alone, and so he hadn't been out with his guy friends in months. But he had needed it. He did, he really did. He hadn't been able to get the memory of that crazy night out of his mind: the man with the machete, hacking away—hacking away casually!—at that guy against the wall.

Every night this week, *every time* he walked home, he would look down toward where it happened on Kent Avenue. Just a few, couple blocks from his building. He felt so guilty about not calling the police. Maybe the guy would have lived. Maybe an ambulance would have gotten there in time to save him.

But Erin was right. She was always right. Why get involved? They were both too busy at work, and then the baby was on the way. And if they came forward now, they would get in trouble. They would get on the news. They'd get interviewed on *Good Morning America*. (Did they pay you to go on *Good Morning America*? They must, because why would you go on otherwise?) And all their friends would Facebook about it, and they would never stop asking them questions. Did you think about helping? Why didn't you go over and do something? Not fight the slasher off—although half the people at work still thought he knew kung fu, the assholes—but at least scare him off, so you could have saved that Stoller guy. Why didn't you do something?

People would hate them.

It would follow them for the rest of their lives.

So they couldn't say anything, couldn't go to the police with a description, with details, because everyone would ask why they waited.

People. Would. Hate. Them.

Bedford Avenue was a beehive of people, a beehive that had been kicked over, and all the people were buzzing. *Buzz buzz buzz*. But when he turned onto North 7th, a mostly residential side street, the crowd thinned out. He was halfway down the block when he thought he heard the ticking of bicycle spokes.

He turned. There were half a dozen bike riders at the corner. It could have been any one of them, although it had sounded closer.

That was the other thing. Had the killer seen them? But even if he had, he didn't know who they were. How would he ever find them? He'd had to stalk around the neighborhood every night, searching and searching through swarms of people. So why was he getting so paranoid?

Steven walked carefully and deliberately down the block, weaving just a little, and heard it again. This time, he could see the bright lights on Bedford Avenue, but the street he was on was poorly lit. He could see nothing on the opposite side. It was draped in darkness.

He kept walking. A little farther along, he thought he saw something out of the corner of his eye, a bike rider on the other side of the street, riding on the sidewalk and not the street. He couldn't see a face, couldn't see the bike very much either.

But his heart began beating fast. He saw a bar a few feet ahead on the right and decided, yes, he would duck in there. Who would follow him in there with a bike? He went in and sat down at the bar and stared at the big front window. Some boy band song from the '90s was playing on the radio.

The bartender behind him asked what he wanted. Without thinking, he ordered another Guinness.

He watched the window. His neck began to hurt, so he turned in his seat, but kept creeping his hand back to pick up the beer. Guinness was so creamy. Like a latte, only better and more loving.

With his eyes on the window—seeing people walking by, one at a time, couples, or groups but no bike riders—he crept his hand behind him to reach for his beer. But instead, he knocked it over with a crash.

"Whoa!" the bartender said.

"I'm sorry. Sorry." Steven blushed. He could feel his face was already flushed from the other beers. Atomic tomato face. "Sorry."

"Don't beat yourself up. It's a bar. Happens all the time, my brother."

Steven helped him clean the mess with wads of napkins. He turned back to the window as soon as he could.

Had he missed something?

Well, sure, he could have missed a whole parade out there.

What was he going to do? Stay there till the morning?

His phone rang. Erin.

"Where are you?"

"I'm at—I don't know the name of this bar."

"How much have you had to drink?"

"Just, just my two pints."

"You'd better! Just kidding! So, when are you coming home, Pancake Panther?"

"I'm having just one more here."

"Uh, one more?"

"Sorry, it's the guys, they're in a partying mood."

"Who's there with you?"

"Oh, you know, the regular group. Phil, Michael, John, Casey."

"Well, tell them you have a wife at home who you knocked up and who needs you home ASAP."

"Okay, I will."

"Tell them now! I want to hear it."

"All right."

"Hey, fellas," Steven said to no one. He saw that the bartender was standing right there, polishing a glass. "I have a wife at home who needs me," Steven said to the bartender.

"Well, then you better go on home," the bartender said.

On the phone, Erin laughed loudly and said, "Who was that? Was that Casey?"

"No, it was Phil."

"It didn't sound like Phil."

"I'm on my way home now, honey. See you soon."

"Yay! Hey, could you bring me a cupcake before you get here."

"The bakery you like is closed. I mean, it's probably closed by now."

"Oh, any old cupcake will do, as long as it's good."

"Okay. I'll get it. See you soon."

He watched the window for a long time. He left a twenty-dollar bill on the bar and didn't look back for his change.

Before he opened the door, he tapped "9-1-1" on his phone and held his thumb over the send button. When a couple walked by, he quickly exited the bar.

He heard nothing and kept walking quickly up the block,

staying close to the couple. They walked most of the way toward his complex.

When he got to his street, he looked all the way down to the area where it had happened that crazy night. Nobody. No killers were there. No one rushing at him on a bike. Just people walking dogs and pushing strollers. Still, he ran across the street and didn't stop until he got to the brilliantly illuminated vestibule of his building. He nodded to the doorman, who was not Angel tonight, for which Steven was very grateful. He didn't need another reminder.

But once Steven was in the elevator, the image of the dead man and the machete man jumped into his mind again. He tried to think of something else and then remembered: the cupcake! But he was not going back out there now. No way. Erin would just have to deal with not having a cupcake. She would just have to.

CHAPTER FIFTEEN

Adam Horvath hailed from a small town called Atlantic in Iowa. He had been raised with fresh air in his lungs and trees, regal and green, on every horizon. He had moved to Billyburg years before, following a swarm of almost two dozen of his peeps from the University of Michigan, happy to be in a city bloated with excitement and money, opportunity and money, and sex and money. But too, too quickly, over just his first summer, he had come to hate the hot, stanking city. How the mosquitoes and the roaches and the fat, green bottle flies seemed to be everywhere, and how during heat waves, the garbage outside restaurants turned sour, chemicals bubbled up through the blacktop smelling like rotten eggs, and what was that funk coming from Newtown Creek?

It got worse every summer, and every summer he considered moving to Colorado, L.A., even San Francisco, or, if every drop of his luck—and his trust fund—dried up, back to the fir-lined roads of Iowa.

He wobbled on crutches along Kent Avenue, just off of North 1st Street, toward the Schaefer Landing, a condo development built on the site of the old beer factory, right on the waterfront. He had busted his foot at McCarren Park Pool the week before.

A stupid show-off dive it was, just to impress Katie, the hottie project manager at his job. They hung out all the time, even though she had a boyfriend. The dive must have looked good, maybe even graceful. But then he bounced off of some obese black dude and did a wild somersault, smacking his right foot into the pool edge. Three out of five metatarsals *snapped*.

It was past midnight and still hot. Flies everywhere. He could feel the crutch saddle fermenting a swamp in his left armpit. And he was drunk, too, very drunk, after celebrating—in the middle of the week—the launch of a new ad campaign he had pitched and helped design—*all while in a cast!* Katie had been there at the bar, egging him on to do one more Irish Car Bomb, looking incredible in a supertight Wonder Woman T-shirt, her hands stroking the wood of his crutches. Her boyfriend gave him dirty looks the whole time, made snarky comments. *Too bad for you, bro.*

Then they finally left, the boyfriend's patience ended, and he dragged a drunk Katie out of there. "See you, Monday," she'd said, wink-winking.

Monday, sure, yeah, yeah, and maybe after a few more late nights with the gang from work and maybe once, maybe twice alone he'd be able to tap that, take her back to his condo, impress her with his uniquely spacious layout and private balcony with a view to die for. That boyfriend of hers was way too much of a douche. She deserved better. At least for a little while.

He was looking forward to getting some *zzzz*s when some dude on a bicycle buzzed him, knocking one of his crutches away, almost pushing him to the ground.

"What the f—?" Horvath said, wobbling. He leaned heavily on his other crutch. In his liquor-lined brain, he grasped that he might possibly be in trouble, and then the first slash came. No way this was happening. The dude had gotten off his bike. In his hand, he had—*Holy shit! Was that a machete? Oh no! Like in the news feed!*

The dude raised the blade.

"Shit!" Horvath said. He threw a crutch sideways and it landed right back next to him. "Fuck off, man. You're not getting any of my shit. Fuck off!"

The biker came close and whispered, "Die, yuppie scum." And then he brought the machete down hard. Like a butcher on a particularly stubborn bone.

Horvath thought that he couldn't die, that this wasn't his time. His parents would be crushed. He would never see his mom again. He would never ever get to tap Katie, the hottie project manager. He listened to the spokes of the bicycle ticking away. He listened to fat bottle flies buzzing around his face.

CHAPTER SIXTEEN

Tony's iPhone rang from way down at the bottom of a dream. He cracked an eye open and reached for his phone, dropped it on the floor, cursed, then picked it up again.

"What?" he said.

"Tony? Hi, it's Ken Stoller. Patrick's dad. I hope it's not too early."

Tony checked the time. It was just past 8 a.m. "Yeah, no worries."

"Sorry to trouble you," Stoller said. "But, you see, we got through at the station yesterday and so decided to get on back home today. We've been staying at Patrick's place and packing things up, but we got to get them downstairs and to our car, try to fit as much as we can in there, though I don't know how."

"Uh huh."

"We were hoping," he said, "well, we'd love for you to come by and help us out if you could. You did say 'Maybe.' And we'd really love to meet you, too."

"Right now, you mean?"

Tony had planned to get freelance work done and then swing by the park for a few rounds of pétanque. He was about to say he wouldn't have the time. But he realized they had just spent a lovely visit to New York seeing their dead son and then spending the night in their dead son's apartment.

"Yeah," Tony said. "I guess I can come by."

"Terrific."

An hour later, Tony walked up to Patrick's apartment building on South 3rd and Havemeyer. Like many of the older residential buildings in Williamsburg, this was a row house, but it had miraculously escaped the false promise of aluminum siding, or siding of any kind, and so its dark red bricks were exposed, looking scruffy and in need of mortar. A warped awning above the front door matched the bricks perfectly, as did the few shattered steps of the front stoop.

Parked in front was a mud-dirty SUV with a Pennsylvania license plate. An older man came out of the building holding a food processor (sleek) and an albino armadillo (stuffed). Following him closely was a sausage-shaped beagle that waddled. The man wore shorts and a polo shirt, topsiders, and had gray hair that was white at the sideburns. Tony recognized his face from the Christmas photo.

"Mr. Stoller?" he said.

"You must be Tony." The man held out his hand from under the food processor. The sausage dog got between them, nudging Tony like a linebacker. "Meet Major Alphons."

The beagle looked up at Tony with doleful eyes. "Hey, dog."

"I was getting worried about you. I called a while ago."

"I'm more of a late afternoon-slash-early evening person," Tony said, wincing internally at his word choice.

"I understand. But I'd like to get going early as I can, you know?" Mr. Stoller unlocked the SUV's side door, put in the box, and locked the door again. "Can't be too safe."

Patrick had lived on the top floor, three flights up. The linoleum on the narrow stairs was old and peeling, the banisters loose and rickety.

As they walked up, Ken Stoller said, "You know, I think we almost had a break-in. Someone was trying to come in through the back window, up the fire escape back there. My wife thinks I'm being paranoid, but then I ask her, 'So why was Major Alphons barking up a storm?' and he was."

In the apartment, Patrick's mother was packing glassware in

the kitchen. Ken Stoller introduced her, and she nodded and then turned back to the glassware. She was taller than her husband by a head, with silver hair and a small, hooked nose that made her look like a bird.

As Tony walked into the apartment he noticed one, two, three locks on the door, a hell of a lot of security and more than he remembered being there. The apartment was the railroad style, long, narrow, opening into a kitchen with a new stove and a narrow stainless steel kitchen island. The floor was new, too, tile in the kitchen, parquet in the living room. The off-white paint on the walls had been peeling last time Tony saw them, but now they were a shiny pastel purple. Patrick must have put all his money into renovating.

Tony had only been to Patrick's place once before, for a New Year's Eve party. He didn't want to go, but when he found himself drinking alone at a bar, he figured he'd just stop by. Big mistake. Everyone at the party was coupled up, and so Tony felt like a thirteenth wheel. The others played video games and nuzzled and teased each other in the small living room, and he hung out in the kitchen by the window, drinking one watery PBR after another. Patrick's girlfriend, Kirsten, must have caught on. She came over and asked him if he was okay. She had eyes a little too far apart, and a button nose, giving her a passing resemblance to a frog. Still, a very attractive frog.

In lieu of a real answer, he'd said, "You know they used to tie real ribbons around every bottle of Pabst?"

"Was that in the nineties?"

"No, about a hundred years ago."

"You don't look that old."

"Wait till midnight. That's when I turn into a rotted pumpkin."

"Oh, I can't wait till midnight then."

He stayed for another couple of hours, getting bored and getting drunk. Which took an awful lot of watery PBRs. Just before midnight, when everyone else was due to smash lips together, he slipped out and sulked home, keeping his rotted pumpkin face to himself.

Well, that was a lousy memory. The living room, just off the kitchen, held a mix of IKEA furniture and old stuff that looked like it had been found on the street. On one side, posters covered the walls—*Mean Streets, The Warriors, A Clockwork Orange* (in velvet), and one of a concert for some band or someone called Manu Dibango. On the other side, over what looked like a brand new couch, were three framed paintings of dogs playing poker.

In the kitchen, Sarah said, "All this stuff is good," holding an aluminum pot and some utensils. "We should save it."

"We don't need it. And we're going to run out of room in the car," said Ken. "Tony, do you need any of this stuff?"

Tony didn't like the idea of taking a dead man's things. It was too close to grave-robbing. "Thanks," he said, "I have all the kitchen stuff I need."

"Well, do you know a place where we can donate this?"

Before Tony could answer, Sarah shot back, "But we should take these home."

"I tell you, there's just not going to be room in the car for all this stuff," Ken said.

"You're not doing that right," she said. "You don't know how to pack."

"Of course I know how to pack."

"Did you find his big suitcase? We could put things in his suitcase? I don't know where anything is. How am I supposed to pack everything?" she said, and then her eyes watered, and she turned and went into the only place you could get privacy in a railroad apartment—the bathroom.

Ken Stoller looked at Tony and then began picking up a box. Tony turned and did the same with a surprisingly heavy box in front of him. Vinyl record albums. He put it down and looked for something lighter. But the next box was packed with books. Hardcover books.

Over the next few hours, going up and down three flights of

stairs, Tony debated which was more lethal to his back, milk crates of vinyl or boxes of hardcovers. He lost interest in the debate when he saw how stoically Ken was handling the burden of crates. Still, if Tony had to guess, the vinyl was the worst.

On the fifth trip back up, Tony saw a woman on the landing talking to Ken. She was one of those genetically gifted people (unusual height, skeletal limbs, high cheekbones) who were destined to be models. Or destined to be constantly told they should be models. She wore shades, a backward baseball cap, and shorts short enough to embarrass a gynecologist. Tony was making a half-hearted attempt not to notice this when he saw that the door next door to Patrick's was open. This woman must live there, must have been his neighbor, and then Tony realized that apartment next door used to be Rosa Irizarry's. As Tony approached the landing, the model turned from Ken and was closing the door, but Tony got a quick glimpse inside. Bright colors, new fixtures. It looked like whatever was left of Rosa Irizarry had been renovated out of existence.

Once the car was packed, Tony sat on the stoop sucking down a bottle of water Sarah had handed him. Ken sat next to him and handed him a small cardboard box.

"Got you a present."

"A present?"

"Not from me. Found this bag with your name on it. Patrick must have wanted you to have it." It was a small ziplock bag with several flash drives in it. "Matter of fact, there's a whole bunch of this stuff we for sure don't need. We're not techie people. You take it. Looks like stuff you could use as a reporter."

Tony was too tired to resist. In it were several mini-webcams, a dozen or more sealed baggies of flash drives, and operating system CDs in their original sleeves. He took the plastic baggie and the box but planned on tossing it all into the first garbage can he came across.

"I found a bunch of those little memory sticks all over the apartment," Ken said. "In the couch, in the medicine cabinet, in his shoes. I bet he must have been sore looking for where he lost them."

Tony found the strength to say, "Thanks."

The Stollers invited Tony down to Pennsylvania for the funeral, but he told them to let him know and he'd see.

"Reporters," Ken said. "Always working." Then he bent down to give Tony an awkward hug. It would have been awkward regardless of the angle. And it didn't help that Tony was covered in sweat and very aware of it. Sarah just shook his hand.

"You can come down to Allentown any time you want," Ken said. "You're like family now."

They drove slowly away, leaving Tony on the stoop next to a few black garbage bags filled with the rest of Patrick's possessions that didn't fit in the car. Including a couch. It was a good-looking couch. But Tony wasn't going to try to move it. It wouldn't fit in his apartment anyway.

He was in no shape to play pétanque, not that pétanque required much in the way of shape. He walked over to the *Sentinel*.

When Tony got there, Bobbert was in his office, talking to someone on his cell phone. When he saw Tony, he yelled him over.

Bobbert Swiatowski was a doughy man in his late fifties who unwisely wore a goatee and kept it and what was left of his hair dyed jet black. He was, as usual, in shirtsleeves with the sleeves rolled out to show off meaty forearms. Bobbert's office was well air-conditioned, but he was still shiny with sweat.

"Sit down, sit down, sit down," Bobbert indicated the guest chair at the side of his desk. It was covered with stacks of the latest issue—the last one Patrick finished, Tony realized.

"Hey, Tony. Hey, listen, how you holding up?" Bobbert

said. He held his hand over his cell phone.

Behind him on a corkboard were well over a hundred printed pictures of Bobbert's family: wife, four kids, two dogs, and two cats.

"You want to finish that call?" Tony said.

"That's okay," he said, holding the phone askew and whispering. "This is Maru, telling me about her adventures with her Bear Bear. You want to say hi?"

"Not at the moment."

"I understand. I can only understand every third word she says." Into the phone, Bobbert said in a high-pitched voice, "*And his teeth were BIG?*" Then, in a normal voice, he said to Tony, "My wife'll kill me if I don't invite you over this weekend. She's making pork knuckles."

"I love her pork knuckles."

"She knows. She knows. *Tell me about the TIGER!*"

"I'll have to see."

"Here, Maru wants to talk to you. She heard your voice."

Tony got on the phone and listened to the child's incoherent story for what he felt was a respectable amount of time.

"I guess I ru ru you, too," Tony said, handing back the phone.

"You love kids."

"I hate kids."

"You love my kids. *Bye bye, Ruru, Daddy has to get back to work.*" After some more back and forth with his daughter, Bobbert kept the phone by his head and said, "Listen, so I want to talk about your future here at the *Sentinel*."

"Maru's still on the phone?"

"Yeah, she's still on the phone. It's about Bear Bear's favorite ice cream now."

"Well, my future is my present," Tony whispered back. "That's the way I—"

"Sure, sure, but with Patrick gone, well, you know, we need you to do more. And to be honest, you know and I know that you could do more. You have the talent."

"But not the patience. And I'd have to be here every day." And no more waking up whenever he wanted, he thought. And no more long afternoons in the park.

"I'll give you Patrick's salary." To the phone, Bobbert said, *"That's terrific, sweetheart. Bear Bear taught you to fly."*

"Can I ask what Patrick was making?"

"Twenty-eight K."

"Twenty-eight?" Tony thought of Patrick's apartment and all the new furniture and fancy kitchen gadgets he had. "Patrick was only making twenty-eight?"

"Hey, I'm not lying," Bobbert said. "Twenty-eight K. I might be able to get you more, but, honestly, things have been touch and go lately."

It was just a little more than what Tony was making now, scraping by. But if he could still do other freelance work at the same time, he could almost be respectable. "Can I think about it?"

"Why are you crying, honey? Tell Daddy what's wrong," Bobbert said to his phone. "Yeah, Tony, but you gotta tell me soon, or, honestly, then I gotta start looking elsewhere."

Tony walked the two feet over to the writers' office and could still hear Bobbert talking on the phone. *"Don't cry, honey. Bear Bear is not flying away."*

Gabby was at her desk, hair pulled back and wearing a thin tank top and tiny terry cloth shorts that Tony made an effort not to notice.

"Ew. Did you not shower today?" Gabby said.

"I just came from helping someone move. Sorry if I offend."

"You helped somebody move? That is so unlike you."

"I'm going over to my desk now. Try not to inhale."

"O.M.G. You got two messages, B.T.W.," she said and waved a neon pink post-it note. "Patrick's ex called. She wants to talk to you."

"Kirsten? What the hell?" He took the pink note. "Kirsten" was spelled "Christen."

"If you don't get a chance, don't worry," Gabby said, "I gave her your number."

"What the hell?" Tony said, and then he muttered to himself, "Everybody's giving out my number."

"She's grieving. Obvs. She probably just wants to talk about Patrick, reminisce, you know. Please. You just don't get people, you really don't."

"I get enough of people, thank you very much," he said.

"There was another slashing last night. Did you hear? What is this neighborhood coming to?"

"Yeah. I read about it."

Because it seemed to give off an air of death, Tony gave Patrick's chair a wide berth, as much as he could given the tight space. He opened a file cabinet and poured most of the contents from the box Ken Stoller had given him into it. He put a camera and a couple bags of flash drives, including the one with his name on it, in his messenger bag.

"O.M.G., are those flash drives? Can I have some?" Gabby said. "They're so handy, and my computer at home is always crashing."

"Sure, these are from Patrick's," Tony said and tossed her a bag of them from the cabinet.

"Oh, that's sad," she said, holding the bag tentatively. "And a little creepy."

"Relax, they're just flash drives, not ghosts." With great relief, Tony sat down at his desk, which was just four feet from Gabby's, and said, "If anyone else calls, I'll be in my office."

CHAPTER SEVENTEEN

This place on Grand Street used to be a clothing store where Petrosino bought his suit for high school graduation, his first suit ever (not counting his communion suit, which was a hand-me-down). It was run by a couple of Jews then, and they eventually got bought out by a couple of Italians. Then the place was turned into the House of Jeans or World of Jeans, something like that, selling all things denim. A Greek guy started it, then it got bought by a Puerto Rican lady, and then a West Indian. Then it closed and stayed empty. And now it was a sushi restaurant. Judging by the manager and the entire staff, it looked to be owned by Mexicans—Hispanics, anyway.

Petrosino and Hadid were talking to the head sushi chef: Stasio Mejias, a dark-complected man of less-than-average height, with a shaved head and several prison tattoos, all of the gang variety. They were just outside the kitchen, in the unshaded backyard behind the restaurant, baking in the afternoon heat along with bags and boxes of garbage. The stink of dead fish and putrefying vegetables was so strong Petrosino could taste them in his mouth. But he was enduring it along with a lesson in street economics.

Mejias sat on a drum of peanut oil and was the one giving the Business 101 lecture.

"It don't go," Mejias said. "It ain't worth the visibility, you see what I'm saying? It's counterproductive. Back in the day, all the rich white customers were in Manhattan, and that was another gang's territory. So we was stuck here with the addicts and the school kids and lots of teachers. More teachers than you'd think, boy! But now—now the rich white people, they're in our own—I mean, the gang's—hood. They be living right next door. Right in our buildings, man. It's great for business. Buy local. Smoke local. It's sustainability."

Mejias had been convicted of second-degree assault and served five years for slashing a man across the face with a machete. Nowadays, he told them, all he cut was spicy salmon rolls on a daily basis.

"Hey, any of you got a cigarette?" he said.

"Great idea," Petrosino said. He offered an open pack to Mejias, who took a cigarette, and he took one for himself, then lit them both.

"Oh great. Now it's a smoking club," Hadid said.

"What's his problem?"

"Health," Petrosino said. "Go on. So what do you think this slashing is all about?"

"Well, I don't know, but maybe a couple of young bucks are wilding out there, not like an organization thing, just to be stupid. From an organizational commercial business standpoint, it don't go to go slashing people, especially your customers."

"You don't happen to be hanging with any of your old friends now, would you?" Petrosino said. "To know it ain't them for sure."

"Naw, man, that would violate my parole. But I don't gotta hang with them. I read the news. I hear the gossip. But it don't go. It's economics."

"Get this guy," Hadid said.

"In fact, in my humble opinion, my bet would be that the gangstas ain't liking this slasher thing one bit. It's gonna mess with their branding. So you know they on the looky-loo for whoever's cutting people up."

"Oh, wouldn't that be nice?" Hadid said. "We got no reason to believe any of the shit you're saying."

"Man, believe what you want," Mejias told Hadid. "Don't be such an ass about it. Be like your partner. He's cool people." Petrosino sensed his partner tensing up and put a hand on his shoulder. "Okay, okay. Listen, we hear what you're saying, Stas. But we need a lead, somebody in the ranks who can give us some confirmation of what you're saying."

"Excuse me, but since when did it become healthy to snitch. No one told me. Maybe I was out buying mahi mahi."

"C'mon. Just give us something, someone else to bother with questions on a hot day," Petrosino said, blowing a huge cloud of smoke out of the side of his mouth.

"Eladio Cortés," Mejias said, looking around. "Talk to him. He's more hooked up than I am. Don't tell him I sent you."

"Right-o. Thanks," Petrosino said. "Keep your hands clean, Mejias."

"'Employees must wash hands before returning to work,'" Mejias said.

Petrosino kept smoking as he walked through the tiny restaurant. Out front, he flicked away his cigarette and got into the car.

As he sat down, his partner said, "What a fat lot of crap. Son of a bitch."

"Don't get your knickers in a twist. The whole day's been a waste. Tuchman's got us on a wild good chase. We talked to five gangbangers today, former and current, and they're all pretty much saying the same thing. And I believe them."

"Yeah, but I don't see how we can trust these people?"

Petrosino took out a handkerchief and wiped his face, trying to get out the smell of garbage with no luck. The smell got on the handkerchief, but it didn't leave his face. "You ever been in a gang?" he said.

"I never had the pleasure."

"Too bad. I was in two. A long time ago when I was very young and full of fire and pizza sauce. Dukes of Williamsburg and then the Brooklyneers. Sure, we got into fights and caused some property damage. But those guys—those guys were my brothers. I would do anything for them, back then and even now, if they ever asked me for anything. I'm not saying the gangs today are like those gangs. But they're not all psychopaths and stone-cold killers. Some of them are just abandoned sons of bitches, people looking for family. Family! Do you know what I mean?"

His partner's phone was ringing. "Yeah, I have to get this."

"I was trying to say something important. Are you friggin' kidding me?"

"Are you serious?" Hadid said into the phone, ignoring him. "Right-o."

"Send me a picture."

"Jesus H. Fucking Christ. Might as well be talking to myself. La di da."

Hadid was writing something down. "Is that right?" he said to whoever he was talking to. "Is that right?" he said again. "And what about the last two? Yeah. Send me a picture." He thanked whoever he was talking to and turned to Petrosino. "Petro, listen to this."

Petrosino ignored the nickname. "Okay, what's the dilio?"

"Hold up...Here." Hadid handed him his phone.

"What's this?"

"I just got a call from Zamorano, one of the patrolmen down by the waterfront. I just joined his fantasy baseball league."

"About which I will never care."

"Anyway, yeah, our first two murder scenes. Victims Hewitt and Nelson. Seems somebody spray-painted this same graffiti near the scenes, on the wall nearby or on the sidewalk, like here." Hadid held up his phone.

Petrosino looked at the picture. "'hipster death rattle.' What the fuck does that mean?"

"Some people have no respect for the dead," Hadid said. "No gang signs that he could see, but still kind of looks like gang M.O., no? Marking territory or taking pride in their work."

"Yeah, yeah, they do that. What about at the latest crime scenes? The Stoller kid."

"He checked. He said there was nothing there. Not yet anyway."

"Make sure Zamorano keeps an eye out. If they start tagging the other scenes, we want to catch them in the act."

"Will do," Hadid said. He relayed the message and then said, "So, this really is a gang thing. It looks like Mejias was bullshitting us."

"Worse than that. It looks like Tuchman might be right."

CHAPTER EIGHTEEN

The bouncer at SubBar looked at Tony's ID for a long time.

Tony said, "I'll save you the trouble: I'm a Taurus."

The bouncer was an oak tree wrapped in black, like a bad art installation. His hair was tied in a knot on top, and he had a blank face marred by a nose so broken it could have passed for a thumb. But what he clearly wanted you to notice was his facial hair, another one of those trendy, Smith Brothers beards, this one tied prettily at the bottom with a tiny bow. A whimsical touch, but he still seemed as friendly as a coffin.

"Not that astrology means anything, of course," Tony added.

The bouncer handed back the ID, and Tony could still feel his gaze as he squeezed past him into the bar.

Located less than ten feet from the Metropolitan Avenue subway entrance, SubBar was a tiny dive, barely bigger than a studio apartment. The black walls were decorated with items snatched from the subway system—L, J, M, and G train signs, a vintage subway map in its frame, a floor-to-ceiling column of "No Se Apoye Contra La Puerta" stickers.

A couple of barflies sat on stools at the end of the bar, and behind it was Kirsten, Patrick Stoller's ex. Or at least he thought she was Kirsten.

The last time Tony had seen her, she had been a freckle-faced and honey-haired young woman who never used makeup and whose wardrobe favored pink and white and orange. The woman behind the bar wore all black, thick eye makeup, and green-orange hair. Her button nose had a spike in one nostril. Her sleeveless T-shirt was loose-fitting (and distracting because of it) and on the right forearm was a passable facsimile of Johnny Cash sticking up his middle finger, and on the left, what looked like a patch for a brand-new tattoo.

The big city changes everyone, Tony thought. *No one escapes unscathed.*

"Tony!" She reached over the bar to give him an awkward, but still warm hug. She gave him a solid wet kiss on the cheek. "It's great to see you, sweetie."

Tony said, "Hey. Got your text just now. Thought I'd drop in for a nightcap."

"Right on!" Kirsten poured a shot of bourbon for each of them.

After Tony had turned in the community meeting story, he wheedled a cash advance from Bobbert. Feeling flush, he had gone to McCarren Park to play a twilight game of pétanque and go out for a few, four, five beers afterward. He was pleasantly buzzed already and would never say no to a free shot.

"To Patrick," she said, raising her shot.

"To Patrick," Tony said. "A good guy."

"Oh god," she said after sucking down the bourbon. "It's horrible what happened." Her pretty face broke, scrunching in a paroxysm of grief that Tony had no idea how to deal with.

I should have texted and not shown up, Tony thought. *Why didn't I just text?*

Kirsten took a napkin from the behind the bar and blew her nose. "I'm sorry."

"Ah...don't be," Tony said,

"I miss him so much. I can't tell you how much."

"You guys were together a while."

"I was with him since before we moved to New York together, yeah," she said.

"Long time," he said.

"Yes, it was."

"Yeah."

It went like that for another hour and two more shots apiece. She reminisced, and Tony agreed with her reminiscence. He was surprised at how many times he had actually hung out with Patrick and her and how good the memories of it were. Although, it was Kirsten he had really liked hanging out with. He didn't remember a damned thing Patrick had ever said or done on those occasions. She was pretty, and she was getting prettier with every beer.

Tony was wondering what the protocol was in such circumstances—ex-girlfriend of a dead co-worker—when Kirsten told the bar patrons in an unexpectedly loud voice that it was getting on time to close.

Then she put her elbows on the bar and hunkered close to Tony. Her face was so close, he could smell the bourbon on her breath.

"Oh, sweetie, there was something I wanted to ask you," she said.

"Sure," Tony said. *Hmm, maybe she's thinking about the proper protocol in these situations as well.*

"I know it's kind of a strange question, so I didn't want to just ask you over the phone. You see, when Patrick and I broke up, it was kind of sudden, and we were both pretty pissed at each other. And when I left, I ended up leaving a lot of my stuff there. Clothes and stuff."

"Yeah?"

She moved away and began working her way around the bar, wiping things down and closing out the cash register.

"I just never got around to getting them," she said. "So, I know it's weird, but Patrick had stuff at the office, I'm sure. He's—he was—very anal, so I happen to know he had a spare set of keys at the office, so I was wondering if you could, you know, get them for me?"

"Keys to his apartment? You didn't keep a set?"

"I didn't. Like I said, I was pissed. I wasn't thinking."

Tony followed her around the tiny bar, helping her put chairs on tables. "I hate to tell you this, but Patrick's mom and dad, they took everything home yesterday."

"What? Wait. The Stollers? They took everything?"

"Did you expect them to leave stuff behind?" Tony said.

"I'm sorry. I meant: *already.*"

"But, listen, I didn't see any women's clothes. But a lot of stuff was packed by the time I got there. They probably have your stuff." He thought it best not to tell her about all the leftover stuff that was bagged and tossed on the sidewalk. By now, any clothes would be long gone, in the garbage dump, sold to a thrift store, or on someone's back.

"Call them again," Tony said. "They can check and send it to you. I don't know if you're going to the funeral—"

"To be painfully honest, they never liked me very much, so, yeah, no, so not going. But you know what? I will contact the Stollers. I should stay in touch with them. They're such good people."

Tony wondered if he should ask her to come to his place for another nightcap, just to be friendly. He was wondering if he had anything to drink at home when a long shadow fell over his shoulder.

"You met my boyfriend, right?" Kirsten said, indicating the colossal bouncer with the bow-tied beard. "This is Gunnar."

"Wonderful to meet you," Tony lied.

CHAPTER NINETEEN

The bone-white dominos rattled on the kitchen table. Tony's mother mixed the tiles under her soft, small hands. It was late on a Thursday afternoon, and she had wanted to play dominos instead of watching TV. The air conditioner was working, and Tony had bought two airplane bottles of Kahlua for her. The previous night's indulgence at SubBar still throbbed in his head and stomach, so he stuck with water.

When the tiles were settled, she and Tony drew from the pile. She looked at her draw and then immediately smacked a double-six tile into the middle of the table.

"You always draw the double six," Tony said.

"Play," she said.

"*Brujeria,*" Tony muttered. *Witchcraft.* He didn't have a single six. He took five tiles from the pile before he found a six-and-four tile to play. "I don't know why I play you. You always win."

"Practice," she said. "You get there."

She threw down a double-four. He answered with a four-five. She threw down a five-three, and Tony realized he had no threes either.

He sighed and said, "Didn't Jerry say anything to you?"

"He said he would send me some money for rent," his mother said. "But that's too much. He already pay for my tickets." Tony's mother went to Puerto Rico for vacation every year, come sunshine or hurricane.

"When do you leave?"

"Two weeks. You should come."

"Maybe next time."

"I hear that every year," she said.

Later, while she watched TV, Tony snuck a twenty-dollar bill in her purse, another in the sugar bowl where she kept change, another in her coat. He knew it was very likely that after the next time he came over, he'd find them all tucked back into his messenger bag, but that was a chance he was willing to take.

In the living room, his mother sat in her recliner, and Tony plopped on the sagging couch. He got out his laptop and read the news. On page four of the *Daily News*, a headline read "B'burg Braces for More Slashing Attacks." On page two of the *Post*: "Murder Is Trending in Wmsbg." Both articles quoted the police as saying it was a "few separate incidents" that were "not linked."

Tony remembered that he still had to look at those flash drives that Ken Stoller had given him. He fished one out of the ziplock bag and connected it to his laptop. In it were countless versions of "KingzCounty.ANovel.PStoller." Tony rolled his eyes and ejected it immediately. Three of the drives had copies of video files, hopefully not porn. He would have to make sure later. Another held documents about street gangs, PDFs of short articles about some gang leader some Eladio Cortés, picture files of same. Snooze.

He put another drive in. There were only a few files, but he immediately noticed a PDF marked "Rosa." He clicked it open. It was a PDF of a news clipping from the *Sentinel*. He recognized Luis De Moscoso right away. Mr. Bathes-with-Cologne. Tony could almost smell him through the screen. It looked like the same shiny suit he wore at the reading and at the community board meeting. What the hell did Magaly see in a guy like that?

The article read:

VIGIL AGAINST DISPLACEMENT AND HARASSMENT
By Patrick Stoller—Family members, community lead-

ers, and local residents gathered to remember Rosa Irizzary, who disappeared earlier this year.

Irizzary should have been blowing out her birthday candles to celebrate her 68th birthday. Instead, family and friends spent hours, days, and then months looking for any sign of her whereabouts.

El Flamboyan Community Human Rights Organization, the Displacement Advocacy Group, and the Southside Development Corporation organized a vigil to mark the disappearance and bring attention to the issue of displacement in the neighborhood. More than 40 people came out in the rain to stand in front of Irizzary's former dwelling, which has since been rented.

Irizzary went missing in May. Police and family say they have no idea what could have happened to her.

At 10:52 a.m. on May 15, her sister, Iris Campos, received a text from Irizzary on her cell phone, telling her she was on her way to Campos's house. That was the last time anyone has heard from her.

Irizzary disappeared in the midst of a two-year battle with her landlord to return to her apartment, which had been damaged by fire.

"She had every right to stay in her apartment, but her landlord wanted her out so he could rent the apartment for more money," said Luis De Moscoso, director of El Flamboyan.

According to De Moscoso, Irizzary was frequently harassed. "She came to us many times, saying she was scared of her landlord and what he would do to her," he said.

No charges have been filed against her landlord, Elias J. Litvinchouk. Local police said there is no evidence of foul play, and a reasonable explanation for her disappearance has not been found. But while there is no evidence a crime was committed, Lt. Kevin Batista said all possibilities are being investigated.

While the family and the community prays for Irizarry's

eventual return, Campos said she is certain something "bad" happened to her sister. Campos said all her sister wanted was to live in her own apartment, which she occupied for more than 40 years.

In a press release, Representative Camila Santiago stated, "Rosa Irizzary's disappearance cannot be forgotten, and we will continue to seek justice for her and for all of our residents who are threatened by harassment and displacement."

As Tony finished, he thought again that the name "Elias Litvinchouk" was familiar. He'd had a professor at Brooklyn College with that same name. A good professor, a bit quirky. Could it be the same guy? How many Elias Litvinchouks could there be?

A picture with the article was captioned: "Friends, family, and neighbors of Rosa Irizarry hold a vigil for their friend. Pictured: Luis De Moscoso, director of El Flamboyan, Iris Campos, Magaly Fernandez, Denise Vazquez, Vivian Romero, Angie Roman, Martha Rodriguez, and Miguel Diaz. Picture by Patrick Stoller."

Each person in the photo was holding up the same picture of Irizarry. She was gray-haired, nut brown, and had small, watery eyes. It was a kind but stern face, just like a thousand other Puerto Rican mothers' faces he'd seen.

"*Que?*" his mother said.

"Nothing," he said. "I'm reading about Rosa Irizarry?" He pulled himself and brought the laptop closer to her.

"Aha," his mother said. "It's about time."

"It's all still a mystery. She disappeared. She left home and then...well, they never found her."

"That's too bad. I told you. The same thing could happen to me. But I don't worry about me."

"Why not?"

"I know you find me."

CHAPTER TWENTY

Some women can run in heels. Magaly Fernandez knew was not one of them. But she was walking as fast as she could because she didn't want to be late, and it hurt—her feet, her calves were pulsing. She had always had an issue with punctuality, something that used to aggravate Chino all the time, and now that she was going to meet him, she didn't want to hear him say, like he used to before, so many times, "Habitual lateness is an unconscious expression of anger and resentment."

Tony had surprised her with a text the night before, asking for a contact number for Rosa Irizzary's sister, Iris Campos. She almost dropped her phone. She happily texted back, told him not to worry, that she would set up an interview for the next day, and that she'd meet him outside Iris's building. Ten minutes ago.

"Why do u have to be there?" Tony had texted.

She had texted back: "Did yr Spanish get better than yr Latin? Iris is Spanish dominant + doesnt know u."

"Good point."

So, she had to be ready on time. Then Luis, her boss—and, oh god, her lover (How did that happen? Well, she knew how it happened, she just didn't want to think about it) called and he was having another panic attack and needed her to calm him down. He'd started having these a few months ago, and now he was calling more often, to vent, to flirt, and—inevitably—to ask her if he could come over. Most times she would balk, come up with some excuse to keep him at bay as long as her willpower held up. But tonight she actually had somewhere to be. Still, she couldn't get him to hang up until she'd promised to text him when she was on her way back home.

She turned the corner and stopped for a second to check her face and hair. The face was fine, but the humidity was murdering her hair. It was blossoming like a bag of microwaved popcorn on top of her head. So be it. Tony just better not make any wisecracks.

Iris Campos lived in one of the older buildings in the Southside. Its entrance had once been classy—marble floors and lintel, cherubs carved above the doorway. But the doors had been covered over with metal bars and grates that were thick with black oil paint.

Tony was waiting inside the front door of the building.

"I'm so sorry I'm late," Magaly said. "My life is so crazy now. I can't begin to tell you."

"No worries. The front door lock is broken, so I got in here to stay cooler."

He looked grumpy. But he always looked grumpy. But something was different—the shirt. He was wearing a collared shirt! Some things do change. She decided not to tease him about it.

"Come on," she said. "It's upstairs."

Inside of the building, the floors and hallways were chipped, gray marble, and there was a strong, familiar smell of frying oil, garlic, *sofrito*.

The bell on the metal door didn't work, so they knocked loudly.

Iris Campos cracked the heavy door open and peeked her head out. More of that *sofrito* smell spilled out into the hallway. She was a tiny woman with black hair heavily streaked with white and huge square glasses that sat like picture frames on her small face. She wore a *bata*—a housedress—decorated with tiny blue flowers, knee-high tube socks, and pink slippers with rabbit ears and whiskers on the front end. She gestured them inside. "*Entre. Entre.*"

Magaly bent down to hug her. She turned and introduced Tony. Iris gave him a hug, too, and he looked as uncomfortable as Magaly expected him to. They all squeezed into the small kitchen. With three of them, there was barely room for the table and a cabinet with what looked like one of the first refrigerators ever made and a microwave that looked big enough to nuke a steer, head and all.

Magaly explained again to Iris why they were there. In his very halting Spanish, Tony said he was happy to meet Iris, that he just wanted to ask a few questions.

Iris led them into the living room dominated by an entertainment center with a big box TV squeezed into its center. On the set was a Spanish-language *novela*, the volume very low. Framed pictures of family covered the shelves on either side of the TV. Rosa Irizarry was in many of the pictures, smiling broadly enough to make her eyes squint. The top of the entertainment center itself swarmed with ceramic figurines of dogs, elephants, Jesus, Mary, and Joseph, as well as clowns in a million states of melancholy.

"*Siéntese,*" Iris said, and as they sat down on the plastic-covered couch, it made a crunchy sound.

Iris offered them coffee and food and then coffee again, but they both refused.

Magaly saw through the open door of a bedroom a man she recognized as Danny, Iris's son. The man turned to look at Magaly, giving one of those lifeless stares you get from ex-cons, killers, and video gamers.

Tony took out his digital recorder and showed it to Iris, saying, "Do you mind?"

Magaly touched him on the knee and then she explained to Iris that the tiny black box was like a tape recorder—*un grabador.* Tony asked her to ask the woman's permission to record her.

Iris picked up the recorder and said it was "*maravilloso*"—

marvelous. Slowly, she said, "I will try to speak from my heart."

Tony asked a question in Spanish, but Iris just smiled at him and then looked at Magaly. She asked the question again, in Spanish—Tony wanted to know about her sister, about her life.

Iris nodded her head and began speaking in Spanish. Magaly translated back and forth.

<"Our family comes from Mayagüez, where I was born. My father used to own a farm, but the government took it away from him. So our parents moved to New York to get work. Mami raised the kids and Papi worked in the Schaefer Factory over here before they closed it. We moved here in 1951 to be close to his work. The Italians and the Irish didn't like the Puerto Ricans. They did not want us here, and Papi used to get into fights all the time.

"We had three brothers, but one died when he was a baby, the other went to Vietnam and never came back. God have him in heaven. And the last one moved away in 1972 and died in California. We all went to school over here in St. Peter and Paul on South 2nd.

"Rosa was my little sister. She was born here, and she was a sweet girl, always smiling, always nice. But she sometimes had a temper, oh Christ in heaven. She used to throw things if she got angry at you. She almost took my eye out once when we were kids with a toothbrush.

"So little Rosa met Jose when she was sixteen, and he had just come out of the army, very handsome in his uniform. They got married and moved to the Southside. They had a little boy, Joselito.

"When the factories closed, Jose could not find work, but Rosa worked as a teacher's aide. But then she got laid off. That was 1973. That was when the neighborhood turned bad. There were no jobs. We all had to go on the welfare. Jose hated the welfare, but we had no choice.

"After, Joselito, he was working on Wall Street. He made good money. He died in 9/11. God have him in heaven. They never found his body.

"After that, Jose, he died of cancer. Rosa was left very sad. She didn't care about anything. She was left all alone in that apartment. I told her to come live with me, but she said that was her home.

"It used to be a very nice building. Always clean. But then they stopped taking care. They stopped fixing things, and then one day she got the roaches and then she got the mice. Not Rosa! You could eat off her floors.

"And then we were going to celebrate her birthday. She was so happy. She liked people. She liked parties. We got the cake, we had the music, I made yuca salad, which is her favorite, and everybody was coming.

"Something happened her, something bad, I know it. I don't want to think what happened, but I know it. I miss her so much, every day. God bless her wherever she is.">

When she finished, the only sound was the TV set and the video game being played in the next room.

Iris turned toward her son's room, and then she told them they should talk to him, that he used to go over to check on Rosa all the time. Magaly had met him once or twice before, and she knew he was intense.

Iris called her son in, as if he hadn't been listening the whole time, and he came in, still staring dead-eyed at Magaly.

He was heavyset, with muscular arms. His shiny hair was cut in severe bangs and he had a razor-thin goatee. On his neck were two tattoos—"Faithfulness to a cause" across his Adam's apple and, on his jugular vein, "God Understand Me."

The man shook Magaly's hand—his grip was surprisingly limp and disturbingly moist.

"*Hola*," Tony said, and they shook hands. "I'm Tony Moran. *Trabajo* for *el Williamsburg Sentinel* newspaper."

Danny smiled with sharp yellow teeth. "What you want?"

Tony said, "Ah. Danny, I wanted—"

"Call me D-Tox."

"D-Tox? Really?" Tony said. Magaly bumped him with her knee and gave him a sharp look.

"Yeah. I came up with that."

"Okay, D-Tox, I just wanted to get some quotes about how you all are doing now?"

"My aunt is dead. How am I supposed to be doing?"

"Well, she's missing, as far as we know. I just wanted to check in, see if you've heard anything new or felt there was something maybe that wasn't covered before."

"Look at this," he said, pointing to his arm. Above a very large tattoo of Al Pacino as Scarface was a tattoo of a cross-eyed blonde angel and above that the words "Rosa. *Dios le protégé.*"

Iris, who had gone to the kitchen, came in and put cups of coffee in front of Tony and Magaly.

"*Gracias,*" Tony said to her, and then to Danny, "But I guess you think she was killed for sure?"

"Yeah, and I know who did it, too. That landlord—he had it in for her. He was trying to get her out of there for years and years. You gotta go after him, ask him some questions. Bring some justice for my aunt."

"What do think the landlord did, specifically? The rats and roaches would be hard to prove. What about this fire?"

"That was done on purpose! She didn't see how the fire started, but the super, he showed up right away to stop it from getting out of hand. Right away—you see what I mean?"

"Yeah."

"They didn't want to burn down the building, you feel me. That's why he showed up right away."

"So you definitely think the super had something to do with it?"

"Had to! Had to! How else would they get in and out of there. You reporters need to do something good for once. You don't do shit against the government. Try to do a little something good for my family."

"Well, justice—you know what justice is?" Tony said, and something in his voice made Magaly wince inside. Please don't make it a long, condescending lecture, she silently told him. She looked at his face. Here it comes.

"Justice," Tony said, "is what's fair and morally right. It's also when everyone gets their due under the law. Now, I'm not a cop, I'm not a detective. I'm a reporter. Part-time. And I barely get paid, and...But that's beside the point and not what you want to hear. What you want to hear is that we can find your aunt safe and sound tomorrow, or if she was kidnapped or killed, find the person or persons responsible. Any of that—that 'justice'—is very unlikely, an impossible long shot. I mean, let's be honest here, I doubt we'll turn up anything."

There was a silence, and Magaly realized she was grinding her own teeth. But to her surprise, D-Tox was not murdering Tony.

"If you don't mind me saying," D-Tox said, "you're kind of an asshole. But that makes me like you more." He took Tony's hand in what looked like a crushing embrace and shook it fiercely. "You'll find my aunt," he said, then he turned to his mother. "*Mami, da mi comida ahora, por favor.*"

Iris asked him something in Spanish, and D-Tox said, "*No, no, ellos tienen que ir ahora.*"

Time for dinner and they weren't being invited, Magaly thought. Rude of D-Tox, but she had no desire to stay and watch him try to eat while staring at her.

Tony picked up his recorder, and they both stood.

Magaly thanked them again, in Spanish.

Iris followed them to the door. In Spanish, she said, <"God bless you. Please find my sister.">

Magaly hugged her. Then the woman turned to Tony and hugged him.

"We'll do our best," Tony said.

Magaly looked at him. Maybe he had changed.

They walked downstairs and stood in the coolness of the vestibule, avoiding the heat of the night until the last possible minute.

"Wow, that guy creeped me out," Tony said.

"You?" Magaly said.

"How much did it hurt to get that tattoo across his neck?"

"Nice speech about justice at the end there, Chino. Couldn't help yourself."

"I was being honest."

"*Oy*. God help us."

"The Lord helps those who help themselves," he said. "Which makes the Lord pretty superfluous. Speaking of which, I need to get a hold of the landlord from the building, Litvinchouk. Do you people at El Flamboyan have his contact information?"

"You bet we do. We have every landlord in our database."

"You know, you're proving to be very helpful."

"What was that? Was that Chino Moran admitting that people—people of the human race, no less!—can help him with something?"

"See, that's not helpful."

Magaly smacked his arm but then let her hand linger on him. "Funny. So, why do you want to talk to that man?"

"Well, it's only fair to let him tell his side of the story. I mean, he's not going to confess to harassing Rosa or say, 'Oh yeah, I have her right here in my cellar.'"

"That's not funny."

"I wasn't trying to be funny."

"Yes, you were," she said. "I'd like to be there when you talk to him."

Tony gave her his scrunched-face incredulous look. "What the hell for?"

"I have some questions for him myself."

"I don't know about that. I'm afraid you'll be a little hostile."

"I don't get hostile. I'm a Buddhist," she said. "Mostly."

Tony shook his head. "Now who's trying to be funny? I saw you punch a man so hard he threw up."

"I was sixteen, and he touched my ass. That's not a fair example."

"Granted. I'll let you know when I go. You ready?"

Magaly pushed the door open and felt the humidity like a slap. And there went her hair again!

Tony said he would walk her to her place, but she told him she had a bunch of stops to make first, people to visit. He said, "All right," and left, and she walked home, knowing exactly what she was going to find. She felt it.

And sure enough, there he was: Luis De Moscoso, pacing in front of her building.

CHAPTER TWENTY-ONE

Jesus Echeverria waited for his wife to come walking down the stairs of the elevated J line at a quarter to two in the morning. As usual, he waited at the corner of Marcy Avenue and Broadway, in the shadow of the elevated train, because he liked to smoke but he didn't want to smoke in people's faces as they went up and down the stairs.

Every day, Jesus walked Carlotta home to the apartment they shared with her sister's family. It could be bad at night, they both knew, and he wanted to make sure his wife was safe. He wasn't worried about the slashing attacks he had read about in *El Diario*. Where he stood, livery cabs whizzed by all the time and buses were always going back and forth. Both sides of the block underneath the train were lined with ninety-nine-cent stores, clothing shops, a *cuchifrito* restaurant, a pizzeria, and a Chinese restaurant where the waiters spoke Spanish good.

Jesus and Carlotta had recently emigrated from Guatemala, and Echeverria was still looking for steady work, instead of the piecemeal construction work he got from time to time. He spent most of his days and nights walking around the neighborhood, waiting for the time to go pick up his wife.

During the day, she worked as a housekeeper in Manhattan, and at night she worked as a janitor, making eight dollars an hour. She usually came down the stairs at 1:30 a.m. She was late. He didn't like that she wasn't on time. Lately, she was laughing a little too much, and he had been getting suspicious that she had a boyfriend at her job.

He waited at the bottom of the steps, looking up. He kept seeing the image of his wife with another man, probably that guy Marco she kept talking about. Marco this, Marco that. With every passing minute, Jesus got angrier. He felt like going back to his wife's sister's house and telling them what he thought of Carlotta. He walked to the corner and lit up a cigarette.

He walked down Marcy Avenue and puffed heavily. Halfway down the block, he noticed someone riding a bicycle, way down on the other side of the elevated BQE. *Delivery guy*, he thought. *They get paid shit.*

Echeverria turned from the wind, away from the bicyclist, to touch up his mullet with his left hand. He was mad now. He was going to yell at Carlotta like never before. This stupid country. You couldn't trust any of the men. He didn't notice when the bicyclist hopped onto the sidewalk and rode slowly, his wheels ticking, coming up just behind him.

Echeverria's hands were still up near his ears, gently tapping the spiky upper ridges of his hair, when the machete cut almost all the way through his left wrist.

Another cut bit into Echeverria's thigh, sending the rings of keys that hung out of his pocket flying.

A third slash, backhanded from the bicyclist, cut open Echeverria's face from chin to nose.

Jesus Echeverria collapsed onto the street, halfway in the gutter. He was trying to hold onto his face with the one good hand he had left.

The attack had taken less than ten seconds.

Twenty minutes later, Carlotta exited the subway station. She waited at the bottom of the stairs for fifteen minutes, checking and rechecking her phone. Police cars and people were gathering at the corner behind her, so she went to take a look at what was going on.

CHAPTER TWENTY-TWO

"What is it you want?" The voice on the other end of the phone sounded busy and a little obnoxious—and more than a little familiar—to Tony. "I'm very busy."

"Look, Mr. Litvinchouk," said Tony. He was at his desk at the office, where he'd just finished a write-up on the closing of Gloria's Spanish Food. He had been spending far too much time at his desk lately, as far as he was concerned, and away from the pétanque court. But he'd done four revisions that morning for Bobbert, so at least more money was coming his way. "I'm calling from the *Williamsburg Sentinel*. I'd like to discuss the disappearance of your former tenant Rosa Irizarry."

"Aha. I see. No need to get testy, sir."

Tony took the phone away from his face and smirked at it.

"To be frank," Litvinchouk continued, "I am not sure I'd have anything new or interesting to say that has not already been reported."

"That's fine," Tony said. "You don't have to be interesting, and it won't take long. I can record you over the phone if you prefer."

"Why don't you come over now then?"

"Right now?"

"Right now, yes. What? Why not? It's Thursday night. I don't like anything on TV on Thursday night. I insist."

Tony looked at the phone again. Then he said he would be there and tapped off. Then he remembered his promise to call

Magaly. Maybe she'd be busy with her crazy life. But she surprised him. She said she would meet him there.

"Don't be late," Tony said, but she'd already hung up.

The night had cooled off from the day, and so the long walk to the Litvinchouk's house was humane. The landlord lived in the Hasidic section of Williamsburg, an area that seemed to exist separate from the rest of the neighborhood. Little trash. Little noise. The Hasidic men walked about in long black coats, hats as big as sombreros, and sideburns that ended in Shirley Temple curls. The Hasidic women went about wearing wigs, plain dresses, and a fear of strangers. The area lay around an open-cut section of the Brooklyn-Queens Expressway, brownstones, projects, and new low-income housing, many with enclosed attachments on the balconies. No Puerto Ricans, no Italians, no Irish, no hipsters. In his shorts, sneakers, and T-shirt, Tony felt out of place.

He looked ahead and saw someone else who was out of place. If he didn't recognize the sway of her hips, or the giant purse she carried, the hair was a giveaway.

"Ms. Fernandez," he said, catching up to her.

"Mr. Moran."

They rang the bell at Litvinchouk's building, a brownstone that matched all the others on either side of it and across the street.

A woman opened the door. She wore a scarf over a dark brown wig. Tony extended his hand for her to shake, but she ignored it. Instead, she turned and told them to follow her.

In not-quite-a-whisper, Magaly said, "The women can't shake a man's hands. Don't you know that?"

"I did know that. Damn, I forgot."

The apartment was in back, beyond the staircase. Old wallpaper peeled off the walls in the hallway. Tony smelled food, something very oniony.

Several children ran in and out of the doorway. The boys wore vests and sported brown curls on either side of their faces.

The girls wore neat dresses that to Tony looked like Girl Scout uniforms.

As soon as they walked into the apartment, into the kitchen, Tony recognized the man sitting at the kitchen table. "Mr. Litvinchouk, from Brooklyn College!"

"Mr. Moran," said that man at the table. "I thought the name was familiar. *Mea culpa.* I didn't know it was you on the phone."

Magaly seemed shocked. "You two know each other?"

"This is my old Latin professor."

Litvinchouk rose to shake Tony's hand. He said, "*Sumpsi te in studiis latinis mansurum.*"

Tony hesitated for moment, then answered, "*Volui scilicet pecuniam lucrari.*"

"*Ergo diurnarius factus es!*"

"*IIuvenis atque stultus eram.*"

"English, please," Magaly said.

"Sorry," Tony said. "Now you know how I felt back at Iris's place."

Litvinchouk was a short man with a thick brown mustache that grew wildly under and, it seemed, from within his nose. He wore a yarmulke atop a head of steel-gray hair, a yellowed white shirt, and black pants with frayed edges. To Tony's eyes, the man hadn't changed an atom since he'd last seen him senior year. A boy in curls sat next to him, and a schoolbook and paper were open in front of them.

"You have lots of grandkids," said Tony.

"Hah. You'd think so," Litvinchouk said. "But these are my own children. Eight are here. Those are the ones at home. I have two more in college and two who are professionals. I have six grandchildren, but they're with their parents."

Magaly said, "Your wife must get exhausted."

"My wife—she's an eternal source of sunshine. She's unstoppable. I couldn't live without her. But you wanted to ask me about Rosa, correct?"

Tony put down his recorder and turned it on. "Yes, well, there were some allegations—"

"Did I ever tell you I grew up in Los Sures?" said Litvinchouk. "I've lived in this area all my life."

"I remember your saying that," Tony said. "So have I."

"Hah! Where?"

"South 3rd and Bedford. So did Ms. Fernandez."

"I was on Havemeyer Street," Litvinchouk said. "We could have been neighbors. My mother was Puerto Rican. Can you believe that? It happens."

"That must've been some courtship," Magaly said.

Litvinchouk nodded. "Let me tell you something—when I grew up, this neighborhood was rotten. Rotten. Gangs, bums, tough guys. And I got it from all sides. The Puerto Ricans hated me. The Jews hated me. There was crime, there was filth."

"And what do you think of it now?" said Tony.

"There's still crime. There's still filth. That's the way the world is, my friends."

"So what happened—"

"I'll tell you the same thing I told the police. She was a good tenant, very nice lady, for the most part. If you got on her bad side, forget about it. One time she threw a broom at me when I was walking down the stairs."

"Why did she throw a broom at you?" Tony said.

"It's been so long I don't remember. But that's neither here nor there. I knew her for many years. But while I co-own that property and continue to receive income from it, I no longer manage it."

"Tomasello Management does that for you," Magaly said.

"You got it, young lady. They've handled the building for more than ten years. All the trouble that Rosa reported, that was from them."

She went on (and Tony heard a sharpening knife in her voice): "So you had nothing to do with harassing her, trying to get her out of the apartment?"

"If I knew they were doing anything illegal, I would have severed my relationship with them."

"Did you ever check up on them to find out?" she said.

"Check up?" Litvinchouk said, raising his voice a little. "Why would I sign a contract with someone I needed to check up on. Understand: Tomasello has been doing business with me for years and years. I felt no need to *check up* on him."

Magaly jumped in. "Rosa reported harassment for years. And then there was the fire. You didn't think you should check up at that point?"

Litvinchouk smirked and looked at Tony. "She's a live one, this one."

"And a half," Tony said. "But she's right—what did you do after the reports of harassment?"

"That I checked. Of course. And I saw nothing amiss. A few roaches, a mouse or two. Nothing out of the ordinary in this city. The fire was a simple accident that anyone of Rosa's age could make."

"How did it start?"

"Something she left on the stove caught fire. A loaf of bread or something. Rosa—"

Again, Magaly jumped in. "She hadn't even been in that room. She just came back from visiting a friend and only went into the kitchen when she smelled the smoke."

"Old people forget. Look at me—I forget things all the time. This morning I forgot where I put my watch and I still can't find it."

"That fire was deliberately caused by someone else," Magaly said.

Litvinchouk shook his head. "A New York City Fire Department inspector found nothing."

"Fire inspectors are bribed all the time!" she said.

"Magaly." Tony put a hand on her knee. She pulled it away. "Mr. Litvinchouk, I have to ask straight out: Did you have anything to do with Rosa Irizarry's disappearance?"

"Absolutely not," Litvinchouk said.

"You would admit though that with her gone, you would be free to rent her rent-controlled apartment at a market rate, which is considerably more than what she was paying?"

"I wouldn't try to lie to you. Yes, I would make more money, but I loved Rosa as a tenant. You can't beat a good, clean, responsible tenant. They're worth more than gold."

Magaly harrumphed dramatically.

"Can I ask you then if Tomasello Management Corp would have any reason of their own to harass her?"

Litvinchouk smiled and looked at an invisible spot on the table. He rubbed it back and forth. Then he looked up. "Listen. I think I answered all the questions you need. We're done, I think. After all, you were a great student, but let's face it, you're not the *Wall Street Journal.*"

"Ouch," Tony said.

When he went to shut off his recorder, Litvinchouk put his hand on his. "One thing, my friend. I'll tell you one more thing. Off the record. Because she was a nice lady, good people, *buena gente,* I didn't tell the cops this."

"What?"

"A few weeks before, she had hit the number—not the legal type, you understand, the local Spanish lottery. She won a lot of money. At least ten thousand dollars."

"How do you know?"

"I loaned her some money, years ago. All of a sudden she paid it all off about two weeks before she disappeared. She was so happy, she let it out how she got it."

"Why didn't you tell this to the police?"

"Well, two things. One, maybe when they found her she'd get in trouble for gambling. Two, I don't want them taking me for a Shylock."

"Thanks. Thank you."

"Remember: Off the record!"

"*Vale,* Mr. Moran! One more thing. *Velim in auribus tuis*

loqui."

"*Quando?*"

"*Te vocabo. Volo tibi soli loqui.*"

"Okay. *Vale.*"

Outside, Tony walked fast to keep up with Magaly, who was walking stiffly and quickly back toward the Southside.

"So, what did you think?" he said.

"Oh, your Latin professor knows more than he's saying. And what was all that at the end?"

"He wants to meet me. Alone."

Magaly threw her hands up. "That sexist son of a—"

"You said he knows more than he's saying. Obviously, there are things he doesn't want to say in front of you. Maybe it's because of your gender. Maybe it's because you came in ready to arrest him. And you work for a local advocacy group, so he probably sees you as an unfriendly adversary."

"I wanted to hit him," she said.

"I couldn't tell."

"You know, even if Tomasello had some reason to harass Rosa, I think this guy would still be liable. I'll have to check."

"Okay," Tony said. "Let me know. Even though, I have enough for a story now."

"Enough? But this is just the start. Don't you want to know the whole deal? Don't you want to find her?"

"Hey, what is this? I'm going to find out what I can, but my job is not to find her but to bring more attention to Rosa's story, so the cops can do their job."

"I can't believe you. The cops are not going to bother. Some little old Puerto Rican lady in Williamsburg. They're more concerned with keeping the white yuppies safe."

"Is that really fair to say? Now who's being cynical?"

"Tony, you've been out of it for too long. You play with your bocce—"

"Pétanque."

"—whatever. You slack around. You don't know what's

going on."

"I know what's going on. I just don't—"

"You don't care, yes. I get it. Like you said, you've always been that way. What can I say? I guess you really haven't changed at all. Listen, I have to be someplace. Good night, Chino. Get home safe."

"Let me walk you home."

"Please," she said, storming away, her hair bouncing. "I've got pepper spray."

"Pepper spray expires," Tony said. "And if the wind catches—"

"No worries. If someone tries to attack me right now, I'll just kick their ass."

CHAPTER TWENTY-THREE

Magaly liked to tell herself that although she was only one floor away from her parents' apartment, she had at least moved out of the tiny bedroom she had grown up in and now lived independently, except for those two, three, four, five times a week she felt too tired to cook and went over for dinner. Her Titi Cecelia had had an apartment upstairs on the fifth floor, a cozy 2BR, heat and hot water included, and, if you leaned your entire torso out the window, a pleasing view of the Williamsburg Bridge. Titi Cecelia knew she and her kids would be moving to Florida, so years before she left she put Magaly's name on the lease, and once she flew south, Magaly inherited the apartment. So now she had a place of her own, a place a whole family used to occupy that was now hers to fill with books and plants and the odd sock or underwear on the floor. She felt slightly guilty to have so much space, but she told herself she needed it, more figuratively than literally, but still.

And now her boss was in that space—her married boss— Luis De Moscoso, dressed in slacks and shoes but no shirt, as he jumped off the couch and walked back and forth.

She loved her job. She didn't know how she felt about Luis, but she did know the situation was stupid and that Luis was not what her friends would call a "catch." She would have left El Flamboyan, but she knew she was doing something important for people who had been forgotten, not just someone missing like Rosa Irizzary, but all the Latinos and Latinas who still lived in Williamsburg while the neighborhood violently transformed all around them. It was just very complicated. *Ai*, she needed a drink.

The floor was bare wood, last varnished decades ago, and his feet made slapping sounds as he paced. He walked into the bedroom, into the storage/law library/office/second bedroom and then back out to the living room—there wasn't any more space to walk unless he wanted to walk into the bathroom, but there was only enough room to take a single step in there. Naked and cold without his warmth next to her, Magaly slouched on the couch, a hand-me-down from her aunt.

Magaly asked him what was wrong. "*¿Que te pasa, hombre?*"

"I can't. I just can't tonight," he said.

She could tell he was warming up for a speech. So much for a quiet night, she thought. He had been acting more and more unpredictable lately, and not in a good way.

His chest, shaved as smooth as his head, was red and heaving, as she worried he would hyperventilate.

"Is this about Jocelyn's closing?" she said. "Because I'm not surprised. I don't know how they were able to stay in business the last few years without any customers."

They had a tradition where he would always bring her a bag of *alcapurria*, *rellenos de papa*, and *morcilla*, all very greasy yet ecstatically delicious deep-fried food, from Jocelyn's, one of the last cuchifrito joints in the neighborhood. He came in tonight empty-handed, saying the store was closed and was now a pop-up shop called Mown that featured clothes made of grass.

"You know, that food will kill you anyway," she said. "It's full of the bad cholesterol, not the good cholesterol—" She stopped herself when she realized she was sounding like Chino.

"Jesus! It's not about Jocelyn's!" Luis said.

Speeches and lectures. What was up with the men in her life? What was that about?

"*¡Carajo!*" she said, losing her patience. "Then what is it?"

Magaly watched him pace and sadly realized how much he

reminded her of her father. Not just the pacing and the ranting, but also the shirtlessness. She realized—for the first time, and she couldn't believe she hadn't seen it before—that her father wore his goatee the same way Luis did. Holy Mother of Sigmund Freud. Here was a whole new series of sessions with her therapist.

"Those slashings, the killing," he said. "Did you see the news?"

"I saw the news, Luis. I read the news every day."

"It's not just white people now. All the other victims were these hipsters and yuppies, and now it's one of us. Not a Puerto Rican. He's a Guatemalan, but he's a Latino."

"So? Do we get a free pass?" she said. "Where do you get them? Because I would like one."

"No, Mami. You don't understand. It was an accident."

"An accident? Wait, how do you know?"

"*Ai,* because this is the Latin gangs. I know what they're doing. They are trying to clean the yuppies and the hipsters out of the neighborhood, not us. They must have thought it was a white guy."

"I don't know, Luis. I think it was only a matter of time before they started killing Latinos. Not that there aren't plenty of white people to slash. But I wouldn't think the gangs were discriminatory."

"No, no, no, you don't understand, they're like us, like me. They want the neighborhood to go back to what it was."

Magaly's face scrunched up in disbelief. "So, wait, their plan is to wipe out the white people so we're all back in 1979? That doesn't make sense."

"It makes perfect sense. This neighborhood, my old neighborhood. You see what's been happening. These white people, they think they can come in and change everything."

Here we go again, she thought. You get Luis lost on a highway, but he would always find his way home to his favorite subject.

"I know, Luis. I don't like it either," she said. "But the mayor only cares about the yuppies and the tourists. Most of all, he cares about the real estate developers."

"Mami, we can't just do nothing while they expect us to go away or die off, so that they can take our homes and our businesses. What we need to do is kick them out and change it back, change it all back."

Why, oh why did he have to call her "Mami?" It was a step up from "Baby," which she had to train him not to use. In another circumstance, it might have been endearing. But now Luis calling her "Mami" sounded more than a little creepy.

"Change it back?" she said. "C'mon, Luis, that's impossible. And don't you remember how it used to be? The catcalls, the harassment, the assault. I couldn't walk the streets at night. I can't tell you how many times I almost got raped, how many people I know got mugged or had their apartments broken into. It was insane!"

"That was a different time. The economy is better now. But our people don't get to enjoy it. We never get to rise above second-class citizenship."

She shook her head, her hair a moving cloud of curls, and got up and padded to the kitchen.

"I don't know, Luis," she said from inside the refrigerator. "We have to work with them, not fight them. That's what I want. I'm having that meeting with the Keap Street gallery. Maybe if we work together, I don't know."

There was no beer, no more wine. Just an old bottle of coquito from last Christmas.

"Work with them?" Luis said. "These stupid, entitled artsy-fartsies. They don't care about art. All they care about is money. Only the rich have the security to pursue a life of art. It's the people with the money who have always had the power."

"Wow. You should talk to Chino. You two could power all the electricity in the city."

"You mean your reporter friend?" he said. "I was meaning to ask you: What kind of friend is he? What's the story there?"

"Oh my god, I'm not going to justify that—"

He grabbed her arm, knocking the coquito bottle out of her hand to smash on the floor.

"Luis! You're fucking hurting me," she said. Great. Another reminder of her father. "Bastard! Go ahead. Treat me like you do your wife."

He raised a hand to smack her, but she was faster and grabbed the first thing in her reach. A metal spatula, two dollars at the ninety-nine-cent store.

"Don't. You. Dare," she said, pointing the spatula at him. "My grandmother used to beat me with one of these until I would bleed, so I know how to use it. Don't even think about touching me. Ever."

He stepped back and took a breath. His eyes weren't seeing her. He didn't see her standing there, naked, holding a spatula, feeling ridiculous.

"I have to do something..." he said quietly, almost whispering, "...I have to help bring the Southside back to the way it used to be. All...all my childhood memories are being ruined by people that don't belong here. They're changing everything."

"Luis?" she said.

"I have to work on articulating this concretely. No one loves the man who has to tell the truth. But my plan has to work. I know it's gonna work," he said. "And please, god, forgive me."

In seconds, he had put his shirt back on and had raced out of the apartment.

Magaly plopped on the couch and realized she still had the spatula in her hand.

"Men suck," she said and threw it across the room, hitting her two-foot-high statue of Christ. "Oh god!"

She got up to do something, anything, and then she stopped and plopped back down. What was she going to do? Soothe the statue? Apologize to it? She rolled over, pushing her face into the couch. But then she mumbled a "Hail Mary," just to be safe.

CHAPTER TWENTY-FOUR

Ah, the summers in Brooklyn. Yogi Johnson loved them. *Energy! Electricity! Passion!* The people had it in spades. And it would all hit a peak on July 4, when things went bonkers on his block. All the guys and the little kids on Maujer Street would set off firecrackers, sizzling sparklers, bottle rockets, cherry bombs, morning, noon, night, for weeks before and culminating on the date. He liked to watch from his front window, but he felt a part of the people down there—*distance avails not*—part of Brooklyn, and on those days it was as if the whole street was on fire, absolutely lit up. And then the morning after July 4, Maujer Street stank of sulfur, and firecracker paper littered the whole block, covered the sidewalks, piled into dunes in every gutter. *Fantastic!*

But a July 4 like that hadn't happened for a few years now. Now there were a few pops and cracks here and there. Where had all the fireworks lovers gone? He watched the street, and it was clean. And quiet. *Boring.*

It was time to go downstairs to check on Mr. McShane. After being rushed to the hospital, the old geezer had been diagnosed with a gallbladder infection. He'd spent three days in the hospital for tests. Yogi had visited him every day because he felt karmically involved.

"Where are your kids? You got kids, right?" Yogi had asked him.

"Gone."

"They're dead?"

"California."

"Same thing, then."

Somebody had to take care of the old man. There was a tube that emptied the contents of Mr. McShane's gallbladder into a bag. Somebody had to help clean out the bag and clean the area where the tube entered the old man's body. Mr. McShane had to watch what he ate, what he drank, how much he went to the john. A nurse came by only every three or four days. So Yogi stepped in, gladly taking on the burden. He checked on him a few times a day. He had taken a spare set of the old man's keys and let himself into his apartment.

"Mr. McShane," he said as he came in.

The old man lay on an extended recliner that looked like it belonged in a junkyard, in front of a console TV set topped with dozens of paperback westerns and with a screen layered in dust. Some baseball game was on, playing too loudly. Yogi lowered the volume.

Mr. McShane looked at Yogi with tired eyes and said nothing. He moved his head toward a side table covered with ancient issues of *TV Guide*, Bill Cosby right there on the top.

Barely audibly, the old man said, "Mail."

There was an envelope on the table with Yogi's name on it. He'd look at it later.

"Time to clean your tube, Mr. McShane."

Yogi raised the old man's T-shirt and examined the bandages. Mr. McShane smelled like a homeless man, a combination of sweat and ass and feet-stink that could fill a subway car in seconds. The old guy needed a sponge bath badly, but brave as Yogi was, he wasn't feeling up to that challenge. He'd leave that for the visiting nurse.

After he finished cleaning the hole and changing the bandages, Yogi emptied the old man's pitcher of urine and then microwaved a turkey dinner and set it out for the old man. Then he went back and microwaved a Salisbury steak dinner for himself.

After what he'd done for Mr. McShane, he figured he was entitled to a cheap meal. Besides, there wasn't anything in his refrigerator upstairs. It was meat, alas, but he didn't feel like being a vegetarian this week.

As he sat on the floor eating, he could feel the old man giving
him the stinkeye. Yogi decided to create some goodwill, lighten
the mood, try to reach across the Generation Gap. He and Mr.
McShane hadn't been on the best terms before, but the old man
and he would have to get used to each other now. He saw a
black and white picture on the wall, just above the TV set. In it,
some farmer types stood in front of a series of horse sheds.

"Where is this, upstate?" Yogi said, standing up in front of
the TV set.

"Devoe Street." Old McShane spoke slowly and softly.

"Devoe?" Yogi said. "That's just over a few blocks from
here."

"Used to be farms all around here. That's my grand uncle's
farm. 1910. Those are all parking garages now. The owner
makes a mint."

"The neighborhood sure has changed," Yogi said. He was
totally reaching the old man with his positive tone and selfless
attitude. "I bet you've seen it all."

"Yeah." The old man leaned over to one side of the recliner.

Yogi settled cross-legged in front of the TV set. "I bet you
think it's changed for the worse."

"No. Well, for a while," the old man said. He leaned over to
the other side of the recliner, and Yogi saw him wince with
what looked like pain. "It's a much better neighborhood now,"
McShane said. "Nicer people."

"I don't know about that," Yogi said. "I'd say the neighborhood was much better ten, twenty years ago, when it was really
for artists."

"You're talking about the hippie artists. I'm talking about
the coloreds and the PRs. Used to be crawling with them. Now
we got nicer people. Much nicer people."

"Oh." Yogi sensed negativity and decided to change the subject. He said, "Oh, hey, let's watch something we can both enjoy."

He took the remote control from where it sat by the old man. Yogi started changing channels. "I don't have a TV set in my place," he said. "I don't even have Internet at the moment. I'm pretty cut off from the world."

Yogi stopped on the local news. He normally would never watch the news—it was all fear-mongering, crime, and product placement disguised as news. But he saw the headline behind the news reader: "Another Williamsburg Slashing."

"...Echeverria is still in intensive care at Woodhull Hospital. This attack brings the count up to five so far..."

Yogi said, "Wow. Really?"

"...local gang members are being questioned in relation to the slashings. Police say they have no suspects at this time..."

"Wow." He turned to look at old McShane. Yogi said, "Well, the more the merrier, I always say."

After the news, and after two very bad sitcoms, Yogi got up nimbly and with purpose and emptied the old man's pitcher of urine again. Then he filled a pitcher of water and set it next to the urine container.

"Now, don't get these two confused," he said.

As he went out the door, Yogi felt Mr. McShane giving him the stinkeye again.

CHAPTER TWENTY-FIVE

Right out of the elevator, Detective Hadid spotted a gorgeous Puerto Rican nurse by the nurses' station. He left his partner, Detective Petrosino, behind, and slid up to her with his best Hollywood smile. In what he considered his decent Spanish, he said, <"Good afternoon, beautiful lady. Please, can I talk to me where Jesus Echeverria's room am?">

The look on her face did not say, as he would have liked, "Hello, Papi." Instead, it said, "I know how to make an enema unpleasant for you." But what she actually did was point to a room across from the nurses' station, where a uniformed cop stood. And toward which Petrosino was already walking without looking back.

Inside the room were several Hispanic visitors, no doubt family relations, all in varying degrees of hysterical crying.

On the bed, the victim looked awful. Jesus Echeverria's left hand had been reattached and was heavily bandaged, his head swaddled in bandages.

Using his decent Spanish, Hadid introduced himself and Petrosino. He told them they'd like to speak to Echeverria alone. The visitors moved out slowly, except for the victim's wife. Hadid looked at Petrosino. He shrugged his approval.

Hadid stood by the bed and leaned over. He got close to Echeverria's face and hoped he could hear behind all the bandages, <"Mr. Echeverria. Can I tell me who hurt me?">

Echeverria looked confused, but then he answered slowly, in

a whisper. <"He...came from...nowhere. Why did he do this to me?">

<"Did I see the man?">

<"No. Too fast.">

<"Was you a white man? A black man?">

"Blanco," Echeverria said.

"White," Hadid said to Petrosino.

"I got that," Petrosino said.

<"I told the officers on the scene that the man ran on a bicycle. Can I describe the bicycle?">

<"No. It was just a bicycle,"> Echeverria said.

<"Do I remember the color?">

Echeverria paused. Then he said, <"I think it was red. I think.">

Hadid took notes. He turned to Petrosino. "Want me to ask anything else?"

"Ask him about the weapon."

Hadid did. Echeverria looked up at the ceiling. His eyes watered. <"It was a big machete. Two feet. Why did this man do this to me? I didn't do anything.">

Petrosino said, "Right-o. That's enough."

Hadid thanked Echeverria, and the detectives left the room. As soon as they did, all the visitors poured back in.

Outside the hospital, Hadid watched Petrosino have a smoke.

"You're outside smoking here, and there are people inside with the cancer," Hadid said. "Don't you see the irony there?"

"I hate irony," Petrosino said. He flicked his ashes. Some of them landed on Hadid's jacket. "So, I didn't know you knew Spanish."

"Oh c'mon, man," Hadid said, wiping off the ashes. Then he said, "Yeah, my wife's people are from Ecuador, so..."

"Is that so? Well, Mr. Echeverria here blows the young and white victim M.O."

"Well, I was thinking, if it's gangs doing this, maybe there's a chance Echeverria's gang-connected somehow."

"Maybe. Although he seems a bit long in the tooth for it. Still, check him out. Did you look into that 'hipster death' thing we talked about?"

"Yeah, Petro. Sorry, I got to it right away, soon as you asked me. I googled around. No link to any gang stuff, but I turned up something on Twitter."

"And?"

"Well, the reason I didn't say anything before is I did find a Twitter user named 'hipster death rattle.' But whoever it is joined way back in 2002. No followers, not following anyone. And just the egg. You know, the egg avatar, means he or she never bothered to put up a picture?"

Petrosino nodded.

"And over on Instagram, fourteen people took pictures of the crime scene graffiti and used it as a hashtag. But that's it."

"All right. Keep keeping an eye on it."

"Sure," Hadid said. "Hey, I was thinking. You want to go get a beer tonight? I want to get to know the local bars, and frankly, I could use a break from the wife. She's getting tired of my big mouth."

Petrosino just looked at him. Hadid again felt like a man being sized up for an enema.

"Yeah, I don't think so," Hadid said. "Back to the precinct?"

But Petrosino was already walking.

CHAPTER TWENTY-SIX

"You start, Mr. Moran," Petrosino said.

Tony was in a windowless room in the 90th precinct. The soundproofing tiles all along the walls and ceiling had been freshly painted avocado green. Twenty years before.

He had called Petrosino, saying he had questions to ask, and the detective had said to him, "I was just about to call you." Turns out Petrosino had questions to ask him. So here he was, playing intrepid reporter. But why did he feeling alarmingly like a suspect?

Petrosino's partner, Hadid, took a seat across from him and said, "So, Mr. Moran. 'Sfunny, you don't look Irish."

"I didn't say I was Irish," Tony said.

"Well, by your last name..."

"There's an accent on the 'a.' Morán."

"I knew that. It was just a joke."

"Is that what it was?"

Hadid got flustered. "Oh...You know what I mean. I didn't mean anything by it."

"If it makes you feel better, I'm Algerian, and people think I'm Spanish all the time."

"They think you're from Spain?"

"No," said Hadid. "What I mean is—"

Petrosino finally spoke. "Okay, guys, enough with the flirting. Hadid, on second thought, get Tuchman in here. Save us a meeting later."

When Hadid left the room, Tony felt it was his chance. "I just had a quick question or two about something."

Petrosino held up a finger. "Let's do this first, champ. Don't worry. I won't forget."

The door opened and in walked Hadid, followed by a man who looked more like a lawyer than a cop. His tie matched the handkerchief sticking out of his pocket. He had a tie clip and cufflinks and a pinky ring that was slightly smaller than Staten Island. He introduced himself as a Lieutenant Tuchman.

They all stood opposite Tony. He said, "Well, now it's a party. Or an inquisition. Which one is it going to be?"

"Not exactly a party, but thank you for coming in," Tuchman said. "I'd like to start off by asking you to tell me, tell us, as much as you can about Patrick Stoller. What kind of person was he?"

"Well, I guess he was a nice guy. A decent editor. He was very organized, I can say that."

"How'd you meet him?" Tuchman asked, leaning forward. His pinky ring threatened to poke Tony's eye out.

"At the *Sentinel*," Tony said. "I was working there freelance, and the editor who'd been there for twenty-five years retired, and they wanted me to take the job, but I didn't want it, so they promoted Patrick."

"So, you didn't want his job?"

"No. The hours suck, the pay sucks, and who wants the responsibility?"

"If I remember correctly," Petrosino said, "you had said you weren't exactly friends with Stoller?"

"Right. Just co-workers."

"You two didn't get along?" Hadid said.

"It's not that."

"Professional jealousy, maybe?" Hadid again.

"You know, this sounds like it's turning from 'some questions' to a barbecue pretty quickly."

"Just a few questions, Mr. Moran," said Tuchman, twirling

Staten Island around. "We don't want to make you feel uncomfortable."

"No worries. I'm having a lovely time. I'm learning so much about police work. To answer your question: Patrick and I got along fine. We didn't exactly hang out. But, I mean, do you guys hang out after work?"

Hadid looked behind him at Petrosino. Petrosino gave him a poker face. Hadid turned back and said, "Nope."

Petrosino shook his head. "Okay, so you weren't best buds. You told us he lived in the other direction, and you were right. So do you have any idea why Patrick would be riding his skateboard in that part of the neighborhood at that time of night?"

"Cardio? Sight-seeing? Geocaching?"

"Mr. Moran, please..."

"Honestly, I have no idea. I did think it was strange, especially since it was hot as hell that night. Maybe he couldn't sleep."

Tuchman leaned back now. "How about this? Was your editor Mr. Stoller working on any particular scoop?"

Tony shrugged. "We're always looking to fill the issue but no, we don't exactly do exposés or get scoops, if that's what you mean."

"No?" said Tuchman. "Maybe an in-depth story on gangs in the neighborhood, something along those lines?"

"Are you kidding? Our crime coverage is a police blotter. We're mostly a lot of gallery openings and bad restaurant reviews."

"Reviews of bad restaurants?" Hadid said.

"No, badly written restaurant reviews," Tony said. "Look, we write nothing negative. We're a supportive community newspaper. We have to be, otherwise we wouldn't get any ads. Can I ask why you think he was doing an exposé? Are you suggesting a gang member didn't like something he might have been working on and then killed him for it?"

Tuchman said, "Perhaps we should emphasize here that we

don't expect you to tell me exactly what story your friend was working on. We understand how journalists operate. Professional ethics and all that."

"Can I ask you guys a question?" Tony said.

"Just a moment. Let us finish," Tuchman said.

Ignoring him, Petrosino said, "Of course, you can. Go ahead."

"So what is your prevailing theory about the slashings? Do you think it's just a repeat of those gang-related slashings we had back in...2008, 2009?"

Petrosino spoke. "2008. Yeah, the police department has—"

Tuchman interrupted. "What Detective Petrosino is trying to say is that the 90th Precinct Gang Task Force has had a near hundred percent arrest-and-conviction record when it comes to gang-related crime."

"Hundred percent?" Tony said. "Is that even possible?" When he said this, he spotted Petrosino covering a smile with his hand, pretending to move his toothpick around.

"It is," Tuchman said.

"Okay, fine. But getting back to my question, what is your prevailing theory? Do you have one that you can share?"

Tuchman smiled now, an oily, politician's smile. "You know we can't give you much detail. But we can tell you this: We are still not saying that Mr. Stoller's death was anything other than a violent attack in a relatively deserted part of the neighborhood. But we are considering every possibility."

"Well, here's what I'm thinking," Tony said, talking to Petrosino. "And mind you, I'm barely one step above a blogger. But this guy says he's the director of the Gang Task Force. But you keep asking questions about Patrick as a person. I think you think this wasn't a random slashing, by gang members or whoever, but that someone killed Patrick very much on purpose."

Petrosino and Hadid looked at Tuchman, waiting for him to respond.

"Very interesting. That *is* an idea we have discussed, Mr. Moran," said Tuchman. "I can't say much more. But since you're being very helpful, I'm going to go out on a limb and be upfront with you, and maybe you can help us a little more. Let me ask you: Do you know who the Southside Quistadoreys are?"

"Sounds like a rotary club."

"A rotary club," Hadid said. "Is this guy some kind of joker?"

Tuchman ignored them both. "Have you ever heard the name Eladio Cortés?"

"Nope."

"Cortés is the current leader of the Southside Quistadoreys. He's a dangerous character. Suspected of fifteen bodies on his scorecard. Never served time for anything but small potatoes though."

"I did know an Eladio Cortés in kindergarten. He picked his nose a lot. Probably not the same guy. Or maybe exactly the same guy. The psychology of the criminal is fascinating."

Petrosino chewed hard on his toothpick. Then Tuchman said, "Can you tell us why your friend Patrick was in touch with him?"

"A gang leader?" said Tony. "Does that mean you found his phone? Or did you subpoena his phone records?"

Tuchman tapped his ring on the metal desk. Somewhere the dead were hearing it and covering their ears. Tuchman talked to Petrosino and Hadid without taking his eyes off of Tony. "Gentlemen, I think maybe it's time for a little quid pro quo with Mr. Moran."

He didn't wait for them to respond. "Understand, Mr. Moran, that what I'm about to tell you has not been released to the press, and we would appreciate your keeping this to yourself until we complete our investigation. If you release it, our chance of getting this killer could go south. I'm sure you want us to catch your friend's killer as much as we do...Are we clear?"

Tony guessed Tuchman's dramatic pause was to show them all how impressive he was.

"Yep. We're clear."

"Tell him, Petrosino."

Petrosino took a toothpick out of his mouth and smoothed down his yellow-brown mustache. He said, "Patrick Stoller had contact with an individual who called himself Eladio Cortés. They were dozens of texts between them."

Tony didn't buy it. "He had a gang lord's phone number? And what were these texts about?"

"Couldn't trace it. Was probably a burner phone. We can't go into detail about the content of the texts, but in any case, here's the thing: Stoller received several texts from that phone number on the day he was killed."

Tuchman stepped in. "We think your friend Patrick was on to something, and it backfired. If you know something about it, it could really help us make this connection."

"Let me get this straight. You think this Cortés guy slashed Patrick—then he took his iPhone because he didn't like the story Patrick was writing? Why did he even bother dealing with him in the first place?"

"Well. We see it this way," Tuchman said. "Naïve white boy from Smalltown, Pennsylvania. From what we understand, your friend wanted to be a big-time reporter, and as far back as two years ago he was talking about doing a story on the gangs. So, somehow he finally gets a contact and then arranges to meet a gang member to get a scoop. Cortés says the hell with the story and takes him for what he's got."

Tony said, "Uh huh. Plus there's the added benefit if you tie Cortés to Patrick's death, then you have a suspect for all the slashings? Case closed. This summer's biggest story neatly wrapped up."

Petrosino stepped away from the wall he had been leaning against. "Mr. Moran, as far as anyone in the press is concerned, we are looking at a wide range of suspects."

"I don't know anything about a gang story. Like I said, we don't run that kind of stuff. If Patrick was after a Pulitzer Prize, he never told me. Like I said, we weren't close, and I only work part-time. Why would Cortés even bother to meet him just to kill him and potentially leave a trail?"

"If criminals were smart, they'd be bankers," said Hadid.

"One thing I've learned is that gang members can be very arrogant, too arrogant for their own good," said Tuchman, standing up abruptly. "Okay, gentleman, I have got to run."

He handed Tony a business card. "If you remember anything else about your friend, please let us know. We're only here to help."

Tuchman left the room with gusto, as if he spent time practicing his exits, and the atmosphere suddenly felt a lot lighter.

"Can't say it hasn't been fun," Hadid said to the closed door. "Because it hasn't."

Tony was about to ask a question when Petrosino stopped him with a raised hand.

"Just a second," Petrosino said. "I have a quick question for you."

"Okay."

"I see you live on South 4th Street. That's not very far from where your friend was found."

"Despite what real estate people say, Williamsburg isn't that big a neighborhood. Nothing's very far from anything."

"Yeah, well, just as a matter of formality, can you tell us where you were that night? Were you at home? At the hospital, I recall you got there pretty quickly."

"I was in Queens. I took a cab. There was no traffic at that time of night."

"Can someone verify where you were?"

"Ummm. Yeah, someone can."

"Why 'Ummm?'"

"It's just...it's just ridiculous. I was with Gabby—Gabrielle—from the office. We were at a poetry reading around here, then I took her home to Queens."

"Poetry reading?" Hadid said.

Tony ignored him.

Petrosino said, "This Gabby, is that your girlfriend?"

"Co-worker."

"Another one of those. Right-o." Petrosino put another toothpick in his mouth. "Now, you said you had questions for me."

"Is it my turn already?" Tony said. "Okay. Thing is, there is a story I happen to be working on—the disappearance of a woman named Rosa Irizarry. As a matter of fact, she lived in Patrick's building. Disappeared about a year ago. Do you know the case?"

"Can't say I do."

Tony went on. "Well, at the time it was alleged she might have been the victim of foul play. She claimed that she had been constantly harassed to leave her apartment."

"That happens all the time," Petrosino said. "Urban renewal, they call it. Look, we got our backs up against it with this slasher all over the neighborhood. This stuff isn't really our department."

"Well, it could be. What if the harassment led to something worse? She did disappear, and she wasn't the kind of lady to disappear."

"Sure," Petrosino said. "Let me guess: She was a nice, sweet old lady with a lovely disposition."

"As a matter of fact, she wasn't that nice," Tony said.

Petrosino smiled. "Well. Be that as it may, I'm sorry. I can't help you."

"Any chance you could point me to someone who can?"

"Give me a call later. I'll see what I can do."

Tony left the semi-cool interior of the precinct and went back out into the heat wave. Being in the precinct had left him feeling dirty and used, like the bottom of a shoe. He wanted air and sunshine. He knew what he needed. He walked toward McCarren Park, aiming for a long afternoon of pétanque.

CHAPTER TWENTY-SEVEN

She had had to sell her car, the one she drove up with from PA years ago, when she first moved to the New York. It was a stinker, literally, so she'd had to sell it. And now Gunnar was being a total pain in the ass. The cheap, stingy sonofabitch. And Kirsten was glad he was stuck checking IDs at the door and looking away from her. They had argued at home and walked to SubBar together in silence. She didn't look at him the whole time, and she did not want to see his face for the rest of the night.

Kirsten stood behind the bar, having a cup of tar-thick coffee, the way she liked it. Above the never-cleaned coffee maker was one of Kirsten's photographs, from her series of women in prayer. The rest of the series was currently on exhibit exclusively in her apartment.

Aesthetically, of course, the women she chose to shoot were not beautiful, not by mainstream society's current definition of beauty. She had been walking down Grand Street one day and noted one neighborhood woman after another, how they were so diverse, so ethnic, so real. She decided immediately that she wanted to photograph them. She began stopping them and asking them to pose, to put their hands together in prayer, even the two or three who said they were not religious at all. She had framed each photo in cheap, plastic frames with broken glass or plastic to emphasize their economic class. The result was a parade of holy women, of saints. It was an extraordinary series, it really was. But she hadn't taken new pictures in a dog's age anyway, years already. What did it matter? Throw a rock in Williamsburg and you'll hit a jillion aspiring photographers.

She chanced a glance at Gunnar. He stood outside the bar's front door, which was jammed open because the owner preferred not to pay for high electricity bills and ordered the AC off unless it got over a hundred degrees outside. He kept his eyes forward. She guessed he didn't want to see her face tonight either. Fuck him.

She decided to start listening to whatever Black Martin had been saying to her the whole time.

"...I'm thinking of moving," he was saying. "I hear the Bronx is getting livable. Well, parts of the Bronx."

"I totally know what you mean," she said, not at all interested, but years as a bartender had taught her how to pretend to be.

"Black Martin" was her secret, unspoken nickname for him, to distinguish him from "Regular Martin," who sometimes came in at the same time.

He nodded energetically, his watery eyes not quite focused on her. He mumbled, "Gotta pee," and walked off.

The bar wasn't packed. It never got packed. Most of the bar stools stayed empty every night. There were five bars within a block, three with better beer selections, two with live music, and all of them better pickup joints for twentysomethings than this place would ever be. SubBar was living on borrowed time.

And so was she. If only Gunnar wasn't such a skinflint. She needed to get down to PA, and she hated buses with a demonic passion. They couldn't try one of those car-sharing outfits because they sucked. So the only option was to rent a car. She had enough, but she insisted that Gunnar chip in half, because it was just as important to him. But he refused. Tightwad! Her parents were the same way. She hated tightwads!

She had no friends with cars to borrow. Hell, she had no friends. The ones she had stopped calling, stopped texting, stopped inviting her to things on Facebook after she broke up with Patrick. So for the moment, she had to deal with the drunks and the losers.

A fat dude kept cursing at the Space Invaders game. If he kept that up she'd have to talk to Gunnar to toss him out, so she let it go on more than she normally would. Some couple made out across a table, half-standing up and spilling their drinks without a care. Ah, to be young and stupid and in love. And around the pool table were a group of guys, and Kirsten played "Gay or European?" in her mind with them until Black Martin plopped back himself onto his stool and then slipped off to the floor. He crawled back up the sitting position.

"You okay there?" she said.

He was in the bar every night. Whatever he did for a living—he had told her once or twice but she had forgotten—the boy had a lot of money to throw at hooch.

"I had this thing today," he slurred, ignoring her question. "Somebody asked me where I live, and I lied and said Red Hook."

"Red Hook? That still seems out in the boonies to me," Kirsten said.

"It used to be cool to say you lived in Williamsburg. Now I find it embarrassing. You know what I mean?"

He was on his fifth or sixth PBR and third or fourth call brand tequila back. He was drinking both like water. And now he was leaning almost across the bar as he was talking to her. She didn't like that.

"Now—now you see I tell people I live on the other side of Brooklyn just so I can dis...dissss...disassociate myself from hipsters and the douchebags."

Black Martin's eyes were glassy under his thick black-framed glasses. Once again, he slid off the stool and went to the john.

When he came back, his zipper wasn't closed. He said, "LemmegetanotherPBR and a shot."

"I think you're done, honey," Kirsten said.

"What do you mean?"

"You want some water? Let's get you some water, okay?"

"What? Fuck no. I want another PBR."

She looked up at the doorway and, like some psychic connection clicking, Gunnar was looking right back. She had to give it to him—he knew when she was in trouble. He always came to the rescue.

All six feet five inches of Gunnar marched in and came up right behind Black Martin and gripped him by the shoulders. She knew that steel grip. No way out of it. Not even if you wanted out.

"What the hell?"

"Time to go home," she said.

"Awww."

"Sorry," she said. "If you can't handle your liquor, you don't belong in a bar, know what I mean?"

Black Martin raised his empty can and said, "Lemme finis'."

Gunnar began to lead the poor bastard out. One day all of this would be behind her. One day all of this would be a funny but sad story to tell.

But then she suddenly remembered something very important about Black Martin.

"Wait. Wait a second. Gunnar! Stop."

Gunnar looked at her. He raised a WTF eyebrow at her, like he was wondering if this was going to be another fight with her today.

Black Martin stood between them in a haze.

"Martin! Listen to me," she said, waving him closer. She winked at Gunnar, who stood behind Black Martin.

"Yyyeah?" Black Martin said.

She cracked open a PBR and set up a tequila for him. "Martin, you have a car, don't you?"

CHAPTER TWENTY-EIGHT

Tomasello Real Estate and Management Corp. was located in Maspeth, Queens, just northeast of Williamsburg. No subways ran there, so Tony could either walk all the way, under a sulky, blackening sky that afternoon and through curtains of humidity.

Or he could take a bus.

And he hated buses.

And he had forgotten to buy a new umbrella after losing his last one.

He waited for the Q59. It was one of those eternal waits when it seems that mass transit had retired and moved to Florida and nothing was ever going to show up ever again.

"Ridiculous," said Tony out loud. He was ungently being steamed to death on that sidewalk. He was grateful at least that it was a lousy day to play pétanque.

When the Q59 bus finally showed, there were two more right behind it. When it took off, it crawled.

It seemed to take a thousand years to get to Maspeth. Five hundred years in, a steady rain began.

In order to get the full story for whatever the hell he was going to write about Rosa Irizarry, he had to interview Frank Tomasello, head of Tomasello Real Estate and Management Corp. and co-owner of Rosa's building. Tony tried calling and got nowh

ere. He didn't know why he was bothering. He was moving on momentum now, but he had to admit the story had been nagging at him. Something to do with Patrick's death—Tony hadn't helped him that night, and, not that he thought Patrick's death was his fault—hell, if he had gone with him, they might both be dead. But he hadn't done anything to help Patrick or the police. But with Rosa, there was something he could do. It might not add up to anything. In fact, it wouldn't be more than a round-up of facts, with some new quotes, but it would keep the case alive. Which was enough, wasn't it? He was in motion now, and it felt better to be in motion than to be doing nothing.

He got off the bus on Grand Avenue. Rain came down in steady, hot sheets. Without an umbrella, Tony was forced to run past the small businesses and staid brick and siding-covered homes that lined the street.

The Tomasello office was a block down from the bus stop. The office was a storefront in a single-floor building, its display window covered in so many real estate placements that Tony could barely see inside.

In front of the door was an awning, but it was narrow, and when Tony ducked under it, rain continued to fall down his back.

As he went to turn the knob, the door opened. He was about to step in, but a living statue blocked the entrance.

She stood over six feet tall, although some of that must have been heels. Her skin was tanned just shy of jerky and she wore enough makeup to embarrass a clown, so it was hard to figure her age. She could be anywhere from her thirties to her fifties. In any case, she kept in shape. The thin blouse she wore emphasized well-developed shoulders and arms, and around each wrist were bangles the size of basketball hoops. She smelled of thick layers of coconut lotion.

"Can I help you?" she said.

"My name is Tony Moran. I work for the *Williamsburg Sentinel*."

"Tony?" she said. She gave him that strange look he got just about every time he said his name.

"Tony, yes."

"The reporter. You left a million messages. Jesus."

"Fourteen, actually. That's me. I'm here to see Mr. Toma—"

"You didn't make an appointment," she said.

"Yeah. That was the whole point of the calling. But that didn't seem to work, so I'm here."

"You didn't make an appointment."

"Like I said, I did make the effort. Fourteen times. But no one got back to me, so..."

"So, you don't have an appointment."

"No, I do not have an appointment," Tony said. "But if I could have five minutes with Mr. Tomasello, I'll be out of here and back out in the rain forever. How does that sound?"

She looked up at the sky as if there would be an answer there. Then she stood aside. It was like a vault door opening.

Tony took off his glasses, which had fogged, and wiped them with his T-shirt. The office was one large room, lit by a few desk lamps. There were several small, empty desks and one large and old wooden desk in the back. Standing behind the desk was a short man with a high head of hair and an angry look on his face. Both seemed set in concrete. He had 360-degree muffin-top paunch emphasized by his pink polo shirt tucked into gray slacks. He wore a gold watch that could be seen from space.

The big woman walked past him and took the seat at the big desk. "Sit down already," she said. She pulled a cigarette out of a vinyl-covered case and lit up.

Tony sat on a metal chair in front of the desk. "Are you Mr. Tomasello, the owner?"

The man in the pink shirt was about to speak, but the woman said, "This is Mr. Tomasello, but he's Junior. He's not the one you're looking for. He's my husband, Frankie. I'm Jackie Tomasello, Mr. Tomasello's daughter-in-law. We represent Frank Senior in all business dealings."

"So, he's not around?"

On the wall behind her was a framed reproduction of a

painting featuring barely recognizable likenesses of Frank Sinatra, Rocky Balboa, Dean Martin, Marlon Brando (from *The Godfather*), and Joe Dimaggio, all hanging together in front of a pizza shop.

"If you must know, my father is ill and has been hospitalized since May first, hooked up to more tubes and wires than I can count," she said. "But he'll be fine. They don't make them any tougher than my father."

"So, can I ask you two some questions then?"

"That's what you're here to do, then do it."

Tony took out his recorder, shaking the rain off his hands, and put it on the desk in front of the woman with a splash. "You mind if I record you?"

"No," she said, using her claws to indicate the recorder with disgust. "That is not happening."

"This is for both of us, to make sure I quote you correctly."

"I'll know what I said. Put that away."

Tony left the recorder on the desk and took out his notebook. "So, you recall Rosa Irizarry, the woman who went missing from one of the apartments you manage in a building you co-own with Elias Litvinchouk?"

"Of course. It was very sad what happened."

"Sad," her husband echoed.

"There have been accusations that your father—that this management company—was harassing Rosa Irizarry to get her to leave her rent-controlled apartment?"

"All lies and gossip," she said. "People don't know what they're talking about."

"The accusation is basically that you wanted Rosa Irizarry out, so you could refurbish her apartment in the building that you co-own with Elias Litvinchouk and rent it for a market rate?"

"You asked that already."

"Okay. So you're saying your company did not go out of its way to make her leave?"

"It's the same thing with you, over and over. Okay, let me

ask you: How do they say we did that?"

"You—or you had someone—harass her, put bugs in her apartment, for example."

"You mean like the CIA?" she said, laughing. Her husband echoed the laughter.

"Good, but no," Tony said. "Bugs as in roaches. Plus, mice. How about the fire? Did you cause the fire that made her leave?"

"That makes no sense. Why on god's green fuck would we do that?"

"As I said, to get her to move out, so you could raise the rent."

"That's retarded. Why would we want to destroy our property?"

"So you're saying you didn't harass her or get someone to harass her?"

"I think I'm going to sue you and your rinky-dink paper for libel. Or slander, whatever the fuck it is."

"You're talking defamation of character, something I'd have to convey to someone besides you and your husband. Which will happen when this gets printed, but at the moment—"

"Screw this." The living statue rose from the desk.

"Take it easy, sweetheart," the husband said.

"Take it easy? Fuck," she said. "This guy's got nothing, and he works for a nothing."

Tony sat back and sighed. "Talk about me all you want, but be kind to the poor defenseless newspaper."

"Get out," Jackie said.

"Before I go: Do you know if Rosa Irizarry is dead or alive?"

Jackie looked again to the heavens for support. "The nerve. Have a nice fucking day."

"Time to go, chief." The old man's son was behind him now. He put a meaty hand on Tony's shoulder.

Tony stood, shrugging off the hand, and walked to where Jackie held the door open. The rain had gotten worse.

She gave him a sour smirk. "Be careful out there. You never know what will happen," she said.

"That sounds like a threat," Tony said.

"I was talking about the rain. But you take it any way you want."

CHAPTER TWENTY-NINE

"Room 3, Petro," Hadid said. He had to pick up his pace to keep behind Petrosino in the station. The guy liked to take big steps. "I mean, Room 3."

"If this is another friggin' nutcase, I'm stuffing him up your ass."

"That's harsh," Hadid said. "Hey, I wouldn't hire this guy to be my lawyer, but he seems on the ball. Kinda."

"'Kinda,'" Petrosino said, stopping in place. Hadid thought maybe Petrosino was doing a ten-count.

"Patrol officer says this guy is a 'crusty.' I don't know what that is. He looks like a hipster, but he smells like a vagrant."

"A crusty? Oh crap." Petrosino turned. "Just for your information, crusties are what they call 'voluntary homeless,' young idiots who travel in packs from all over the states, even Europe. They freeload off the city during the good weather months. And they're usually heroin addicts, so not the most reliable witnesses."

"There are whole groups of these guys?" Hadid said. "Anyway, just wait till you hear what he has to say."

As they got to the interrogation room, Hadid said, "Hey, need a toothpick before we go in? I got gum."

Petrosino gave him the granite face he had become very familiar with. "I'll live."

James Marton Cook was in his late twenties, nose ring, checkered shirt, baseball cap. He had matted hair, a matted beard, and scratch marks on his face, arms, and legs. The skin of his face appeared tight, and his eyes were glassy and unfocused. On the floor next to him was a pit bull wearing a scarf and panting loudly.

Cook said, "Like I told your beefy little buddy—"

"Beefy?" Hadid said.

"—I saw this young guy—I'd say 24, 25, 26, 27, 28, something like that, with red, curly hair—and he had a skateboard, and he was all by his lonesome waiting at that corner."

Hadid said, "Kent and South 3rd, you said."

"That's the spot. And he was just waiting there, checking his phone and all."

"Right-o," Petrosino said. "What were you doing there?"

"Doing my thing. Camping out. It was hella hot that night. And I was hella high." Cook smiled shyly, showing green teeth. "So I just decided to lay down right where I was. It wasn't my usual spot, but it was just as good as any."

"Which was where, specifically?"

"Up against a wall, tucked right into the corner between the wall and the concrete pavement."

"On South 3rd?"

"No, on Kent. By that old factory. I've been staying there since I kind of broke up with the group I usually hang with. We had a falling out and—"

"Okay, okay, so tell me all about what happened next," Petrosino said, leaning forward.

"Well, a truly horrible thing. A man comes along on a bike, and snick, snick, snick, cuts that poor young guy all over. There was blood everywhere. It was awful."

"Mr. Cook, can you repeat what you told me about what the man on the bike looked like."

"Well, that's just it. The guy wore a hoodie, but tied up. He must have been hella hot in that thing. I guess that's why he took it off at the end."

"He took it off!" Petrosino said. "Did you see what he

looked like?"

"Nope. He was in the shadows too. But those other people must have, that couple."

"Other people?" Petrosino said.

"Wait'll you hear this," Hadid said.

"Yeah, they passed right by me, you know, didn't even see me. So they got closer, you know, to the man with the machete."

"So the killer must have seen them, too," Petrosino said.

Hadid couldn't help himself. "Exactly!"

"I'm sure he did. He did like this." Cook did a dramatic double-take in his chair. "He did like that when he saw them."

"Can you describe them?" Petrosino snapped at Hadid and made a motion for him to write it down.

"Yes, yes, I can. The man was Chinese, well, Asian, not sure what kind, you know, don't want to offend anybody."

"That's pretty good for...what were you, a block away?"

"I was high but I wasn't blind," said Cook, then he laughed at his own joke for a full thirty seconds. During this time, Hadid smiled at Petrosino, and Petrosino gave him a reluctant nod.

When Cook finished laughing to himself, he said, "And they were in the streetlamp light. Plus, I've got great vision. My doctor told me I had 10-10 vision when I was in college. I didn't finish though."

"And this person with the Asian guy?" Petrosino said. "What did they look like?"

"Oh, the woman was white, pretty, blonde. Oh, and I can tell you this: She was totally pregnant. Very pregnant."

CHAPTER THIRTY

Detective Petrosino was flabbergasted at the amount of pregnant women living in Williamsburg, particularly along the waterfront, where he and his partner had spent the last two days ringing bells and knocking on doors.

"Maybe there's something in the water," Hadid said.

"Nothing good ever came from the East River."

"Then it must be all those lattes."

The heat wave had returned with a vengeance, and so they happily entered the frigidly air-conditioned lobby of the Verge, the tower condominium complex on Kent Avenue. Parking available, rivers views, closet space.

"Sure, sure," Angel Flores, the doorman told them. "I know that couple. The Chinese guy and the pregnant lady. They live upstairs. Apartment 607."

Petrosino wiped the cooling sweat off the back of his neck. "Are they home, do you know?"

"Nah, nah," said the doorman. He was in street clothes, having just gotten off duty when they came in. "They work regular jobs. But hold up, let me check."

Flores yelled across the wide vestibule to the doorman currently at the desk. "Hubert. You seen Mr. Steven and Ms. Erin leaving this morning?"

"The guy did," said the other doorman. "She did too, but not to work."

Hadid stepped toward him. "How do you know that?"

"She left here just a little while ago, but with her dog. You know, Mr. Pee Pee."

"Deeogee," Flores said. "That's the name of their dog. We call him 'Mr. Pee Pee' 'cause—"

Petrosino held up his hand. "I can guess why. Does she have a regular place she walks the dog? Maybe along the waterfront park?"

Flores and the other doorman said they had no idea.

"How long does she usually take to walk the dog?"

"Hours sometimes," Flores said.

"All right. We're going to do a circuit around the area," Petrosino said to Hadid. "See if we can't find her in the crowds."

"Too bad we can't stay in here a few more minutes, huh?" Hadid said. He had his arms out, letting the cool air run over him.

"I'd love to, but we're not going to."

At that moment, Petrosino's phone rang. He looked at the caller ID. "Dammit."

"Morning, Lieutenant," Petrosino said.

"We just got a lead on our ganglord Cortés's location," Tuchman said over the phone. "We're having a meeting in a half hour to work out our game plan. I'd appreciate your presence."

"Right-o. It's nice to be appreciated."

Petrosino moved to hand signal to Hadid to get names and details from the doormen. But he saw his partner was doing that already. They'd have to let talking to this Erin lady wait till later.

"Yeah," he said, turning his attention to Tuchman. "We'll be there."

CHAPTER THIRTY-ONE

Because of a particularly convoluted resume he had to edit, Tony couldn't get to McCarren Park for pétanque until later in the afternoon. But he got to play two games and sweat three gallons under the fierce sun. It was hot enough to fry a chicken on the sidewalk, so he was tired and smelly and, since he had just paid rent, he rejected an invite for beers and decided to go home to shower and enjoy the best ninety-nine-cent ramen money could buy.

He had just walked out of McCarren Park when a station wagon with fake wood paneling pulled up alongside him on Union Avenue. He would've kept walking, but suddenly he heard Latin.

"*Salve,* Mr. Moran."

Tony leaned down to the open passenger side window. "*Salve*, Mr. Litvinchouk. How did you find me?"

"It's a lovely day. It's a park. *Homines transiliunt ubi saepes inferior est.*"

"Okay. So *why* did you find me?"

"There's nothing good on TV again, so I figured I'd get back to you."

"Get back to me?" Tony said. "I thought we were done."

"Yes, it seems I neglected to add that we had a super in the building at the time of Rosa's disappearance. A man named Jorge Marte. He had the keys, and he certainly was capable of doing what you were saying."

"And?"

"Come, take a seat. Take a load off."

Tony opened the door and sat down. The seat was warm. The car was warm. Papers littered the top of the dashboard. There was a bag of water bottles in the well of the passenger side, and in the doorway armrest was a peppermint candy and a large and gaudy bangle, decorated with a fire-breathing dragon.

"I'll drive around," Litvinchouk said, "to get a breeze going."

Litvinchouk moved the car up Driggs Avenue, but the car wasn't getting any cooler. Tony was conscious of the stink of his own sweat. And he smelled something else in the car—something he couldn't place.

Litvinchouk said, "I told you I wanted to talk with you privately, but you never called."

"Had a few things I wanted to look into first."

"I'm sure. By the way, who was that vivacious young lady you were with? A girlfriend?"

"An ex," Tony said.

"An ex, huh? Did you love her or were you in love with her?"

"Is there a difference?

"*Amor gignit amorem.* Of course. I'll tell you the difference. When you love somebody, all the little bullshit small talk she makes, how her day went, her new shoes, her new haircut, all that sounds like a knife in your ear. But when you're in love, it's music."

"I'll remember that."

They were stuck at an intersection. The light was green, but there were too many people crossing the street for the station wagon to move.

"Look at this. So many people," said Litvinchouk. "It's as thick as Manhattan with the people. And with the traffic."

"Well, I wonder how it got this way."

"Is that intended to be a jab at me for my dabbling in real estate?" Litvinchouk smiled broadly. "You can't stop change, Mr. Moran. One group replaces another group, and then that group is replaced and so on and so forth. 'Twas ever thus back to the Neanderthals. Why blame me for making a living on the way of things? Do you have any idea how much money they pay professors? That's why I got into real estate."

Tony kept his eyes on the crowd. "So, you were saying about Jorge Marte?"

Litvinchouk laughed and eased the car across the intersection.

"Listen," he said, "before I get to that, I wanted to say that I personally, as well as the entire very small Latin Department at Brooklyn College, was very disappointed that you did not major in Latin."

"That was fourteen, fifteen years ago."

"Yes. I understand this journalism you do is nice, I guess. I can understand the desire to right wrongs and change the world. I was young once, too. As my mother used to say, '*De poetas, tontos y locos, todos tenemos un poco.*' But, let me put it this way—you have a very small apartment on South 3rd, yes?"

"Now, how did you know about that?"

"Building owners talk. Yours was a one-bedroom basement apartment that got chopped in half, did you know that?"

"That explains the plastic standing shower."

"Wouldn't you like to live in a bigger place, say a two-bedroom, full bath, laundry in the building, and maybe pay even cheaper rent? A place for a man, a place for a grown-up. And your mother, I understand she is having to leave her apartment that she's been in very many years, am I correct?"

Tony gave Litvinchouk a long look. "You know you are."

"It would be marvelous if she had a place, maybe in one of the new senior citizen housing facilities, where they have nurses come visit every day. That would be marvelous, wouldn't it?"

"Mr. Litvinchouk, I hate to say this, but it sure does sound like you're working yourself up to a bribe."

"A bribe!" Litvinchouk honked at the car in front of him. "Ha! A bribe is saying I could give it to you. No, I was just conjecturing. 'Wouldn't you?' I said. 'Wouldn't you?' That said, I could probably *help* you find places for you and your mother very, very easily."

Litvinchouk took a right on Metropolitan Avenue and drove toward the waterfront. But just before they got there, he took a left onto Wythe Avenue.

Sweat poured down Tony's back against the warm seat. "So, tell me, why are you doing all this 'conjecturing?'"

Litvinchouk stopped the car at the intersection, although there was no signal and no one crossing. "I'll be honest with you. You were a mediocre Latin student. I remember most that you were lazy, you didn't want to do the work. But you did seem to enjoy the language. That year the dean told us we had to have a certain amount of declared majors or we'd have to share our office. We came up one short. We've been sharing with Mandarin and Russian for fifteen years now. I needed you then. I need you now. Don't be a putz. Leave this business with Rosa Irizarry. You know she's gone. You're not going to find her."

"I know that. That's not what this is about. I hate to sound corny—" Tony couldn't believe he was going to say what he was about to say "—but there's an element of justice i—"

"Listen to yourself. Justice? Are you still so righteous so long after college? A knight in shining armor?" Litvinchouk started the car again, taking another turn. "Let me tell you what life is about, my friend, because it's clear that no one else has. Life...life is eating well, having good things, and enjoying the good things you have. We're all rats. The point is to die the happiest, fattest rat of all. Justice is nothing. All our labors are for nothing, Mr. Moran, not in the end. Surely, you're old enough to know this by now."

Tony said nothing. He stared out ahead at the heat rising off the station wagon's hood.

"I can tell you haven't had many golden opportunities in your life," Litvinchouk said. "Here is one. I'm giving it to you."

They were passing under the Williamsburg Bridge, an erector-set-looking bridge Tony had seen every day of his life. He and his brother used to play stickball in its shadow. He hadn't really gotten very far in the world, had he?

"I just..." Tony said. "I just need to know if there's anything else you can tell me about Jorge Marte."

It was a good thing he didn't care about getting very far in the world.

Litvinchouk sighed and made a turn and then another. Then he raised his voice. "He was a drunk. He was capable of anything when he was drunk."

"Where is he?"

"Dead in an alley, probably. Believe me, I wish I knew."

Tony looked out the door and realized they were in front of his apartment.

Litvinchouk waved his fingers and said. "*Vale,* Mr. Moran. Think about my conjecture."

"*Va*...thanks for the ride."

Tony opened the door to his apartment. It stank in there. Socks mostly. Maybe the garbage. Books, TV, three pairs of sneakers, more books. A tiny stove. A miniature fridge, mostly empty. A narrow closet he stopped using because of a leak from upstairs. He hadn't ever taken the time to realize how absolutely shitty his apartment was. How absolutely shitty his life was. He could do nothing to help his mother. He had succeeded at nothing, had not garnered praise nor millions. He had done nothing with his life.

Tony opened a bottle of beer and turned on the shower and sat down on the plastic shower floor under the spray to drink it.

CHAPTER THIRTY-TWO

Erin's boss had told her, "What are you doing here? Go home! Take a day."

And so Erin Cole had done just that. She was nearing her time to pop, to bring a new life into the world, and she had been feeling totally super crazy the last few days, and it must have totally showed. Stevie Weavie, her little Turkey Cutlet Lips, her Husband of the Century, had texted that it was a great idea for her to relax and go home during the day, and that she should just stay inside and catch up on their Netflix queue. So she went home to the Verge and was about to inhale a family-sized bag of sweet and salty popcorn.

But then Deeogee, dear Deeogee, whined to be outside, and for the life of her she could not deny that dog! Plus, she had had enough of central air conditioning and needed to feel warmth on her skin, even heat-wave warmth.

Plus-plus, she had something special planned for Stevie Wonderman. She would go to the supermarket and get him a nice filet mignon and cook it up for him just right tonight. She had always been a major carnivore, but the idea of a steak had been making her nauseous for months. But all of a sudden she was in the mood for red meat again: thick, rare, juicy with blood. Steveroonie had been such a worryhound the last few weeks, she wanted to do something nice for him.

He had come home the other night, covered in sweat and smelling like beer, and he kept apologizing—"I'm so sorry I forgot the cupcake! I'm so sorry!"—but she barely even remembered asking him to get one, and she had brushed her teeth already, so what did it matter.

And he had been so weird about seeing that attack—what was it, a month ago now already?—they had almost come close to having an argument. But it was past them now, and she just wanted to make him smile.

She didn't cook much—she liked to say the best thing she made was reservations. But she knew her way around the basics. She'd also get him some wine from that nice wine store on Bedford Avenue. So she packed her purse, with her gift-from-Daddy Taurus PT-111 sidearm tucked neatly at the bottom, leashed the dog, and left the apartment, armed and doglicious.

When she got there, she saw there was a long line in the wine store, and she just wasn't in the mood to wait.

So, she kept walking on Bedford, knowing there had to be another liquor store, what with all the alkies in the neighborhood.

She was approaching Metropolitan Avenue when she realized something. The bicycles. Steven had said something, but she was fading in and out of sleep at that point. All the bicycles had scared him. What a silly idea, she had thought. Everyone rides a bicycle around here, so why bother worrying?

And if it was that man, the one with the machete, well, she was prepared. Daddy had prepared her.

She realized that if he had seen them, she'd be the one he'd recognize. The pregnant blonde! Steven was cute, sure, but he wasn't distinctive in any way. He didn't have anything to worry about. She did.

But she was prepared all right.

But anyway, it was daytime. Nothing like that ever happened in the daytime. In this neighborhood! With this many people!

Still, all the bicycles, it did make her wonder. That man could be any one of them. Look at that guy with the messenger bag. Oh, but he was black. Although she wasn't sure if the man she had seen had been black or white, was she? Look at that guy with—what was that, a tuba?—on his back—oh god, call a taxi if you have to haul that thing around, that's just not safe for the rest of us. Look at that asshole over there looking like Where's Wal—

The slash came across her face.

Erin was shocked, didn't believe it. It was daytime! The biker had come out of nowhere, stopped right in front of her. He had on a ski mask. A ski mask?

She heard herself screaming. Why was no one helping? Why was no one stopping this? She heard Deeogee barking, but all his barks were just little yips and they never scared anybody ever ever.

The man held his arm high. *Not the belly,* she thought. *Not my baby, no no no.*

Then she thought about the Taurus PT-111 in her purse. The gun that was fully loaded. "Not heavy or gritty and easy to conceal." The gun that was, despite advertising, a weight in her purse. The purse that was there on the sidewalk, two thousand miles away.

CHAPTER THIRTY-THREE

"Mr. Pak? Mr. Pak, I'm sorry for your loss, sir."

Detective Petrosino stood over the man who sat on the floor in a hallway in Woodhull Hospital. An officer had brought in the ugly dog, and Steve Pak had grabbed it from the officer and was now hugging it tight to his chest.

Pak picked up his head. "Have you found him?" he said. "Did you catch him?"

"Mr. Pak, we, unfortunately, the perpetrator fled the scene..."

"So, no, then. But how did he get away?"

"After the, uh...he was up on his bike and away before anyone knew what was really happening. Some people thought they were filming a movie."

"Erin..." Pak buried his face in the dog's fur.

"I'm sorry for your loss," said Hadid, who had just walked over to stand next to his partner. "But your son is alive and well, and he's waiting to see you."

The dog squirmed, but Pak said nothing.

Petrosino leaned against the wall and slid down on to the floor next to him. It was going to cost his back tomorrow.

"Mr. Pak," he said, "listen, I know this feels like...like the end of the world. But it's not. I know it's going to sound like...I can't think of any other word but 'bullshit,' sorry, but that's what I'm going to say will probably sound like to you, but, really, you'll get past this because you have to.... Listen, you may not think I understand, but years ago my own wife was killed.

By a very bad man. I loved that woman very, very much, more than life itself. And I didn't want to go on. But I did. And so will you."

"What happened to the bad man?"

Petrosino said, "Oh. He's getting punished. He's in jail for life."

Pak looked into Petrosino's eyes for the first time. "You should have killed him. That's what you have to do to the man who did this to my wife. You have to catch him, and you have to kill him."

Petrosino muttered, "Right-o," and didn't know what to say next. Hadid must have caught on and so he said, "Mr. Pak, rest assured we are doing all we can to make sure justice is done. And it'd be a good idea to talk to one of our counselors."

Petrosino nodded at his partner. "Mr. Pak," he said. "I hate to do this now, but it's important. We think your wife may have been attacked because of what you both saw, when a young man named Patrick Stoller was killed. I need you to recall as much as you can of that night."

"I barely saw his face."

"White guy? Black guy? Latino?"

"White guy."

"Anything else? Facial hair? Tattoos?"

"He looked white."

"Okay."

"He was wearing a hoodie. He took it off. But it was dark."

"Anything else you can remember?"

Pak looked up. His face was crushed with pain. "He had an expensive bike, a suspension bike. It looked like a Sommet, very expensive. Black and silver."

Petrosino and Hadid looked at each other.

"I know bikes," Pak continued. "I did a triathlon before we got—before Erin and I were married."

"That's good. That's very helpful."

"It had a suspension fork and a dual suspension frame."

"Very good," Petrosino said. "Can you tell me anything else?"

"No," he said. "Please."

Petrosino wiped his face with his hand. He didn't want to push. "All right. I understand." He stood and dug in his wallet for a business card. "Call me when you feel you can talk some more. In the meantime, for your safety, we're going to post an officer with you at all times."

Pak took the card and looked at it for a while. "We should have talked to the police sooner. I knew it. And then you could have stopped him."

Pak said nothing and continued to hold the dog close, as it whimpered to be set free.

Hadid tapped Petrosino on the shoulder.

"Petro. C'mere, c'mere. We gotta go."

"What is it?"

"Not here."

Outside, it was mid-afternoon and the air sizzled with heat. Petrosino pulled out a cigarette and asked what the hell Hadid was so excited about.

"We gotta go," Hadid said. "They just found another one."

"Two in one day? That's a complete change of M.O."

They began moving toward their car.

"Yeah, two and both daytime. But get this: There was a witness this time. Some guy getting a blowjob in a car twenty feet away."

"Modern romance," Petrosino said. "Did he see a face?"

"No, but you know what Mr. Pak in there just said, about the hoodie?"

"Yeah, matches what that screwy guy Cook said."

"But not what witnesses today said about Mrs. Pak."

"Yeah."

"And this new vic, the witness says it was a guy in ski mask."

"Okay. Time frame?" Petrosino said, worrying his cigarette.

"About an hour after Mrs. Pak," Hadid said.

"What, did he go home to change?"

"Maybe he was covered in blood."

"Maybe. And witnesses get cock-eyed. Mask becomes a hoodie. Hoodie becomes a baseball cap. I've seen it happen. Anything on the color of the bike?"

"Didn't say, but I'll double-check when we get to the scene."

"Now, we got a killing spree," Petrosino said, chucking his cigarette and getting in the car. "But is it really gangbangers having a field day, or is it one particular guy in a ski mask going wacko? Or, even, for Christ's sake, copycats?"

"Or all three?" Hadid said. "The Internet's going to love this shit, and everyone in this 'hood is going to be looking over their shoulder."

CHAPTER THIRTY-FOUR

Hours before, Vishal Raghavan had been walking toward his house on Havemeyer Street, but he stopped in the underside of the BQE. The expressway ran aboveground through the northern part of the neighborhood, and people who lived on the second or third floors in housing adjacent to the expressway enjoyed a charming view of streaming vehicles all day long, if they bothered to raise their smogged-over windows. The underside of the expressway was used for parking as well as for ersatz housing for many homeless, since the width and height of the expressway provided good shelter from the elements. Like shade on a hot day. Which was why Vishal had stopped there to text.

"U must try new Sardinian wine bar," he had texted his friend, Caitlyn. "They have raw cheez."

"Im lacto intolerant," she had texted back.

"Wine select is 2 dye 4."

He wore cutoff jeans, vintage sneakers, and a new T-shirt that read "hipster death rattle." He had stopped by a large steel column to retype the word "artisanal!" which the autocorrect on his phone had turned to "artificial."

Vishal had moved to Williamsburg from Illinois two years ago. His first apartment was a $2,100/month decrepit railroad underneath a woman whose kids seemed unable to walk without stomping their feet. The whole family hung out on the stoop at all hours of the night, being loud, and playing Spanish music constantly. Did those kids not have to go to school? He had called the city's complaint line thirty-five times on them. But the cops would come around and the neighbors would shut up and go inside, and as soon as the cops were gone, sure enough, they'd go out again. And they knew that he was the one who had been calling the cops, so they called him what sounded like nasty names in Spanish whenever they saw him. He moved from there to a $4,700/month, one-bedroom box with a remodeled bathroom and new kitchen fixtures. Next door was a guy who screamed about every kill he made on whatever video game he played all day and all night long.

He had been looking to move again.

As he texted, he sensed more than heard something approaching nearby. Some part of his brain registered that he would have to step out of the way, but he didn't because he was busy trying to attach a picture of what he called "outRAGEous amarelo da beira baixa," words that had somehow escaped autocorrect unscathed when he realized the lower left part of his screen was getting all "hinky" again. But then he finally got it to send and—

When the cut came it had been well aimed. It went clean through Raghavan's neck, banging into the steel column. His last thought had been blissfully of cheese.

CHAPTER THIRTY-FIVE

Danny "D-Tox" Campos was listening to his girlfriend, Zoila, screaming over the phone. She was begging him to take her to McCarren Pool. He lay in bed, groggy, hungry, and hot. He would have gone to the kitchen to get his mother Iris to make him some breakfast, but Zoila would get louder if she didn't think he was listening.

"It's such a hot fucking day, Pa," she screamed. "Me and the kid are fucking getting cabin fever. We gotta take this kid to the pool or something. C'mon, Pa."

"Okay, okay, okay," he said, then he threw on his swimming trunks, got his keys on their keychain, and was leaving when his mother asked him where he was going.

"I gotta go out. I can't stay cooped up in here no more taking five showers a day to stay cool, no joke. I'm going to the pool."

"*Con quien?*" his mother said.

"With Zoila and her stupid kid, Mami. C'mon, don't be like a parole officer." He laughed and kissed and hugged her, and she wasn't happy, but she smiled and told him to be careful.

He slammed the door and was out into the blaze of the day.

D-Tox picked up Zoila and her rambunctious, spoiled shit of a son, LeJuan, and they walked from her house to the pool. Even though the sky was mad cloudy, it was still humid as hell, and D-Tox couldn't wait to jump in when they got there.

First thing, though, he took a long drink of rum and pineapple juice that Zoila kept in a thermos. Then he was checking out

Zoila, who stripped down to her bikini on the side of the pool, those sexy globes of hers 'bout ready to bust. He was about to give her a little sugar and whisper something nasty in her ear, when that freaking *huelepe'o* stringbean LeJuan ran and jumped right into the water, and Zoila said, "Go watch him, Papi. Please! I don't want the kid to fucking drown."

So, D-Tox turned from his lady and cannonballed right into the pool, splashing everywhere and ending up right by the stringbean who told him, "Do it again. Do it again."

After a while, Zoila got in, too. She didn't swim or anything. She just splashed herself a little and then got out of the pool quick.

"*Ai*, Pa. Do me a favor," she said. "There's too many people. I'm going to lay in the sun. Could you watch LeJuan for a little while for me, please?"

Then she went back to her towel and started working on bronzing up that fine skin of hers.

"D-Tox!" the kid screamed. "Look at me! Look at me!" The spoiled stinker was doing backflips into the pool, getting out and doing it again.

The lifeguard nearby started giving them shit, blowing on the whistle.

"What?" D-Tox said. "Let him have a good time. That's what the pool is for, for the kids."

The lifeguard backed down. *That's right.*

But then there was this little white kid, pale as milk and freckled like a motherfucker, and with those inflated things on his skinny little arms. LeJuan did a backflip and landed on the kid, just a little. LeJuan didn't mean nothing by it. But then the kid went crying, "Oh, mommy, mommy."

And then she went to the lifeguard and told him to do something.

The white lifeguard came to D-Tox and had the nerve to say, "Sir, I'm going to have to get you to remove yourself and your child from the pool."

"This shit ain't happening," D-Tox said. "This is our pool. You can't be telling people how to have a good time."

Whitey lifeguard backed down. "Please, sir, please make your child behave."

So, then LeJuan goes back to having a good time, and then he does his backflip again, and again, he lands right back on the milky freckled white boy, who again started crying.

"Shut up," D-Tox said, "You're not bleeding or anything like that. You're a kid. You get bumped and bruised. Deal with it."

And that was when a big white guy, not the kid's father, it didn't look like, shaved head, sideburns thick like fur, came over to the edge of the pool and pointed a finger at D-Tox.

"Dude," the guy said. "Get your kid to play nice."

"What if I don't? What you gonna do?"

"Come up here and I'll show you."

D-Tox pulled himself out of the pool. This shit was on.

CHAPTER THIRTY-SIX

The feast must go on.

No matter that the heat wave had hit record lethal highs for the fifth day in a row. No matter that the local weather personalities had forecast deluge-level thunderstorms for that Sunday, and that the dark churning clouds above Brooklyn seemed poised to prove them right. No matter that the Williamsburg Slasher (*New York Times*) or Southside Slashers (*Daily News*) or Hipster Slashers (*New York Post*) were still at large, eight incidents reported, the last five fatal and one just a block from the twinkling kiddie ferris wheel.

The feast must go on.

Just as sure as Tony "Chino" Moran had to be there to cover it. The bad food, the teenagers in heat, the loud *morra* players ("*Quattro!*" "*Cinque!*" "*Otto!*"). But the annual street carnival was always good for a cover article and an inside spread in the *Sentinel*. It had to be covered.

He had his digital recorder out, ready to collect the usual candid quotes: "It's a great tradition that will never die." "It gets better and better every year." "I don't live here anymore, but I always come back."

Gabby followed him, digital camera in hand. As they waded into the crowd, Tony told her to take lots of pictures, especially of the food.

"Especially the zeppoles," he said. "People love the zeppoles."

While she was there, he introduced himself to the zeppole

vendor and asked her about the feast.

"It's a great tradition that will never die," she said.

"Thank you," he said. "And I'll have a bag of half a dozen."

When she gave him the bag, she added, "I was worried about the slashing man. But he won't come here. There's too many people."

As they walked away, Gabby said, "How can you eat that? It's not even lunchtime."

"It's just like a beignet, better than a donut. Just about every human culture has some sort of fried dough food. Don't eat the fried Oreos, though, they're amazing but deadly in the gut. Hey, get pictures of those kids on the rides."

"All right! I know, Tony!"

Tony knew, from almost thirty years of going to the fair, that they could almost use the same pictures every year. But there were differences every year. Besides the sizzling sausages and mounds of peppers and onions and the endless pizza, there was now Mexican corn, fresh hot falafel.

But some things didn't change. The creaky rides still threatened to break and send little children flying. Sleazy carnival barkers still inveigled people to throw basketballs and shoot water at clowns, all for the glory of stuffed corporate merchandising. Or a tiny bear.

"*Tre!*" "*Nove!*" "*Sette!*"

And the *morra* players were still there.

The sky rumbled. Things had better get going soon.

"Looks who's here."

Oh no. In mid-bite, Tony turned, dropping a cup of powdered sugar on his T-shirt. There was Magaly walking straight toward them with Luis De Moscoso. She had a nervous smile. Her boss looked constipated.

"Hi, Magaly," Tony said. "You've met Gabby."

"Yes, your co-worker."

"Assistant editor at the *Sentinel*," said Gabby. "Oh my god, I love your hair. How do you get it like that?"

"Thank you," Magaly said. "It takes a lot of TLC and the right conditioner."

"That's just it—I don't have time for TLC."

"Do they work you too hard at the *Sentinel*?"

"Oh my god, no, it's easy work. Actually, it's kind of boring."

"What do you mean, boring?" Tony said.

Magaly turned to Tony and said, "Oh, Chino, you remember Luis, right?"

"Checking out the feast for a story?" De Moscoso said, shaking Tony's hand.

"Yes. It fills pages, creates goodwill, gets advertisers."

"Then I hope you do a story on the Three Kings Parade we have every year."

"Of course," Tony said. "It gets a full spread. We quote you every time. You make sure of it."

Magaly gave him an angry look. "We do have an information booth here, in case you wanted to find out about our community programs," she said. "And we also have one set up by McCarren Pool all summer long."

"You should do a story on us," De Moscoso said.

"We'll put it on the list," Tony said. "Gabby, put it on the list of stories we have to do."

"What list?"

"It was good to see you," Tony said. "We have to get back to our boring work now."

"Us too. Take care, Chino." Magaly and De Moscoso turned back into the crowd.

"She's pretty," Gabby said. "So, you used to date her?"

"Pictures," Tony said, pointing.

He stopped in front of a booth that sold T-shirts lettered with slogans like "Not Only Am I Perfect. I'm Italian Too," "FBI: Full Blooded Italian," and "Leave the Gun. Take the Cannoli." He'd seen those for years. But one T-shirt looked different. It read: "hipster death rattle." What the hell did that mean?

Tony introduced himself to the vendor and asked how the

fair was going.

"It gets better and better every year."

"Okay. That's great. Hey, how much is that T-shirt?"

"Yeah, that's a big seller. Twenty dollars, but I only have extra large."

"Tony." Gabby interrupted them. "The priest is starting."

The vendor said, "I have a few in small for the lady."

But Tony had to go cover the dance.

The Our Lady of Mount Carmel's Feast of the Giglio, or what the neighborhood called the Italian Feast, was held every summer on the streets around Havemeyer and North 8th. The highlight of the feast was the Dancing of the Giglio, the Giglio being an eighty-foot-tall structure that rose above the three-story row houses that lined the streets. The structure was dominated by a tower decorated with papier-mâché representations of flowers and religious icons, and at the very top of the tower stood a statue of Saint Paolino. At the bottom of a tower was a twelve-piece Italian marching band. All of this, five tons' worth, rested on a platform. The Dancing of the Giglio involved the lifting—and agile movement—of this platform by one hundred and twenty men. After the Giglio was blessed, and the national anthems of the United States and Italy played, the *capo parranza* went to work. The muscles and the wills of the one hundred and twenty lifters had to be bound together. So it was up to the short man in the front, the *capo*, to be the conductor of the Giglio, using a cane to direct the lifters up, down, forward, backward, in a circle, around corners. To make them dance.

It had been a long time since Tony had really paid attention to the whole thing. The band played "*Funiculì, Funiculà,*" brassy and loud. The crowd around the Giglio, even the very probably non-Italians, seemed engaged, not cynical or blasé. And there was joy—and serious, strenuous effort—in the faces of the lifters as they performed a gently swaying dance in unison. Despite himself, Tony was impressed. Even after the band launched into a brassy version of "Eye of the Tiger."

Little drops of rain began to peck at his face. He went to wipe away the rain and noticed something ahead, behind the Giglio.

The crowd was surging forward. There was a sound like a scream, but it was hard to tell with "Eye of the Tiger" filling the air.

Gabby noticed the movement and said, "Something's happening. Tony."

"Pictures," he said, but he was looking, too.

The scream had come from down the block, where Havemeyer Street meets Union Avenue. The crowd surged forward again and began to part.

Tony saw what was causing the commotion.

Cutting through the crowd was a man on a bicycle. He had an arm held up high. In his hand was a machete pointed straight to heaven.

Two burly guys tried to stop the man, but they jumped back as he slashed at them.

He kept coming, heading for the Giglio. Or rather the men under the Giglio. He was behind them, and they couldn't see him coming, and they blocked the capo from seeing what was happening.

How fast could a mass of one hundred and twenty humans react? There was no way they could just jump out of the way.

The man on the bicycle struck one lifter after the other on the left side of the Giglio. He was laughing a giddy wild laugh the whole time.

The lifters turned away, broke their concentration, broke away from the single mindset controlled by the capo.

The crowd that had once been unified by the sight of the Giglio broke into chaos.

The mighty Giglio began to wobble.

The band, however, never missed a beat.

The capo was yelling for the lifters to lower their burden to the blacktop, but the man on the bicycle was swinging wildly and people were screaming like children and everyone knew there was a slasher in the neighborhood killing people and it looked like there he was, chopping right through them.

The sky cracked again, and the rain began to pick up.

The man on the bicycle made his way around the lifters and began to speed off.

Tony noticed something then. Something that he had been grimly looking for was not there. Where the man on the bicycle had hit at the lifters—there was no blood.

A papier-mâché Virgin Mary fell to the street in front of Tony. A trombone player slipped and fell on his back. The *capo* kept yelling, and the lifters strained. But the Giglio held.

Meanwhile, the man on the bicycle had kept going, slicing through the crowd.

The guy with the machete kept going. But some teenager stepped forward and, with a large inflated bat, clotheslined the biker off of his bike.

A crowd quickly surrounded him.

Tony grabbed Gabby and led her to a street light. He pulled her up to stand on its base, which was about a foot and a half above the concrete.

"Take pictures."

"I don't know if I'm tall enough."

"Just raise the camera in the air and start clicking."

She took picture after picture. "Oh my god," she said. "They're going to kill him."

"What's happening?"

"They're kicking the shit out of him. Now the cops are coming."

"Get down. Let me see."

The man who had had the machete curled up in a ball. He bled from his mouth and knees.

"That's a souvenir," some man was yelling. "That's a souvenir."

A cop picked the machete up and sliced it across his own arm. Then he held it up to the crowd. "It's wood," he said. "It's a fucking souvenir."

The man who had had the toy machete looked old. He had a shaved head, a grubby, toothless face. He wore work pants, unlaced work boots, and a wifebeater decorated with the Puerto Rican flag.

"Shit," Tony thought.

When they brought the man to his feet, he wobbled. Tony could see from his eyes he was lit up bigger than Christmas.

Tony jumped off the street post. The rain had begun to drive down.

"Listen," he said to Gabby. "If you can wait around, get more pictures. Meanwhile, I want to talk to the cops."

She was about to ask him a question when his phone rang.

"Yeah," he said.

It was Magaly. "Chino. I'm at McCarren Pool. You have to get here. There's a riot going on."

He was going to say, "A riot is exactly why I don't have to get to McCarren Pool." But she'd hung up, and he found himself running.

CHAPTER THIRTY-SEVEN

The sky flickered and flashed, and thunder cracked like a bomb, setting off car alarms. Tony ran to McCarren Pool. Police cars, sirens blaring, passed him, heading in the same direction.

The rain had picked up again and came down in curtain after curtain. Tony ran through McCarren Park, past the pétanque court (now better suited for mud wrestling). Swimmers in swimsuits ran down past him, using beach towels as umbrellas. There was a terror in their eyes.

On Bedford Avenue, police cars were parked in front of the pool entrance. More swimmers were running, and there was a mass of people on the steps, gathered around something.

He didn't see Magaly, so against his better instincts, he ran toward the mass of people on the steps. It was where she would be—where the trouble was.

He pushed into the mass until he got to a ring of police. In the middle of them was one man, wearing only baggy swimming trunks and keeping them at bay by swinging a large wet towel.

"Come at me, motherfuckers!" the man said, whipping the soaked towel back and forth. "Come on!"

The man looked like and sounded like—yes, it was the son of Iris Campos. Danny. *D-Tox.*

He was doing a good job at keeping the police back with just a towel. But Tony knew it was only a matter of time before they got him. He supposed tasers were not a good idea in the rain, and in such a close circle. Then one cop tried to grab the whirling towel. D-Tox was strong enough to pull it out of the cop's grip. But this sent him off balance on the wet stairs, and he fell back onto the steps. The cops were on him in an instant.

The crowd yelled: "Stop them!" "Oh my god!" and "Get him! Stomp him!"

Tony pulled out his *Williamsburg Sentinel* ID card and thought, *I can't believe I'm doing this.* He squeezed through the phalanx of cops—then, as loud as he could, he yelled, "Hold up, hold up, hold up! I'm a reporter. Keep this up, and I'll put you bastards on the news."

In his other hand, he held his iPhone, with the video app turned on to record. It was pointed at the cops. His heart was pounding, he could barely breathe. This could go very badly. It wouldn't be unheard of for them to kick him, too, or grab the iPhone. But he gambled on the fact that there were too many people, and other phones out, in the crowd.

One cop heard him and turned. That cop tapped another, and soon they were all looking at Tony. A giant cop took a step closer. Tony backed up, but kept the ID and camera in the air. He wasn't scaring them in the least. But his shouting had broken whatever atavistic spell they had been under.

Two cops took hold of D-Tox, who was conscious but bloody. They cuffed him, picked him up, and led him away. As he went, D-Tox craned his neck and looked at Tony.

"Danny!" Tony called. "D-Tox! Are you all right?"

Two more of the officers leading him blocked Tony's view. They moved toward him as he moved back. They said, "Get back," about seventy-five times.

They pulled D-Tox in the back seat of a cruiser.

As the crowd parted, he saw Magaly. She and Luis De Moscoso had been on the other side of the crowd. Luis De Moscoso held his jacket over her head to keep her from getting wet.

Tony went up to them. "What happened?"

"Oh my god, Tony. It was crazy. People were fighting, shoving, yelling. And it looks like Danny might have started it all.

They say he was punching some guy and there was blood everywhere. Half the crowd was cheering him on. The other half wanted to lynch him."

De Moscoso said, "You can't blame him. These people think they can take over the neighborhood and change it. They can't be allowed to do that."

Tony said, "Well, you can't punch the neighborhood back to the old days."

"Listen," Magaly said. "I'm going to help him get a lawyer. You need to write about this for the paper—a big paper."

"She's right. They're going to crucify him," De Moscoso said. "You have to bring attention to this situation."

"Did you get it on video?" Magaly said.

Tony checked his phone. It showed a jumpy scene of Tony's frightened face. He'd forgotten to switch the camera's view.

"Can I see it?" she said.

"Nah, it's way too blurry, I'm afraid," he said.

"*Ai*, Chino. At least you tried." Her face softened. "That was very brave. You could have got your ass kicked, too."

"It's more likely I'll get pneumonia standing in this rain."

She laughed a quick laugh. "You're right. We better go," she said. "I'll see you. Soon."

She and De Moscoso left, running on Bedford toward the BQE underpass.

Tony went in the opposite direction. He cradled his messenger bag, hoping not everything in it was as drenched as he was. He walked home as quickly as he could, hugging the walls of buildings, praying for awnings and balconies.

CHAPTER THIRTY-EIGHT

Magaly couldn't hide the fact that she felt like a disappointment, to her parents, to herself, to everyone.

She had dreamed for years of being a lawyer. But law school had taken the bloom off that dream, and graduating law school was the happiest day of Magaly's *parents'* lives. When she got a job within a year, they couldn't have been more proud. So she didn't feel like telling them that she was miserable, that every minute of every fourteen-plus-hour day of billable hours (broken into tenths) was killing her, that she didn't feel like she was helping anyone (justice being not only blind but cruelly so), and that more than the specters of her parents' disappointment and her own guilt, she feared the humongous debt she had accrued (despite some financial aid), a debt she knew would linger on her shoulders for the rest of her life. She had made a mistake. She floundered at other jobs for a while, even one at a Starbucks, until the position of general manager at El Flamboyan Community Center opened up.

She thought she was good at her job. They held GED classes, gave tutoring, had food drives, blood drives, advocated for the poor and the homeless. Though she had to admit it often felt like a losing battle. She had begun to feel their best bet was to reach out to the people who were coming in. Unlike her boss, she thought they should work with the newcomers, not against them. But they didn't make it easy.

The Keap Street gallery, for example, had announced a big

exhibition called "The Soul of Williamsburg." But not one of the twenty-four artists they would be featuring was a Latino or Latina, and not one of them had been born and raised in the neighborhood. "That probably would have been a good idea," the gallery owner had said. "We'll definitely keep that in mind for next time." Magaly almost screamed when she heard this.

Still, when someone in the community center needed legal help, as often happened, she stepped up, giving advice, helping to fill out forms. She never went as far as a trial—the very idea of it made her nauseous—but to some extent it made her feel her law degree wasn't a complete waste.

Danny Campos would end up with a court-appointed criminal lawyer, but his mother Iris called that night saying he wanted Magaly to come by in the morning. And to bring Tony.

So she dressed up in her one-and-only pants suit and got to the jail early and found herself waiting for Tony. She talked to Danny about the charges and explained his options. But he didn't seem to worry about his troubles. He only seemed concerned with talking to Tony.

When he showed, the guard let him into the interrogation room. He wore cargo pants that needed a wash, but at least he had a collared shirt on.

"You made it," Danny said. He reached over to shake Tony's hand, but stopped when he realized he was handcuffed. Danny tried to laugh it off. He held up his hands. "See how it is."

Tony smirked and sat down. Magaly could tell he was nervous.

"Listen," Danny said, "I asked Magaly to ask you to come because I wanted to thank you. I really appreciate what you did for me out there. Those cops coulda beat me to death, and I'd end up on YouTube for sorry-ass nerds to look at."

"I didn't do anything, really," Tony said.

"This guy. Look at this guy," he said to Magaly. Then to Tony: "You saved my life, bro. You saved my life. God bless you, bro." He covered both Tony's hands with his, despite the cuffs. She could see Tony was shocked by the contact.

"You did good, Tony," she said. "You did."

"Well, okay," Tony said. "You're welcome."

"Do you got any updates about my aunt? Did you find out what happened to her?"

"I've been going over a lot of old ground, just trying to see if I can uncover anything new. But let me ask you something: Did you happen to know the super of her building?"

"You mean Jorge? What about him? You think he did something to my aunt?"

"I don't know. I just wanted to ask him some questions."

"Ahh, I would say hi to him and shit. But I never *talked to him* talked to him, you know. I knew he was going with one of the ladies in the building."

Magaly hadn't heard this before. "Who was this?"

"Yeah, this lady, Angela. She lived in the apartment below my aunt's. They were friends. They used to go shopping together."

"Does this Angela still live there," Tony said. "Do you know?"

"Nah, I think she moved back to PR or to Florida, one of those. PR, I think. Last year. A little while after my aunt went missing."

"You don't happen to know her last name?"

"Let me think. Yeah. Her last name is Roman. I know 'cause I dated her daughter Vivian for a little while."

"You don't happen to know where the daughter is?"

"Nah, she ain't talking to me anymore. I love 'em and leave 'em and then I forget 'em, know what I mean?"

The proverbial Latin Lover, Magaly thought. Did all men, not just Latinos, think they were that way, or did they just wish they were?

Tony said, "Did you hear about your aunt's having any extra money around the time of her disappearance?"

"You mean when she hit the number?"

"So she did?"

"Yeah. She hit for, like, ten thousand."

"Why didn't you tell me this before? This could be important."

"I didn't want you thinking my aunt was a criminal, a gambler, shit like that. People judge, you know?"

"Everybody plays the numbers, Danny," Magaly said. "It's the same as Lotto."

"Without the taxes," Tony said. "Do you have any idea what happened to that money? Do you think it might have anything to do with her disappearance?"

"Wait up. You think someone robbed her for the money?"

"That's where I was going, yeah."

"Nah, nah, nah. She hit the number a while before she disappeared. Like a month. I think she spent most of it."

This surprised Magaly. "Spent it? On what?"

"I don't know. I know she didn't have none before she disappeared."

"How do you know?"

"Because I asked her for some, and she said she didn't have any."

They were wrapping up. Magaly said she would find out who Danny's court-appointed was and see if he or she was any good.

"Before you go, there's one more thing," Danny said. "Come close." Magaly and Tony leaned closer, and Danny whispered, "I was thinking of you when I heard these gang guys talking in here. I thought maybe you could do a big story. I mean, after my aunt's."

Magaly looked over at Tony and he seemed more annoyed than curious.

"What big story?" Tony said.

"You know the SQs, right?"

"The what?"

"The Southside Quistadoreys. The gang. There're like six or seven in the lockup with me last night, and they was talkin' about the slashin'. You know, first he be mowing down white people like they was sugar cane. More power to him. But now he's doing everybody. Anyway, they were saying they know who this guy is, the real guy, and they're going to get him because of all the hell he's bringing down on them, you know. The police have been on their shit like crazy, which is why so many of them were in the lockup last night."

Magaly saw Tony's eyes pop open. Now he was excited.

"So, who is he?" he said.

D-Tox looked at the door and then back at them. "It's not like they have his home address and social security, Papi. Jesus! But they know his bike. It's a funky-looking bike. Red, they said, but it looks like it was put together with duct tape."

"Well," Tony said, "that's something, I guess. Thanks, D-Tox."

They all shook hands, and Danny was escorted out. As they were leaving, Magaly picked up Tony's messenger bag to hand to him.

"Damn," she said. "What do you have in here, encyclopedias?"

Tony took the bag and stopped in the hallway. "Only essentials."

"And your balls, I assume. You carry your balls with you everywhere."

Tony smiled. "Well, I need them." He reached into his bag and came out with a bag of flash drives and one of the minicams. "Hey, you want these?"

Magaly held the mini-camera up her eye and felt like a cyborg. "Chino, aren't these for online dating?"

"Um, not just," he said, but she caught him not looking at her. "You want them? You can help me lighten my load. Take the flash drives, too. I don't need them."

"Hell, yeah, I'll take them. I love free stuff," Magaly said. "You know how tough it is to get supplies in non-profit? Hey, by the way, you know you were pretty good in there. You might almost be learning to accept nice things that people say to you."

Tony shrugged. "I don't know. Maybe. It happens so rarely I don't worry about it."

"So, what's your next move?"

"Next move? My next move is an afternoon in the park and then a night of beer."

She shook her head. "The park? How about Angela Roman?"

"Are you kidding? Talk about a long shot. Mr. D-Tox thinks she went back to PR. Or Florida. Maybe. And maybe she went with the super. What have I got to start with? *Nada. Simplemente nada.*"

"Your horrible accent kills me. Can't locate her in PR? There is the Internet!"

"But then what am I supposed to do?" Tony said. "Give her a call, send her an email, post on her timeline? If she's shacked up with Marte, she's not going to say, 'Oh, yeah, let me put him on the phone.' It's a dead end."

"So you must think they have something to hide?"

"Yes, I do. The coincidence is weird. Rosa disappears, and then they leave the state quickly after. Something is fishy." He stopped himself and rolled his eyes. "Listen to me. What am I saying? Statistically, it's just as likely they had planned to retire into the sunset years ago and it has nothing to do with Rosa. Coincidences only seem meaningful because we try to explain them."

"But your gut is telling you something is weird here. My gut says the same thing."

"My gut is telling me it's lunchtime. I have enough for a story. I've got plenty for a nice retrospective article just in time for the anniversary of Rosa's disappearance. It'll be respectful, have some nice pictures—"

"But what about what you told D-Tox—Danny? You said you would keep digging."

"C'mon, Mags, I was just trying to be nice. You used to say I didn't know how to be nice, but *quod erat demonstrandum.*"

"You son of a bitch. I thought you had changed."

"*Quod cupio mecum est,*" Tony said.

"Oh my god, you have to stop with the Latin shit. What

does that mean?"

"I'm happy with the life I have, thank you very much."

Outside of the jail, Tony went his way and Magaly went hers. She had been hoping to have lunch with him. She had thought he was different, and she had been looking forward to getting to know who he was all over again. But he hadn't changed at all.

She was disappointed in him, and now she knew she was going to binge at the first fast food place she found on her way.

CHAPTER THIRTY-NINE

Black Martin's car smelled like French fries, beer, and feet cheese. But it ran fine.

It had taken Kirsten and Gunnar four hours to drive to Pennsylvania. Things were smooth until New Jersey, as expected. Traffic and shitty drivers from end to end. And they had taken a while to get started because Gunnar always took forever to decide what to wear. And then he wore all black again anyway.

Gunnar was typically quiet during the ride. He never said much, her Gunnar. But that's not what she liked him for. She'd met him at a bar in the East Village, where his band Franzbrötchen was playing what they called "death metal rap-folk." Kirsten couldn't give two shits about the music either way, but she loved the way he held his like a giant cock.

He'd come over from Germany to find himself, *i.e.*, to find a band to play in. She'd heard the same story a thousand times over as a bartender. But Gunnar was a big man. And he liked strong women. And she liked big men who liked strong women.

Patrick had been different. Very different. He liked a strong woman. But he was frail, almost feminine. They grew up together in Allentown. She was his first lay, and, as far as she told him, he was hers. They came to New York to NYU and journalism school. After a year of school, she'd run out of money and interest. But Patrick had hung in there, got his degree. Had to give him credit for that.

Too bad he turned into such a weasel.

When they saw the exit for Allentown, Gunnar asked her if she wanted to visit her family.

"Nope," she said. "We have to stay on mission."

She knew why he had asked. Eight months together, living together. He probably wondered if she was ashamed of him. He had written several songs to that effect. He was a sensitive one, that Gunnar, under that curly 'stache. But he had nothing to worry about. He was her man. Her right arm. She wasn't going anywhere without him.

Not for the moment anyway.

When she pulled into town, she looked back on all she had left behind. The trees, the wide open sky, the used car dealerships. So green. So boring.

They pulled up to a picturesque orange-and-red brick corner house on Whitehall Street, with a little chimney, a matching garage, and guarded on two sides by perfectly trimmed hedges. Only two blocks from the cemetery.

"Good morning, Mr. and Mrs. Stoller," she said. It had taken them ten minutes of Kirsten's buzzer-pressing to open the door. "It's great to see you."

They stood in the doorway, as American Gothic (sans pitchfork) as ever.

His father spoke up first. "Can we help you, Kirsten?"

"Well, hello. It's so good to see you guys again," she said.

They said nothing, just looked down at her, which made sense since she was on a lower step, but still it made her feel like they were looking at her like dog shit on their driveway that they had to walk around and would have to clean up later.

"This is Gunnar," she said. He stood behind her, as imposing and talkative as a sequoia. No need to say he was her boyfriend. This was all about diplomacy. *Keep it nice. Keep it cool.* "Um, I heard you were in New York recently to pick up Patrick's stuff from his apartment. But, well, when I moved out there was still some of my stuff there, and I think, when you came to get his stuff, you took some of my stuff. Look, I'm sorry we didn't connect while you were in town, but I kind of need to go through his stuff to find my stuff."

Patrick's mother said, "We didn't see anything that was yours."

"You probably didn't recognize it. It wasn't clothes or underwear."

"Well, what was it?" she said.

"It was personal. Something very personal."

"We've seen everything there is in there," Mr. Stoller said. "If you tell us what it is, we can help you find it, and then you can be on your way."

Nosy suburban bastards.

"A camera, a miniature video camera. It was with a memory card and some flash drives. I had bought it a long time ago and lent it to Patrick, and he was supposed to give it back, and I need it for my work."

"As a barmaid?" Mrs. Stoller said.

"I'm also a photographer and an artist."

"We gave that away, didn't we, Sarah?" Mr. Stoller said. "To that nice boy, Tony, who worked with Patrick."

"Yes, that's right. We thought he could use it. He's a journalist."

"Oh, Tony, yeah. I know Tony," Kirsten said. She balled her fists. *Fuck!* "Well, I'll ask him then. Sorry to bother you."

Fuck. Fuck. Fuck.

"Patrick's funeral was last week," Mrs. Stoller said. "I'm not sorry you missed it."

Kirsten looked down at her black boots. Counted slowly. Breathed. Still, she couldn't get the image of something very bad happening to the Stollers out of her head. Something very, very bad.

Just then, another old couple chirped out as they exited the house next door. "Hello, Sarah. Hello, Ken." Clones of the Stollers. *Old. Boring. Feet in the grave.*

"Well, goodbye then," Kirsten said, backing up, taking Gunnar by the hand and walking him away.

Mrs. Stoller called after them. "You've always been an unpleasant girl. Always!"

Kirsten climbed into the car without looking back.

"Don't come here again!" said Mrs. Stoller, at the top of her lungs. "Don't you dare come here again!"

CHAPTER FORTY

"Carreau!"

Few tourists were crawling around McCarren Park, the air was warm but tolerable at twilight, and Tony had just knocked Yogi's ball away from the cochon. So he was feeling pretty damned good.

He walked off to the side of the court and told Yogi, "That's my *qi* working."

"Easy, champ," Yogi said, tossing his dreads back, which gave off a skunky whiff of ganja. "Easy."

The last chance for Yogi's side rested with a new player named Brandon. The guy wore a wifebeater, orange shorts, and calf-high black socks. He had holes in his earlobes large enough to flick quarters through, and he stopped to vape between each round. Brandon crouched and held his arm out straight to aim.

"Okay, Brandy, my boy," Yogi said, "you can do it."

Brandon tossed and his ball came up short, showering sand.

"That is not the way the ball bounces," said Tony. "And that is the game."

They had played three games, Tony's team winning two. The light was fading as they packed up.

Yogi was smoking a hand-rolled cigarette he had bummed off of the new guy. Tony noticed that he wore one of those odd T-shirts he had seen at the feast.

"That 'hipster death rattle.' Is that the name of a band?" Tony said.

"Oh, this?" Yogi said, pointing to the shirt. He laughed. "No. It's—" Suddenly, he yelled. An ash from the roach-sized cigarette had burned his lips. "Holy mother of a fucker! That hurt," he said, but then he seemed to brush off the pain. "Oh, hey, you want to go get a beer at Tim Riley's? I need to quench the heat off my lips for sure now."

"Yeah, I don't know."

"Just a quick one," Yogi said. "Or two. Don't let me drink by myself. C'mon, I'll buy you a round."

Magic words. "Okay," Tony said. "All right."

"Hey, you guys going for beers?" It was the newbie, Brandon. "Can I come?"

Yogi rolled his eyes. "Yeah, sure, why not?"

Tim Riley's was a short walk from the park. It had friendly, dark wood paneling, modern pop trash on the jukebox, and a pinball machine based on a video game.

"Oh, this place looks all right," said Brandon.

They took a seat in a narrow raised area near the front windows. Yogi said, "This used to be a good bar. One of them real blue-collar bars with a lived-in feel, you know, really authentic. Now look at it. New tables. Fake sports bullshit on the walls. It's practically an Applebee's."

"Before that it was a strip joint," Tony said. "Did you know that? Belinda's Lounge."

"I did know that. It was still here when I first moved in, years ago," Yogi said. "Decades ago."

A waitress with tattoo sleeves and a nose ring like a bull's brought their beers.

"At least the beer is still good," Yogi said.

Tony said. "Actually, it's a little flat."

"Curséd be the ungrateful. That's a free beer in your hand, pal."

"Just making an observation. And I appreciate the beer, believe me."

"Tony, you're a beer snob. Now I know something about

you, besides your exceptional skills at pétanque."

"How's the food here?" Brandon said.

"Abysmal," Tony said. "But I'm getting a burger. I'll pay for it."

"Make sure she knows that. Me, I try to eat healthy," said Yogi. "I've been clean, vegetarian, vegan, raw food, paleo, you name it."

"I eat anything," Brandon said. When he spoke, his earlobes wobbled like soggy onion rings. "I don't care."

Yogi ignored him. "It's like I was saying, fakeness ruins everything. Like this neighborhood. It's not pure anymore, man. It was a place for artists, you know? Like all artists, I left behind troglodytes back home and came here to congregate with the creative."

Tony sipped his beer. "Theoretically leaving behind a higher percentage of troglodytes."

"That's why we get these elections like we do," Brandon said.

Yogi ignored him again. "And then these hipsters moved in to Williamsburg, and they moved in because it was cheap and close to the city and ruined it all!"

"Hey, man, I'm, like, a hipster," Brandon said.

"Impossible," Tony said. "Hipsters never admit to being hipsters. Although those ears are a clue."

"See! I got the look. I got the clothes. I don't mind the term. It's just a stupid label."

"The term 'hipster' derives from the term 'hip,'" Tony said, "which derives from an African word meaning 'enlightenment.'"

"Bullshit!" Yogi said. "That's not enlightenment. Why not call a douchebag a douchebag? I'm no hipster, man. I'm an artist. There's a difference. Right, Tony?"

"Don't ask me. You all look the same to me."

Yogi almost spit out his beer. "Wait, wait. What the fuck? I don't care what this one thinks, I am not a fucking hipster, all right?"

Brandon smiled. "Like he said, a hipster would never admit to being a hipster."

"I'm not a fucking hipster. You got that?"

"Whatevs, dude," Brandon said.

"By the way, Yogi, you say you were here when Belinda's was around. How long have you lived here?"

"I've been here twenty-five long years, man."

"How old were you when you moved here?"

"Twenty-one, twenty-two. Younger than this one—"

"I'm twenty-eight—" Brandon said.

"—I was one of the first pioneers here."

"Well," Tony said, "I think the Iroquois might have pioneered before you."

Yogi laughed. "Yeah, but you know what I mean. I figured, make it here, make it anywhere, right? But when I moved in, I wasn't like these guys. I respected the character of the neighborhood, the people, the buildings. I loved the Italians and the Polocks and the Puerto Ricans."

"My people," Tony said.

"Really, I thought you were Chinese, Filippino, something."

"I get that a lot."

"Well, your people are great. Great, salt-of-the-earth people. Genuine people. So fascinating and so colorful, you know what I mean? Not like where I came from?"

"What, do you come from Mars?"

Yogi laughed again, stroking his dreads. "I come from all over the place. I've lived everywhere. What I'm saying is look at the finger buildings we have all over the place now. They're horrible. They don't go with the character of the neighborhood, the brownstones and old apartment buildings."

"What's a finger building?" Brandon said.

Tony looked at his empty pint of beer. "Condo developments. They demolish old houses, and on their small lots, they put up these thin buildings that jut above the buildings around them."

"Yeah," Yogi said, "so they looked like they're giving the

middle finger to the old neighborhood." He said this while sticking a middle finger right in Brandon' face.

Brandon put his hands up, as if in surrender. "Dude!" he said. "I think I lived in one of those, and I had to leave because the building got condemned."

A woman in denim short shorts squeezed behind Yogi to take the next table. Behind her came a man and a toddler.

"Isn't it progress?" Tony said.

"Progress! It's backwards," Yogi said. "The dictatorship of the almighty dollar."

"Down with the developers, then?" Tony said, raising his empty glass.

"Death to the developers!" Yogi said, and he and Tony and Brandon clinked pints.

After that, they seemed to have nothing else to say to each other. The noise of the bar filled the space—the jukebox, the pinball machine, the hum of conversations at other tables.

"Hey," Brandon said, "what do you guys think of all these slashings going on?"

"Isn't it awful? Terrible even?" Yogi said. "No one is safe on the streets."

"I had a friend," Tony said, "a co-worker—he was one of the victims."

"Which one?" Brandon said.

"Two weeks ago. On a Saturday. He was skateboarding—"

"None there is who loves a skateboarder," Yogi said. "They should all be cut off at the ankles."

"Hey, man, that's his friend."

"No, I agree. Skateboarders are horrible people," Tony said. "But cutting off their feet might be a bit extreme."

Brandon said he had to go outside to vape, so Yogi moved into his chair, closer to Tony. "You know, if you asked me," Yogi said, "I think there's a lot more to what happened to these slashings. That guy Patrick was an editor at a paper. Does that mean you're some kind of reporter?"

The toddler at the next table began to complain about not having a window seat. The father apologized to the toddler and explained that there were no window seats available. The toddler began to bounce on his chair.

"Some kind," Tony said.

"So now I know three things about you!" Yogi said. "I have an idea for a story. About how there's more than meets the eye with these attacks."

"Thanks, but no thanks," Tony said. "I've got enough on my desktop as it is."

The toddler began to throw fries at its mother, who wore shades and seemed to be trying desperately to concentrate on her Kindle. The mother explained to the child that throwing fries was not nice.

"Listen, man," Yogi said, then he signaled the nose-ringed waitress for another round of beers and said they were on him.

"Let me put it to you this way," he went on. "And it may sound strange, so hear me out: I think this may be good for the neighborhood."

"What? In what way?"

"Well, it is. Just listen—*listen!*—for a moment. I didn't mean that it was good that Patrick was sacrificed, whoever did that. But, but, what I mean is, it could turn the people off, the other people, the people making this neighborhood into the Times Square of Brooklyn. And not the good, old Times Square either. Then these new people won't want to come here anymore. Like these fucking yuppies. You know what I mean?"

"I guess," Tony said. He thought "sacrificed" was an odd word to use. But Yogi was an odd one.

"Like this. Look at this. Real people should know better than to bring a kid into a bar. Only entitled white yuppies do that. Know what I mean?"

"Hey, buddy, you got a problem?" the father from the next table said. He had the soul-beaten look that all parents with toddlers had.

"Me?" Yogi said.

"Yeah. Why don't you stop looking at my kid?"

"What's your kid doing in a bar? People curse and drink here. You think your kid belongs in a bar? Aren't there enough fucking playgrounds for your fucking kid in this fucking city?"

"My kid can go where he wants. It's a free country, buddy."

Yogi stood up. The father stood up, too. Tony stood up and put his hand on Yogi's shoulder. "Easy," Tony said.

The kid whined even louder, and then the father turned to the mother and said the kid needed to eat, and the mother said the kid didn't like any of the food they'd got him. So they gathered their things and left, and, without asking for the check, left money and most of their food untouched.

"That's better," Yogi said to their backs as they left. "That's much better."

Later, Tony was too buzzed to go home. He wanted to keep talking, and he realized the person he wanted to keep talking to was Magaly.

But since he had to pass near her house anyway, would it be such a bad idea if he just stopped by? She had always been a night owl, right? Even when they were teenagers, he used to see her on the train, dressed to go out, high-haired and heavily made up, just as he was getting home. And it didn't mean anything for him to stop by so late. What time was it anyway? Almost midnight. Maybe he should apologize for the way he acted at the precinct.

Tony was across the street from her house and down the block and then he saw a couple. It was obvious, even from the back, that the woman was Magaly. That wild burst of hair. But just so he didn't make a mistake, he backed into a dark corner between a wall and a stoop. He felt creepy, standing there in the dark. But if he popped out now, and she saw him, it would only make it weird and worse. He watched them, and she laughed.

And as she laughed she turned and he saw for sure that it was her. The man was Luis De Moscoso.

No pain, no pain.

Tony walked home. He checked his phone and saw there were seven texts from Kirsten. What was that about? He'd check later. Maybe there was some booze left in the fridge.

Just as he got to his gate, he stopped and shut off the music on his iPhone. His front door was wide open. The wood near the jamb was split. It looked like it had been kicked in.

As he took a step down to the doorway someone came from behind him and pushed him into the gates on his front window. He felt his lip bust. He was about to turn when a cover was put over his head. All two hundred pounds of him was lifted into the air and carried a few feet, then dumped onto the metal floor of a moving enclosed space. A van.

Its tires screeched as it roared away from his apartment.

CHAPTER FORTY-ONE

It was just before eight in the morning and Petrosino tap-tap-tapped his walkie-talkie on the steering wheel of his PT Cruiser along to a song by the Genies. He half-sang along: "'Boom boom boom, bang bang bang.'"

"That is certainly a blast from the past," Hadid said. "Like Jurassic past. Like, maybe it should stay in the past."

"'Cause you don't appreciate good music," Petrosino said, tapping away.

They were parked around the corner from Le Jolie Somme, one of the new boutique hotels in Williamsburg. Convenient to the hottest bars, restaurants, shops, and residential areas, it boasted personalized service and luxurious accommodations. At only $400 a night and up, minimum two-night stay. The hotel also happened to have been built on the site of a former live poultry market, a live poultry market that stank of chickenshit and death from blocks away and that Petrosino's mother used to send him to every Saturday.

Petrosino looked over at his partner and asked for chewing gum. Hadid was rocking back and forth in his seat.

"Jeez, you look like you need a cigarette more than I do," Petrosino said.

"I'm just, just anxious. I get the feeling this is going to be big. I've never been part of something this big."

"They're all big to somebody and small to somebody else."

"What the hell does that mean?"

"I have no fucking idea."

Eladio Cortés, king of the Southside Quistadoreys, had not checked in with his parole officer but had checked into this hotel three nights before. His room came with thirty complimentary premium movie channels and an ergonomic bed with an orthopedic mattress. He had paid for the room for a week—in cash. A housecleaning woman had called the police, having spotted a gun in his room. And because he didn't tip.

"The balls of this guy to hide out in this fancy schmancy hotel," Hadid said.

"Pow-pow-pow-pow," sang Petrosino along to "A Little Too Long" by the Wanderers. Then he said, "He ain't a suspect yet. We just need him for questioning."

"He don't know he's practically got an army waiting for him."

"That's Tuchman overcompensating."

The doo-wop song filled the car, and Petrosino sang along until it trailed off.

In the brief silence, Hadid said, "You don't like me very much, do you?"

"What's not to like?" Petrosino said.

"There Goes My Baby" by the Drifters came on the radio. Petrosino looked at his partner and then lowered the volume. He said, "You've been getting better."

"I have? In what way?"

Petrosino sighed. "All right. When you came in, you were a big-mouthed, fast-talking, indiscreet son of a bitch. But you learned, you changed. Like with Mr. Pak, not blabbing about the second vic right in front of him, waiting till we got outside. Good thinking. You might actually end up a half-decent detective."

"As half-decent as you?"

"You little sh—"

Tuchman's voice barked over the walkie-talkie. "We are a go, gentlemen. We are a go."

When they rushed into the hotel, Tuchman took point, of

course. Petrosino and Hadid were right behind him.

Tuchman banged on the door and shouted, "Police! Open up!"

From behind the door, Petrosino heard yelling, a man and a woman. "What the fuck is going on, Eladio?" "Shut the fuck up!"

"We just want to ask you some questions," Tuchman said.

"Oh my god! Eladio!" "Shut the fuck up!"

Even though the squad had the room key, Tuchman yelled, "Bring it down."

Petrosino's first thought was that it was a tiny room for something billed as a boutique hotel. There, less than twelve feet away and backed between the front wall and the king-sized bed that took up most of the room, stood Cortés. He was in a little spot away from the window—which made him out of the reach of the police snipers outside. Cortés held a Glock .40 in his right hand and, in the crook of his left arm, a baby, who looked calm and angelic, as if none of this was happening. Petrosino knew the infant was Cortés's daughter, the woman with her head peeking out of the john with the wet hair was Cortés's girlfriend, who went by the name "Beyoncé" (birth name: Awilda Fuentes).

"Don't fucking shoot!" she said. "Don't nobody fucking shoot! Don't hurt my baby!" She moved out from the bathroom and tried to grab the baby away from Cortés.

Tuchman said, "Ma'am, please step away!"

"Give me my fucking baby!"

"Chill out, chill out, chill out, chill out," Eladio said, holding on tight to the baby.

"...please step away."

"...my fucking baby!"

The baby wailed. Then there was a shot.

Someone, Petrosino first thought it was one of the younger cops, must have got nervous and fired. The young woman was clutching her chest. Cortés, instead of shooting back, held his gun up and dropped it to the floor, staring wide-eyed at his girl-friend, and cradling the baby so tight he could have suffocated it.

A moment later, just as Tuchman rushed in to cuff Cortés, Petrosino turned and saw his partner on his knees, his head down and his service weapon on the floor in front of him. The officers next to him in the doorway looked at him in shock.

It was Hadid. He was the one who had discharged his weapon.

CHAPTER FORTY-TWO

The van drove for a while. Wedged between two sets of legs, Tony rested his head on his bulky messenger bag. They had roughly tied both his hands and his ankles with what felt like plastic zip-tie restraints.

The bag over Tony's head made it hard to breathe. This could his *tempus mortis,* be how it ended, kidnapped on the street, then imprisoned and tortured forever in some hidden location, dumped in the river or buried in a shallow grave. His mind spun a million different deaths. To stay focused, to stop from panicking and soiling himself, he tried to listen to the sounds and feel of the streets they were on.

Judging by their first turn, they had taken Kent Avenue, but then they took a few quick turns and he lost track.

But then they moved with speed and without stopping frequently—that meant highway, and the closest one was the BQE. But which way? North, which meant Long Island or even upstate, the kind of places with plenty of areas to dump a body. Or south, toward Coney Island and the Atlantic, or over the Verrazano, toward Staten Island—he would be able to smell if they went there—and farther on toward Jersey and the Pine Barrens, another popular destination for corpse dumping.

The van had stopped after about half an hour. Too soon for the Pine Barrens.

He was pulled out and lifted high and then bent over onto someone's shoulder. Somebody very strong and tall. It was harder to breathe bent over that way, and blood rushed to his head. He knew his brain could hemorrhage or blood could pool in his lungs. He found himself wondering who would tell his mother, if Magaly would ever find out what happened to him, and how his apartment would be superficially renovated and rented again for a few hundred more dollars a month.

He was carried through doors—temperature change, echo of steps—and up a short flight of stairs. A big empty space that smelled of piss and beer. Warehouse? An empty dance club? Citi Field?

They walked into what felt like a smaller space (less echo) with metal floors, and the room began to move up. Elevator. Metal doors moving in slots. Lots of clacking.

The door slid open, and he was moved a short distance. A door opened and there was sound and wind. He was outside again. He was placed down, not on concrete, but on something that had a slight spring to it. He felt underneath him.

Roof tar.

He decided to play it tough, to show he wasn't scared. As if this kind of thing happened to him regularly and it was merely an inconvenience. As casually as he could, he said through the bag, "So, we're in a new neighborhood, I guess. what's the rent like here? Are the schools goo—"

"Shut the fuck up." Someone kicked him hard in the ribs, knocking out his breath.

Stupid tactic. Okay, no more Mr. Tough Guy approach.

He was dragged up against a vertical surface, maybe a wall. His hands were still bound behind his back, and his feet were still bound tightly together. A rope was tied around his chest. Someone searched his pockets and took out his phone.

A second later, he heard a sad crunch. A sad, three-hundred-dollar crunch.

Someone spoke. "Here is what is happening to you and why." Male. Brooklyn accent. "This is to teach you a lesson. To mind your own business. That blackmail is unacceptable."

"That's two lessons," Tony almost said. Then he remembered his ribs. At least he knew it wasn't some bizarrely random kidnapping or some government death squad.

Someone to the right, another male voice, said, "Should we take off the hood at least?" A different kind of Brooklyn accent this time. Yiddish?

"Fuckin' kiddin' me?" said a whole other voice, male. Brooklyn Italian. Or Irish. Or Greek. "So then he can see our faces? Fuckin' kiddin' me!"

The first voice began to read again. "Just so you know, you are now sitting on a roof with no shade and up on which no one can hear you. No one knows you're here." Then the voice turned in another direction. "Get that tarp."

Tony heard footsteps and then the sound of rough cloth unfurling. They covered most of his body but not his head.

"You're a smartypants," the voice said, "so you can guess how it's gonna be. Tomorrow we got another heat wave, and you're gonna be one microwaved enchilada."

And no traffic or police helicopters would see him under the tarp. Clever. Tony stopped himself from telling them he was not Mexican, if that's what they were getting at with the enchilada crack. Again, it didn't seem useful to speak at the moment.

The tarp was placed over his head and tucked behind him, and from what he could hear and sense they were laying cinderblocks on the edges of the tarp, lots of them.

"Check the bag," he heard, muffled.

"Is it there, Norm?"

Or was it "No" or "Noah?" Tony couldn't quite make it out.

"No names, asshole!"

"Sorry. Shit. Sorry. He can't hear us. He's got more things to worry about."

"What are these things? Weights?"

Pétanque balls, you idiot. Pétanque!

"They look almost like bocce balls."

Tony rolled his eyes under the hood and tar. He heard the

muffled sounds of metal balls thudding on the roof. And then the metallic sound of one being kicked.

"Oww."

"Idiot."

"Fucking shit. Hey. Look here. Got 'em. And a laptop."

"Smash it."

Tony heard a loud crack. His laptop. And one whose hard drive he'd never had the energy to back up. A thousand dollars to replace. *Bastards.*

"Let's go," one of the voices said.

Then he heard, close to his covered face: "*Adios,* asshole."

CHAPTER FORTY-THREE

Litvinchouk's station wagon was, for the most part, a utilitarian vehicle, a mobile office loaded with responsibilities. As a landlord, he drove it almost every day from building to building, and then from schools to shopping malls to synagogue.

But she, the lovely she, by her mere presence could transform it from pragmatic dullness into a den of erotic splendor.

"You're incredible," Jackie Tomasello said. Her leather skirt was hiked to her waist, showing off her sculptured thighs, her Neanderthal hips, and her blouse was open, revealing a half-open fire engine red brassiere.

For his part, Litvinchouk's zipper was open.

They lay panting, side by side in the back compartment, on an old picnic blanket that smelled of mayonnaise. They were close, partly because they wanted to be, but also because they were surrounded by a toolbox, two brand-new fire extinguishers, a box of toilet paper, and a menagerie of children's toys.

"*Ego sum*," Litvinchouk said. "I cannot lie."

For the sake of privacy, the windows of the station wagon were covered in black garbage bags, hastily, sloppily, duct-taped into place.

"But I gotta say, Eli, this car is a fucking sauna," his beauty said. "My makeup is running. I'm dripping everywhere."

Her wonderful legs were so long, her feet threatened to dangle over the driver's seat. Those wonderful legs had just been wrapped around him seconds ago, and he knew he would have to make an appointment with his chiropractor because of the pain he would feel in a few hours. But it would be a sweet pain.

"Would you prefer a room at the Ritz-Carlton, my dear?"

"No," she said, kissing him. "What I love about this is that we don't have to act like solid, respectable citizens in here. We can be crazy, lovesick teenagers. Just like we used to be."

"Well, you were the teenager."

"And I was the pretty young thing you broke in."

"Forbidden fruit is sweetest. Frank Jr. would have killed me if he found out."

"You always worry. He didn't know then and he doesn't know now. He's harmless. That's why I married him. That and his daddy's business."

Litvinchouk hated to spoil the mood, but they had precious few moments to be genuine, to really talk. "Speaking of Frank Senior..." was all he needed to say.

"Ah, that," said Jackie. She didn't seem upset about the return to present matters. She didn't even button up her blouse, allowing him further appreciation of her prognosis for her father-in-law. "Still in critical condition, so it looks like any day now. So he won't be around to stop us either."

"Now we just have to conclude this little business here, and then we can be free."

"I don't trust that little number. She's a piece of work."

"She's on our side. That is, the side of money. She won't upset the money train."

Litvinchouk took a surreptitious look at his watch. She caught him looking and gave him a sad smile.

"My love," he said, "I'm afraid I have to meet with a congressman in half an hour."

"Back to business then."

Jackie fixed her bra and blouse and hiked down her skirt. Litvinchouk zipped up. They shuffled into the front seats. They each took off the garbage bags from their sides. It was still morning. They were parked outside of an old warehouse.

"This is a nice spot," he said. "It's a quiet spot. You can't find too much of them in New York anymore. Certainly not in Williamsburg."

"Tell me about it."

"Remember our spot outside the Navy Yard?"

"Mmmm, yes. Don't get me started again, unless you want to be late for your congressman."

Litvinchouk pointed to the warehouse. "So how long are you going to leave him up there for?"

"Another day, maybe two."

"What if he doesn't survive?"

"So what? No one will raise a fuss. He'll just be another missing person."

"He does have friends. Like that social activist girl he hangs around with."

"Don't worry. We know where she lives."

CHAPTER FORTY-FOUR

To Gabby Vasconcellos, the subway was totes obnoxious. What was it with people today anyway? Everyone pushing and shoving. And grabbing. Men totally taking advantage of the close quarters. *Disgusting.* She had had a long day at the *Sentinel*, finishing up her story on the Italian feast. Tony had written up the incident with the fake slasher guy, some somehow-still-alive Vietnam vet/addict who told police it was just a joke, but it wasn't time to be funny, no-oh—but after she pleaded a little (surprisingly little), Tony let her write up a general overview of the feast, which really meant a lot of captions, but some of them were paragraphs-long, so. Plus, she would be getting a byline again, and she'd had a byline a few times in the paper already, but every time it felt amazing, every time she saw "By Gabrielle Vasconcellos," she felt proud and professional and powerful. Her Hunter College degree shining for the world! Now if only she could get the men on the subway to stop grabbing her ass.

After work, she had decided to hang out with the girls because the girls were hanging out. Her BFF#4 Lala had decided to quit her job—she hadn't actually quit yet, but the deciding was good enough reason to get together. But Lala lived on the Upper West Side, so that meant going to a bar in the Upper West Side because Lala just couldn't. It was just for dinner and a few drinks anyway, and then she would bounce back home.

Three hours later it was—what time was it anyway? Funny thing, it was supposed to be dinner and drinks, but they had forgotten about dinner somehow. Gabby checked her phone. Low battery, yes, fine. 2:30 a.m. O-M-G, five hours later. How was she going to wake up in the morning? She better get the coffee machine ready before she went to sleep. She was getting so organized as she adulted, she really was, and she liked the feeling. But maybe she should also make herself puke a little to make sure she didn't have too much of a hangover tomorrow.

She got off the 7 train, which was never not crowded. She plopped down the elevated stairs and then suddenly remembered the slasher. *Stupid, stupid.* She should have taken an Uber. But Uber drivers were rapists. But the slasher had never slashed in this neighborhood. Still, he might want to branch out to Queens, to Woodside, what with all the cops on the streets now in Williamsburg. And if not that, or just that, all the slashing might give new people ideas...

She looked up and down the street. It was dead empty. Quiet. She thought about running the three blocks home but worried that it would totally make her throw up.

Gabby lived in a pre-war walk-up with a kitchen with full stove, microwave, full refrigerator, and "granite" countertops, and two bedrooms—shared with three roommates, tight, but each got a closet. Her keys were at the bottom of her bag again, and she stopped in the middle of the sidewalk to dig down to get them. That is when she heard the footsteps. Not so much stepping as stopping. That is why she noticed them. They had stopped the same exact time she stopped. Behind her. To the right.

No! All her fears and worries actually coming true. *No!* That's not the way things happened in real life, was it? *No, no, no!* You worry about something and that means it never happens—that's the way life works. That's the way it was supposed to work.

She took a step. She heard nothing.

She took two steps. She heard steps.

She ran.

CHAPTER FORTY-FIVE

Petrosino parked his PT Cruiser in front of the apartment building on Conselyea Street. Aluminum siding, three stories, no pets. It looked like a quiet block, a good block, nice place to live. He walked up the short stoop and rang the doorbell.

It took a while. He was thinking about lighting up when, through the glass in the front door, he saw Hadid coming down the stairs. From what he could see, the guy looked awful.

"Petro. This is a surprise. How's it going?"

"Same old, same old," Petrosino said. "How you holding up?"

"So so," Hadid said. There were dark bags under Hadid's eyes. He was wearing a stained wifebeater and dirty sweatpants. He hadn't shaved in days. "They say I should consider modified duty a mini-vacation. But I think riding a desk all day is hell. Come on in."

They went up two flights of stairs and entered the kitchen of a small railroad apartment. Two walls were painted in orange while the other two were in blue.

"Somebody's a Mets fan," Petrosino said and whistled.

"That's from the last tenant. I gotta paint over that. But the floors are in good condition," Hadid said, taking a pair of socks off a chair. There was a card table in the kitchen, cluttered with cereal boxes and takeout food containers. "Cop a squat."

"Gonna need lots of primer." Petrosino handed Hadid the bag he was carrying.

"What's this?"

"Eggplant parm with linguine. From that place on Frost Street I was telling you about. Been there for years. Nobody does it better. Cono's used to, but they closed."

"Why'd you—"

"Man's gotta eat, and you said you didn't cook."

"Thanks," Hadid said. "How'd you know?"

"Thing about living with a woman. They won't let you leave the house with shaving cream in your ear. Not that often anyway."

Petrosino looked around at the tiny apartment. Underwear lay on the floor, porno DVDs were stacked three feet high against a wall, and the whole place smelled of armpit and damp socks.

Petrosino said, "You told me she wanted to be close to her family."

"Yeah. Thing is, they all live in the Bronx."

"Right-o."

"So, uh, she never actually moved here with me. She refused. Which is why I live like this. By myself. Alone."

"Yeah, I kind of got that."

Hadid opened a fridge that had survived the 1970s, maybe even the '60s, and brought out two beers. "Last couple of days the neighborhood's been going crazy, huh? I heard about the bodega fight. And that bar fight that turned into street brawl. Then there was that scuffle at the Bedford Avenue station."

"Yeah, two males fighting themselves onto the tracks," Petrosino said, cracking open a beer. "It's getting to be a regular war zone, for sure."

"Our slasher's or slashers' bringing out the best in people." Hadid cracked open a beer and sat in front of the takeout bag. "And how's the case going?"

"It's going," Petrosino said. He took a long sip of beer. "I've been working it over in my head. I wanted to run some stuff by you."

Hadid looked surprised. "Is that copacetic?"

"Sure. Why not?" Petrosino said. "Let's just, for a minute, take our heads out of Tuchman's ass."

"Okay."

"We've been looking at gangs for this whole mess, right? Now Cortés's in lockup, and he ain't saying nothing. Fine. But now: Let's look at the patterns. First few slashings, before they got fatal, up until Maxine Channing and Elijah Sackler, seemed like tryouts, going back months. All at night. And all white vics. Then we get Nelson, Hewitt, Stoller, and Horvath. All at night."

"And all white again."

"And all male. Then: We get Echeverria and Horvath, who was on crutches."

"Yeah? So?"

"Keep up," Petrosino said. "And then, in broad daylight, two more in quick succession: Erin Cole, our first woman. And then Vishal Raghavan—within an hour."

"A Span—Latino, another white guy, a woman, and an Asian. So our boy or boys are branching out. So?"

"Branching out? It's practically a rainbow coalition, especially if you count the guy in crutches as handicapped."

Hadid shook his head. "What? Maybe the first ones were all just opportunistic, and white guys are more likely to be out late. And then these gangbangers got hair on their balls, and start going after whoever in the daytime. This eggplant parm is excellent, by the way."

"It's the best," said Petrosino. "I thought the same thing. Just random. I mean, rainbow coalition of victims, no gang is going to be that organized."

"But you think someone is being that organized, someone's being very specific."

"Right-o."

"You tell this to Tuchman?"

"No, and anyways he's had reporters coming out of his ears since the Cortés thing."

"Yeah, that." Hadid got up to get two more beers.

"About that," Petrosino said, "what happened with Awilda aka Beyoncé, it was a million-to-one freak accident."

"You're saying I couldn't've shot her in the head if I actually tried to do it."

"No, you moron. It's just—it was a tense moment, we all had our guns drawn, she was yelling, Tuchman was yelling, you guys were squeezed in by the door. It's not something you should eat yourself up over."

"Yeah, well." Hadid sucked down his beer and stared at the mess on his table. He looked miserable. Through the uncurtained, unshaded windows, the summer light in the room was starting to fade. Hadid got up and turned on the kitchen lights.

"I don't know what else to tell you," Petrosino said. "You have to hang in there, kid. You know, when I was just starting out as a detective—"

"Back up a second," he said. "I know you don't like to talk about yourself, but I gotta ask: Back when you were talking to Steven Pak, was it true what you said, about your wife being killed and all?"

Petrosino gave him a long serious look. Then he smiled. "My wife is fine and fat as a Buick. But sometimes you have to say something. People like that guy, they're just miserable. They need to think people understand what they're going through. It's a lie, but it's also human courtesy. Know what I mean?"

"Yeah," Hadid said. "So were you just about to tell me about some time you accidentally shot somebody."

"Right-o," Petrosino said and he laughed.

Hadid caught it and laughed too. After a little while, he said, "Do you mind if I finish eating here? I'm starving."

"Dig in. You mind if I smoke?"

"Knock yourself out," Hadid said, sliding a small, used microwave container stained with brown sauce over to him.

CHAPTER FORTY-SIX

Tony thought he knew what it was to be hot.

He thought he knew what hot was as a kid sharing a bed with his brother on August nights with no AC in a small room. He thought the Union Square subway station in July was hot, when the platform gets overcrowded and sour as rotten milk. And he thought he knew what hot was at that club he went to—*once*—where he felt like he was dancing in a sauna. He went to the bathroom and practically showered in the sink and when he got out, his date had evaporated. That was real heat in action, he thought.

But none of that was hot.

He had never known *hot* before now.

Sweat rolled off of him, soaking his tee shirt and shorts. His sneakers felt wet all the way through.

As soon as he thought the goons who had dumped him there had gone, Tony yelled for help.

"Hey! Guy stuck on a roof here! Hello! Help! Help already!"

But the sound of his own muffled voice bit into his ears, and his throat went dry.

He tried to wiggle the plastic restraints off his legs. His sweat gave him enough lubrication to get his left shoe and sock off. It took a very long time.

But the restraints remained. He decided to take a break and contemplate a barrel of iced coffee. Poured over his head or with a straw. Either was fine.

How long does it take to die of thirst? Three days? Five

days? Three to five days? He would trade that bucket of iced coffee for a chance to google-confirm.

Tony wiggled his legs some more, and the restraints dug into his flesh. In frustration, he pushed hard, slicing off a long piece of skin.

"Dammit!"

No pain, no pain, no pain, no pain.

Tony had figured out why he was there, the answer was obvious: Jackie Tomasello and/or Elias Litvinchouk. This was a stupid bogus Mafia bullshit kidnapping stupid bullying threatening garbage thing, and it seemed straight up her alley. She had threatened him. Litvinchouk had been less cartoony, had offered him a bribe. Was it Tony's refusal to take the bribe what got him up there? It didn't matter. They had done their job. He was done with the whole Rosa Irizarry case, done trying to play intrepid reporter, even in the half-assed way he had been doing it.

He wanted instead to swim inside a vat of ice cream.

He wanted to slide down a snow-covered hill and plop through the ice of a frozen lake. Naked.

Were they going to leave him to die? That didn't seem to be the point. The thug with the list had said it was a lesson. Again, two lessons, really. Technically, lessons meant something you took away from an experience. And you had to survive the experience to take something away.

How long could he survive up there?

Tony's skull was covered in sweat. It was not easy to breathe, but if he didn't move, he could just avoid the nagging feeling of suffocation. He tried to get his mind off of it, tried to let his thoughts drift. To his job. Pétanque. Magaly. His mom. Williamsburg.

He found himself thinking of his stepfather, Raul. Raul had been a decent enough guy who treated Tony's mother well and had stuck around, unlike his father. When Tony was a kid, Raul used to bring him along on the odd jobs he did. Like roofing.

"It's like making a sandwich," Raul would say, "with the old roof as one piece of bread and the new paper as the new piece, with the tar in the middle like jelly."

Tony had been too small to lift any roof paper or buckets of tar, but his stepfather would ask him to bring him beers from a cooler or to walk back and forth on the newly laid roof paper to pat it down.

One time, on one of those roofs, Tony stood on the side, playing with his stepfather's radio to get WKTU in just right, when he saw a patch of something fuzzy and brown on top of a tarred-over chimney. It looked like feathers, but then he realized that it was hair, and in the hair were sticks that looked like chicken bones, but they were too small and thin to be chicken bones. He asked his stepfather what it was.

"*Carajo!*" his stepfather had said. "You know what that is? That's kittens. Little kittens. Some son of a bitch put them on the roof to die. I swear to god, people are animals."

And that's why Tony hated reminiscing, and—suddenly, he realized: Coconut lotion. That's what he had smelled in Litvinchouk's car. What the hell did that mean? Litvinchouk's wife didn't seem the type to wear coconut lotion, at least not so heavily scented. He hadn't smelled any at Litvinchouk's apartment. Of course, he and Jackie Tomasello knew each other, but why would they be driving around together? Litvinchouk said he left all the management to them. Maybe they viewed new properties together. "Let's tear down this charming building over here." "Yes, an ugly co-op for yuppies would look lovely there." And that gaudy bangle in the car. That couldn't belong to Litvinchouk's wife, could it?

Why was he even thinking about this stuff anymore? What did it matter when he was slowly being turned into a mummy?

He tried again and again to break the restraints and to force away the pain he kept repeating: "*Dolor hic tibi proderit olim. Dolor hic tibi proderit olim. Dolor hic tibi proderit olim.*"

This pain will be useful to you. This pain will be useful to you. This pain will be useful to you.

CHAPTER FORTY-SEVEN

At some point, the quiet of the night stopped, and Tony could hear, muffled through the bag on his face and the tarp, the sounds of the city waking up.

Soon after that the heat came. Subtle at first, warmth at the edge of the tarp.

Then it came on full, heating the air under the tarp with him, making him a corn kernel waiting to pop.

How long were they going to leave him here? What if they forgot him? What if they were on their way to get him out and traffic on the BQE was horrible?

He'd be a microwaved enchilada indeed.

Damn, it was hot.

He should have had to urinate by now, but he was surprised that he had no urge. What he did feel was nauseous. But he didn't want to vomit, not with a bag over his face. That would not be cool in any way, shape, or form. Even if the vomit was lemonade or iced tea, which it was not likely to be.

Punchy. He was getting punchy.

Then he remembered something he had read once about zip-tie restraints, one of those how-to articles he may have even written himself a thousand cooler years ago, in a past ice age.

Instead of trying to slide them off, he spread his ankles apart with as much strength as he could. And then he slammed them into the ground. Nothing.

He did it again. Nothing.

Again.

Again.

And one restraint popped. He could feel it—one less band around his flesh.

Time for the second one. He lifted his legs up—good workout for the abs, he thought.

He slammed. Nothing. He would have to revise that article.

The bag over his head became caught up in his mouth. His tongue felt like he'd swallowed a wool sweater. He never wanted to wear a sweater ever again. He bit into the bag and began to chew at it. He had no spit left and the bag tasted of his own breath, which was awful. He chewed—and he could feel the bag tugging slowly, inch by inch off the back of his head.

But he couldn't eat the whole bag, his mouth wasn't big enough? So he began tugging, tugging, and turning his head, wedging the cloth of the bag against his neck.

It slid off.

He spit out the bag, hacking, almost vomiting.

But he could breathe more easily. No light came through the tarp, but he could better sense where he was. Light came from a space in front of him—he must have kicked a brick or two slightly while he was wrestling with the leg ties.

It took another half hour of slamming to set his legs free. Both his shoes were off by then. His last sock was on and red with blood. He was able to kick up into the tarp.

The blocks were heavy but once he got one loose, the tarp came away—letting the blazing noon sunbeam directly into his face.

Maybe not the smartest move.

He did get a decent look at his surroundings, though. Low horizon, no skyscrapers except that green Citibank building topped with a ziggurat. It was a long way off, but judging from the distance he was likely on a rooftop in Queens. They hadn't driven him very far at all. But of all the places to die. Fucking Queens.

At some point, he dozed off again. Or just plain fainted. Is this what dehydration did? The roof was spinning, and it was highly unlikely that there'd be an earthquake in the New York area. Although not impossible. They happened, but not like in California. He hated Los Angeles. Went to visit once. Smog. Traffic. He would never move there. Why would he want to leave Brooklyn?

All around him were the wrecked remains of his laptop and near and far, his pétanque balls. *Look on my works, ye mighty, and despair.*

With his hands behind his back and a rope tight around his chest, he couldn't slam his wrists free of the restraints. He tried standing up, but there was not enough slack. He tried again. Again.

He screamed in frustration. And realized he had shaken the tarp off. Maybe someone would hear him. He screamed again, but his throat was so dry it came out like muffled and croaky.

What a way to spend a summer day.

That's when he heard the voices. Distant. Giggling.

And then footsteps closer. Were they coming for him? What were they going to do next? They couldn't let him live. They couldn't.

Then he heard: "Oh shit, that dude is tied up."

"He's homeless."

"What the fuck would a homeless man be doing handcuffed here?"

"Kinky sex games?"

They were hipsters, young. Three of them. Floppy hair. Skinny jeans. Why would you wear skinny jeans in this heat, that's what Tony wanted to know.

"Oh shit. Mister, are you okay?"

Tony smelled weed. They had come up to the roof to get high. Two of them had huge cameras around their necks. One of them was on a cell phone calling for an ambulance.

"Hey," Tony heard his voice croak out. "Anybody got some water? Or a beer. A beer would be nice."

CHAPTER FORTY-EIGHT

The West Indian nurse gave Tony Pedialyte to drink and an IV drip. She told him not to worry about his laptop, that it was just a thing and that he should thank the lord above that he was still alive after what he had been through.

He shared the room with two other patients. Neither knew the other but both of them had happened to be impaled with street signs. "Must be the newest meme," he said to the nurse, who looked at him like he belonged in a different kind of hospital, the kind where patients wore jackets with wraparound sleeves and the rooms were decorated in rubber and rabid foam.

A pair of uniformed cops had come by to take Tony's statement. What could he report? He knew it involved Tomasello and Litvinchouk somehow, but he was sure there would be nothing to tie them to the thugs. So he didn't mention them.

He did ask the cops if they knew who owned the building he had been dumped on—just in case Tomasello and Litvinchouk had been that stupid. But the cops said the city owned it, that it had been abandoned for decades.

The nurse gave him cool compresses for his face and slathered him with aloe vera lotion. He slept most of the time because of the painkillers they gave him. When he was awake, he stared at the ceiling and thought a lot. The doctors wanted him to stay one more day but he had had enough of hospitals for a while. *Piss. Disinfectant.* He was getting up very slowly when Bobbert came in. He looked worried. White hair showed at the edges of his very black hair shining.

"You're alive! You look great," Bobbert said. "Thank god."

"I'd rather thank the nurse. But I think she thinks I'm crazy."

They shook hands. Tony's hands were slippery with lotion. "Sorry," he said. "Awkward."

Bobbert took tissues from the nightstand and wiped his hand.

"I didn't expect to see you," Tony said. His throat was dry, and he felt like he could never drink enough water. "How's things?"

"I know. You probably expected Gabby. But, er, something happened."

"What?" Tony moved to sit up, but his ribs still ached from where he was kicked.

"Well, one thing—we had a break-in at the *Sentinel*."

"Oh crap."

"Yeah. Uh. Through the bathroom window. Nothing much was taken. Just a bunch of electronic stuff."

"The computers?" Tony privately wondered if that would mean all-new computers, finally.

"Oh no," Bobbert said, "probably too heavy for them. Just some recording equipment, a DVD player, cameras, and flash drives, stuff like that, easy to carry."

"Flash drives?"

"Yeah, um, nothing important. Nothing to worry about. Insurance will cover it. But what's really important is Gabby. She was assaulted."

"What?"

"Someone robbed her, took her purse, knocked her to the ground."

"Is she okay? Stupid question. Where is she? I want to call her."

"She's home. I told her to stay put and take time off. She's in a bit of shock, as you can imagine."

"Hey!" someone yelled from the door, and Tony was surprised to see Gabby standing there. "How's the roof man?" she said. "Talk about a stupid way to get a tan." She had a big smile on her face, but there was a good-sized bruise on her forehead and her lip had a scab.

"How are you?" Tony asked, feeling stupid for asking.

"I'm fine. It looks worse than it is. Some guy fucking ripped my bag and spilled everything on the sidewalk, but my neighbors, these big-ass Albanian guys, chased him away. But look at you, you look a little gross," she said. "Your face is all shiny and red and stuff."

Bobbert looked embarrassed and perplexed, the way he usually looked, only more so. "Gabby, what are you doing here? You should be resting."

"Hold on, I have to hug Tony," she said. She did and then said, "You smell like my grandmother's lotion."

"It's my new fragrance," Tony said. "It beats the scent of sweat."

"Lolz. Anyways, listen, I came to bring this to you," she said, and she took out the bag of flash drives he had given her. "I had these in my apartment and went to save something on them, but then I noticed there was a bunch of video files on here. You have to see it."

"What is it?" Tony said, taking the bag.

"It looks like surveillance video. But there's something weird going on. Where did you get these?"

"Patrick. Indirectly."

"Oh, you know, maybe I should take those for safekeeping," Bobbert said. "If you think they're important. And I'll give them back to you when you're feeling better."

"Nah, thanks. I kind of want to hold on to them."

"But what are you going to do with them now? You're still recovering. I can keep them safe."

"No offense, Bobbert," Tony said, "but you said the paper just got burgled. So it's not safe there. I'd really rather keep them with me. Besides I'd like to see these right away. As soon as I get to a laptop, that is."

"Are you sure?

"Yeah, I'm sure."

"Well, okay, if you're really sure then, I guess I'd better go. Okay. Stay strong!"

Bobbert left, and soon after Gabby stood up to leave. She said, "I was going to bring flowers, too, but I forgot. Is that okay? I didn't think you liked flowers."

"I'm indifferent to them."

"Okay then. I did the right thing."

"Thanks for coming though," Tony said.

"Of course. We're friends."

"Okay, so just FYI: Friends bring flowers."

"Asshole!" she said.

"I *love* flowers!" he said. "*Love* them."

"I really am sorry to see you like this. But you'll be fine."

"Thanks, Gabby. Thank you. And can I ask you a favor?"

"If it's money..."

"No, it's an assignment. Give me a piece of paper."

"Hello! I don't carry paper with me."

Tony sighed. "Hand me your phone."

She unlocked it, and Tony could see the screen was cracked. He said, "Was this because of—?"

"Oh, no, it was always like that. I should just buy them pre-cracked."

"Good idea. Okay, I'm writing this in your Notes. This lady Angela Roman may or may not live in Puerto Rico. Her name is not uncommon, so you may find a few. But get me as many addresses, emails, phone numbers, pictures, whatever. Check social media, and I'm pretty sure the paper has an account with one of those address lookup services. Use that."

"Oh wow," she said, "another assignment."

"You're racking them up," Tony said. "Listen, I can't call you at the moment, so better yet call this number when you have something."

"Magaly? Look at that. Is she your girlfriend again?"

"I'm not the story. Get on this ASAP."

"So, what is the story?" A voice walking in.

It was Magaly. She hugged him tightly. Her curly hair was still wet. He felt it cool against his face. "You look horrible." Then she quickly turned to Gabby. "How is the job?"

"It's getting a little more interesting," she said.

"Do you have your heart set on being a journalist?"

"I guess."

"You know, I almost died," Tony said.

Ignoring him, Magaly told Gabby: "Listen, if you want to talk about other career choices, call me. We have career counseling, too. Free of charge."

"Oh, I have your number already, but I'll keep this."

"You do?"

After Gabby left, Magaly said, "I like her. She seems sharp."

"She actually is. When she tries."

"Wow. That's a high compliment coming from you. You must have a crush on her."

"Did I mention I almost died, up there, on the roof?"

"Yes, I know. It must have been terrible, and I'm sorry."

"But you didn't bring flowers?"

"Why would I bring flowers? You'd just tell me it's bad for the environment or something."

"It is, and, yes, yes, I would."

"Listen, I went to your apartment—it was a mess, the super was fixing the lock, and got you the clothes you wanted—but there was this note stuck to the door."

"From who?"

"Your brother. He was looking for you."

"What's the matter?"

"Something about your mom. It sounds scary. Here."

"From Jerry? Let me see."

He took it. It read: "EMERGENCY: MOM. CONTACT ME ASAP. JERRY (YOUR BROTHER)."

CHAPTER FORTY-NINE

"You're a prick, Jerry."

"I felt it was the best way to get your attention."

Tony's brother Jerry spoke in the calm, robot-like voice he always used. Over the phone, Tony got the impression Jerry was multi-tasking and that whatever else he was doing was much more interesting than their conversation.

"I was stuck on a roof!" Tony said. He coughed into the hospital room phone. He signaled to Magaly, who stood next to him with wide eyes full of questions. "Ma's okay," he mouthed to her.

Jerry droned on. "Tony, come on, I was not aware of that. I was in Brooklyn, making sure Ma was ready for her trip, which is tomorrow, by the way, and you usually check in on her apartment, when she's away, and I need to confirm that with you, and I thought you were ducking me. So I figured the old-fashioned way was the best."

"You're a real sack of stupid." His throat still felt tight and dry, and, having lost so much weight through sweat, he felt smaller, thinner. And a lot less patient, if that was possible.

"Why do you get so riled up?" Jerry said. "I thought you would think it was funny. It is your sense of humor."

"Funny? You think leaving me a note implying our mother is dying is funny?" Tony got that out and coughed again for a while.

His brother did not let the opportunity to lecture go by—he

never did. "You know, you have to get your life in order. Look at what happened: Getting kidnapped and tossed on a roof? Who does that? What is happening to your life? Are you getting mixed up in drugs and bad people? You have to face the fact that your whole life is a mess. You need to give your heart to Jesus. Jesus loves you."

"Then Jesus is gay."

"That is unkind, Tony. That is unkind."

Tony took a deep breath and let a wave of nausea go by. During his time in the sun, as he liked to refer to it, he had turned his thoughts to his family and his mother, partly because he worried that he was never going to see them again, but he also thought that if he did, there might be something he could do—if he were to accompany his mother on her impending trip to Puerto Rico.

"Jerry, hey, look," Tony said. "I've had a rough couple of days. Too much heat on the brain. It fried out my filter."

"You're always like this, Chino."

"That's true. But, you know what? Listen, I think what I need right now, what I could really use, is a vacation."

"Where? To Iceland."

Tony rolled his eyes but kept his voice controlled and suppliant. "Good one. But I'm thinking on a more practical level. I have an idea. Instead of you going with Ma to PR, like you always do, why don't I go?"

"You?"

"Yeah. I really want to go this time."

"You never want to go. You always complain that Puerto Rico is too hot and that you cannot afford it."

"This is true, but I want to go now, I need to go."

"But you just said you can't afford it."

"Well," Tony said, "you could give me your ticket."

"You are crazy."

"Jerry. Listen to me, please, it's not crazy. When Ma gets back from this vacation, she's going to be preparing to move in with you, right?"

"That is not decided."

"C'mon, you know it's the best thing for her. And then you're going to have her all to yourself, with you and the wife and your wonderful kids. And let's face it, I don't get out to your house that much. This is maybe my last chance to spend a large chunk of time with her. And who knows how many years she'll be around. Do you know what I'm saying?"

Tony wasn't sure, but he thought maybe his brother was crying on the other end. His brother was an ass. But he was also a very sentimental ass. Tony also knew his mother was tougher than steel and would probably outlive them both.

"You have a good heart, Chino. I have always known that in my heart, no matter what they used to say about you."

"And you're my favorite brother."

"I am your only brother."

"When does she leave?"

"Tomorrow."

"Oh crap. I gotta get packed."

"But I did not say—"

"Just call and put the ticket in my name. My regards to your wife and to Jesus!"

After Tony hung up, he gave the phone to Magaly and put on the shorts Magaly had brought him from home.

"I have to get out of here," he said.

"What's this about you going to PR?"

"Oh yeah. I'm going with my mom for her annual vacation."

"But do you feel recovered enough, Chino? You look like your old skinny self again. You lost your beer gut. Well, almost."

"A few pints will get me back to speed," he said, taking off the hospital gown and patting his belly.

"And your calves look like pencils." She saw his ankles then, the bandages around both of them she hadn't seen while he was on the bed. Her eyes welled up with tears.

"Are you okay, Magaly?"

"Chino, you could have died up there."

He wondered if he should hug her, and he guessed he'd better, and so he wrapped his arms around her, and only then was he conscious that he had no shirt on and that his bare skin was touching her. He could feel her warmth and smelled the jasmine of her perfume.

"They didn't want to kill me," he said. "They said I was there to learn a lesson."

"And what happens when they come back and find you disappeared. They're not going to think you just dried up in the sun."

"All the better reason to get out of town for a few days."

He broke the hug, feeling exposed and quickly put on the black T-shirt she had brought him.

"I think you have another reason you want to go. And it's not to spend more time with your mother like you told Jerry. That was a load of baloney."

"Yeah, maybe."

"You're going to try and find the super."

"He's the key to everything. The harassment. Maybe even the missing money."

"You're taking advantage of your brother, too."

"I'm only slightly taking advantage. I still get to spend time with Ma. And the fact that it's paid for by my brother is a double plus."

"That's brilliant, Chino. One question," she said. "Did your Spanish improve on that roof?"

"Not in the least."

"Then I think you'll need a translator. A translator who needs a vacation."

"Oh no, you're saying you want to come along? That's ridiculous."

"Ridiculous but brilliant."

He picked up what was left of his messenger bag—it was empty except for two of his pétanque balls, which the pot-

smoking hipsters were kind enough to recover from the roof.
"Last-minute tickets are very expensive."

"I live on credit. Admit it, Chino, it's a very good idea."

"You know what? I like it. It is a very good idea. We leave
tomorrow."

"What? I have to pack!"

CHAPTER FIFTY

They took car service from the hospital. Magaly got off at her apartment building, and Tony stayed in the car for a few more blocks and got out in front of his apartment.

He could tell a new lock had been put in and the door had been patched up by the super and sloppily repainted.

But that shiny new lock was broken, hanging in its slot, and the two-toned door was wide open. And from outside, he could see his living room/bedroom/home office lights were on.

His old AC chugged and dripped, which meant it was doing its best. And in the dim light from the windows, he saw someone on his futon.

Tony's first instinct was to call the police, but he hadn't gotten a new phone yet. He considered running. *What the hell*, he decided. At this point, what could be worse than baking on a roof for a few days? He eased his door open the rest of the way and went in.

"You need a new air conditioner," said a familiar voice. "That one is useless. I have a brand new one in my basement I could get for you."

In the dimness of the room, wearing a black suit and an askew yarmulke, sat Elias Litvinchouk.

"*Salve*, Mr. Moran."

"*Salve*. Did you come to drop off a get well card?" Tony looked around at the mess of his apartment.

Most of his clothes were on the floor. But someone had tried to fold some things. Magaly. Two tall shelves worth of books

235

had been tossed to the floor, forming hills. His desk drawers were open, and the papers and files in it had been tornadoed. His two pétanque trophies had been smashed against the wall. And the flat screen TV had been knocked to the floor and cracked. Magaly had been there that morning. All this had just been done in the last couple of hours.

"Was that necessary?" Tony said, pointing to the screen. "I got that on sale." There was nowhere else to sit but at his desk on a creaky chair he'd found on the street.

"*Infeliciter*, yes. Mr. Moran, I am afraid we have to talk."

"Was breaking the lock necessary? It was brand new."

"I tried to jimmy it, but I'm not as good with those things as I used to be. So we had to get a sledgehammer from my car and whack it open." Litvinchouk patted the sledgehammer on the futon next to him. "It's part of the landlord's toolkit."

"You say 'we?'"

Just then the toilet flushed and a large Hasidic man stepped out of the bathroom looking like a black and white monolith. He wore the requisite beard, payot, yarmulke, vest, and dangling tzitzits, but his white shirt was sleeveless and showed off a pair of bulging arms.

"This is Noah. My son-in-law. Impressive, am I right?" Litvinchouk said. "And let me tell you, that's not all schmaltz. Search his bag, Noah."

The monolith went to Tony's duffel, opened it, and turned it upside down.

"I'll make this quick, Mr. Moran," Litvinchouk said. "I know you have a lot of straightening up to do. First of all, I want to apologize for what happened to you on that roof, a very, very sad thing, done against my advisement. My business associates are a little too proactive, but not without reason."

"Do tell."

"Frank Tomasello Sr. is an elderly man of means, has been blackmailed for almost two years now by certain individuals. He does not need to be blackmailed by someone new. By which

I mean you, of course."

"Say again? Maybe I'm still back on that roof hallucinating, or maybe my brain really did get boiled. What's this about blackmail?"

"Mr. Moran, I don't know you very well. I don't know how well you lie. But I do know that you knew Patrick Stoller for several years and that, after his death, you went to his apartment, and it is there you got the flash drives. You had some on the roof, and now you have more of them."

"The flash drives. Are you saying Patrick was blackmailing Tomasello?"

"I've already said too much, Mr. Moran."

The Yiddish hulk grunted, holding up the bag of flash drives that Gabby had dropped off at the hospital.

"Ah, the kewpie prize," said Litvinchouk, taking the drives. "This negates my previous offer of new residences for you and your mother. However, if you like I can replace the flat screen TV. I can call my guy and he can bring a new one here in ten minutes."

"What brand?"

"Top of the line. Though what you really need is a new AC."

Tony shook his head. "Thanks, but no."

"Fair enough," Litvinchouk said. "One other thing: Your friend Patrick liked to make copies. I trust these are the final bunch of them."

Tony said, "If you worried about my blackmailing you or the Tomasellos, you already know I'm too lazy for that. As far as any copies, I haven't bothered. I'm not even sure what's on them. You can trust me."

"Despite my best interests, I do trust you, Mr. Moran. However, my business associates, especially Frank Jr., are much more prone to...action, for lack of a better word. I would be careful, if I were you."

"Thanks for the heads up."

Litvinchouk smiled. "*Vale*, Mr. Moran. *Vale*."

"Goodbye," Tony said as they went out the door. "And thanks for flushing."

CHAPTER FIFTY-ONE

Magaly was almost finished packing. She had made sure to bring along her laptop and those flash drives Tony had called and asked her (three times) to bring. For no reason, she threw in a couple of pairs of her sexy underwear. She didn't know why. This was an innocent trip, after all, an investigative trip. Sure, Tony was an ex, but he hadn't shown any interest in rekindling anything but their friendship. Had he? She cleaned out the fridge. She had already spoken to her neighbors to check on her jungle of ferns, spider plants, and succulents. After that, she found she had nothing else to procrastinate with.

Fine, then. It was time to break up with Luis.

She had broken up with him six times already, and he had always found a way to worm himself back into her life and her bed. He was around her at work all the time. He called her obsessively. She gave in because she was weak and she was lonely. And she was stupid. She had been stupid. But now things felt different. And now she had to kick Luis out of her romantic life, once and for all. Which had nothing at all to do with this trip, right?

"No, I don't want to discuss it and I can't see you tonight," she told him over the phone. "Honestly, I'm going on a little trip, a short vacation. I need it. I need a break."

"Wait. Vacation? With who?" he said.

"I didn't say I was going with anyone. Why can't I be going by myself?"

"Who are you going with?"

"Fine. I'm going with—with my friend Chino. But we're just friends."

"Your friend? I knew it. I knew there was something going on! You can't do this to me. I care about you. I love you, *querida*. We are soulmates." His voice broke and she could hear his sobbing.

"Luis, listen to me. I don't even know what 'soulmate' means. If you want to cry, cry to your wife. Don't cry to me. I really have to go now. There is a taxi outside waiting, and he's charging me by the minute. Bye!"

She walked out, really *ran*, of her building, her luggage rolling behind her, and took the J train to the AirTrain to JFK airport.

Tony's mother hadn't seen Magaly in years but as soon as she saw her, she said, "*Mira la pelu'a!*" and hugged her.

"*Bendición*, Anna. It's been so long. You look terrific."

"I went to the beauty parlor," Tony's mom said. And she'd dressed up for the flight.

Tony asked her if she had brought the flash drives and her laptop, and she told him she had, and he looked weirdly happy.

But then inside the terminal, Tony became more himself and grumbled about the long lines, and when they got on the plane he talked about how narrow the seats had become and how there were no more frills to flying because the terrorists had won. But when the plane took off, Magaly reached for his hand and he held it.

They landed in San Juan and walked into the coolness of the airport. It took almost a half hour to get Anna's luggage from the carousel. Outside, as the doors slid open, the heat felt deadly.

"You okay?" she said to Tony.

"It's not exactly the temperature I would have chosen after recent events," he said. "But I am glad to be here. Can I borrow your laptop and the flash drives?"

"Sure. What's the big deal with this anyway?"

"I'll show you later. Promise."

Magaly was going to ask him more questions, but then his mother interrupted. "He looks so skinny. Isn't he skinny?"

Magaly knew then that Tony had not told his mother about what had happened to him on the roof.

Tony's Titi Delia picked them up at the airport. Along the roads were a parade of palm trees, a sight she was always happy to see. The sky above was a sharp, clear blue, and at almost every traffic light stop, a man would come out from the side of the road, selling *quenepas* or mangoes or oranges, ripe and ready to eat. Everyone seemed to drive with lead feet on the gas, and Delia was speeding right along with them, zigging and zagging, and, if there were no oncoming cars, right through any red lights.

Titi Delia drove them to her house, a modest single-floor house made of concrete and painted lemon yellow. There were gates on all the windows and the front door, but still it felt cozy.

During the drive and seven times that night, Tony and Magaly were asked when they were getting married.

They ate a late dinner, *bistec encebollado* with fried sweet plantains and boiled yucca and rice and beans and a salad of iceberg lettuce topped with peas and carrots. It was a good thing she had brought a wardrobe of baggy shorts and oversized shirts.

That night she slept in the guest room with Tony's mom, while Tony slept on the living room couch. The woman snored like a cannon, but Magaly found it weirdly soothing because it reminded her of her own mother's snoring.

The next morning at four a.m., she woke up to the sound one of Tony's uncles arriving in a truck with a freshly slaughtered pig.

* * *

While the pig roasted over half of a steel drum in the backyard—the smell of meat clinging to Magaly's hair, her clothes, and filling her mouth and making it water—and after she had had far too many coconut-water-and-rums, served in actual coconuts chopped in half, and after Tony had stood up on a chair and told everyone no, no, absolutely not, they were not getting married and everyone should just stop asking but they just laughed and whistled, after all that, when some man who Tony said may or may not have been another of his uncles took out a *cuatro*, which looked like a midget's guitar but it could make the happiest and at the same time the saddest music in the world, and another man, who may or may not have been Tony's cousin, set up conga drums and two other guys, one with a tambour and the other with maracas, came out and soon an entire band was playing in the backyard, at that point Magaly reached out and took Tony's hand.

"C'mon," she said.

Tony said, "First of all, I don't dance salsa."

"You do today."

He was awful, but his feet got the one-two-three when he was just letting go and not thinking about it, which wasn't easy for him, she knew. Every once in a while he would get it just right and then sometimes hold his body close to hers as they spun around on the blacktop.

"You know this is just going to make it worse for us with them."

"Shut up and dance," she said.

Later, bloated and greasy-fingered with pork, Magaly sat with Tony away from the swarm of relatives, or maybe the swarm had moved away to give them space. The palm and mango trees framing the backyard gently nodded in the night breeze, and the *coqui* frogs—nearly invisible in the thick fauna—began a chorus of their distinctive whistles.

"That was the best roast pork I've ever tasted," she said.

"Pork! It's good for you," he said. "It's a high-quality protein."

She was going to tease him, but instead she said, "It is, and it's delicious. When was the last time you came to PR, Tony?"

"Me? Maybe fifteen years."

"Wow, you shouldn't go too long without getting in touch with your roots."

"My roots are in Brooklyn, embedded in the concrete."

"Grumpy," she said.

"True," he said, and she knew he was going to kiss her and he did.

"Hmm," she said. "I was waiting for that."

He smiled. It wasn't something he did very often, but it made him look good.

"Maybe I've had too much coconut water and rum," he said. "I should have asked you to marry me when I had the chance."

"Actually, you did."

"Oh, you remember that?"

"I remember. But I thought you were just joking."

Tony frowned. "Maybe I was. I was an ass. An ass!"

"You were still upset I dated your brother."

"You dated the whole block."

"Oh my god, not the whole block," she said. "Well, half the block."

"That didn't upset me," he said. Then he raised his hand. "It doesn't upset me anymore."

"I'm glad."

"Never mind that. Come with me," he said.

In the living room, they could still hear people outside but they were alone.

"Tony. I don't know—"

"Look at this." He had her laptop out. "With my relatives all around, I didn't get a chance to watch this until last night when everyone went to sleep. I've been dying to show you all day."

He patted the space on the couch next to him and put the

laptop on her lap. He reached over to click "Play." In the slight coolness of the room, she was conscious of the heat emanating from his body.

"There's no audio," he said.

The little screen showed a grainy and unfocused picture of a kitchen. She saw a sink and a stove.

"Is that—?"

"—Rosa's apartment."

"Yes, I recognize the linoleum! It's a really creamy yellow that always reminded me of banana pudding."

A figure—a man—came into the room. He had what looked like a potato sack. The resolution was not good at all but she could still see a green workshirt and working pants. His hair was curly and dark. Something was moving in the sack he carried. The man opened the refrigerator and took out a piece of something—maybe a piece of meat or cheese—and bent down and threw it under the stove.

"Oh my god, Marte, the super, right?" she said.

"That would be my guess."

The man picked up the sack and, standing up, opened it and upended it. One, two, three, maybe four mice spilled out and ran in different directions. The tape stopped.

Magaly screamed. "That's disgusting!"

"Keep watching," Tony said.

"This guy, oh my god, oh my god—"

"Wait, that's not the best part. There's a pause and then another video starts."

There were two men this time. One wore the green workshirt and pants. The other was fat and wore a blue polo shirt and a gigantic gold watch.

"Who the hell is this guy?" Magaly said.

"It took me a minute to place him. But the watch stood out in my mind. That's Frank Tomasello Jr."

The light in the room was weaker this time. It might have been late afternoon or early evening. There were dishes in a dish rack by the sink when before there had been none. Junior lifted the top of the stove. He turned and Marte handed him something—Magaly couldn't make it out. The man bent into the stove, like a man checking under a car hood. He was screwing something in. He closed the stove and wiped the top down with a rag. He said something to Marte, then he threw the rag onto the floor and then dragged it with his feet, taking measured steps, walking backward out of the frame. Wiping away footprints.

"Okay," she said. "Oh my god! Did you see what he did?"

Tony got up and brought her another beer. "That's evidence of harassment. We could go to the police with that."

"I need to get a copy of this, Tony. How the hell did you get this video?"

"It was in Patrick's stuff, in a couple of those flash drives I gave you. There are also a lot of documents I've just started looking through. But it looks like Patrick loved to make copies, for some sort of insurance."

"But why was he making a video in her apartment in the first place? Was he a peeping tom?"

"Peeping in her kitchen? Knowing Patrick, my guess is that he was videoing it for her."

"But why?"

Tony stood up and paced around the room. Magaly liked watching him think, liked hearing him talk.

"Well, according to Rosa, the abuse had been going on for a while," he said. "Maybe she wanted evidence to catch somebody in the act. Or maybe she talked to him, friendly neighbor, and offered to do this for her."

"I never thought of her as overly friendly. But it's possible. So he put a camera in her place to catch the super?"

"Yep. It looks that way."

"But why didn't he show this to the cops or the Housing Authority or to me and to El Flamboyan. We could have done something."

"Well, I have a theory. But now I know for sure this is why they broke into my apartment and why they threw me on the roof."

"This still doesn't explain what happened to Rosa. Do you think that Marte and this Frank Jr. guy, you think they killed her?"

"I don't know. Can I borrow your phone?"

"To call the police?"

"Not yet. I want to call Gabby."

"Your 'niece.'"

Tony waved a finger at her. "Be nice."

She had to go find her phone. Once she did, she gave it right to Tony. After he made his call, he gave it back.

"Hey, you got a few messages on there," he said.

Magaly checked. They were thirty-seven texts and four voicemails. All from Luis.

CHAPTER FIFTY-TWO

When Tony said that Magaly and he were going to go do something, his mother gave him a saucy smile.

"Have fun," his mother said and winked.

"It's not what you think. Are you going to be okay here?"

"I be fine," she said, and he knew she would be, staying at his aunt's house all day, sitting on the porch. It was her idea of the perfect vacation. His mom said, "Hurry up! I want grandkids!"

Tony and Magaly got a ride to the car rental company, and he got the keys from the rental agent and began to hand them to Magaly.

"What are you doing? I don't drive," she said.

"I don't drive either."

"*Carajo,* one of us has to drive."

"Well, I mean, I do know how to drive," Tony said. "I just haven't driven in years."

"Exactly. Who needs to drive in New York City?"

Tony twirled the key fob in his hand. "Okay. Let's say I drive now, and then on the way back you drive?"

"God help us both. But if I drive us off a mountain road, I want you to take the wheel."

"By that point, we'll be dead."

"I just don't want to be found dead at the wheel. They'll say, 'Look, I told you women can't drive.'"

"You're insane," he said.

"Let's go, chauffeur."

When he had called Gabby that morning, she told him she had found more than twenty-three Angela Romans who lived in Puerto Rico. It was boring, she had said, but she crosschecked their names on social media. In less than an hour, she had eliminated sixteen who were teenagers or very young, four who were elderly and had died, and two who enjoyed superhero cosplay. On Instagram, she found an Angela Roman who was older, #semiretired, and her location was tagged as Williamsburg, Brooklyn. But there were several recent posts and pictures about problems moving to a house in Cayey. It was a solid lead, and Tony hoped that by finding her, he would be able to find the super, Jorge Marte.

A town surrounded by verdant mountains, Cayey was in the southeastern part of the island, about an hour's drive from Ponce. The roads were often narrow, but no one stopped to politely let the other car go. Everyone seemed to zoom by each other, almost kissing door handles. It made Tony very nervous. He missed the crowded simplicity of subway cars.

"I'm so glad my relatives are on the other side of the island," Magaly said.

"Don't you want to visit?"

"Even more fatty food and everyone asking me why I'm not married and have kids—no thank you. When I get it from your family, it doesn't irritate me so much."

"Understood."

"So, what are we going to do when we get where we're going?"

"We don't have an exact address yet."

"We don't?"

"But I have a plan."

They parked in front of the post office in Cayey. Parking requirements were apparently lax—cars faced each other on the sidewalk outside the office. Tony stood behind Magaly, looking as sad and concerned as he could. She told the postal clerk they were looking to find Angela Roman.

<"Angela's grandmother is very sick,"> she said, hoping this postal clerk didn't know Angela Roman. <"She could die any minute now. We have to hurry. Her grandmother sent us to find her because they have not spoken in so many years, too many years, and it is so sad, so sad when families have problems. She just wants to make peace with her favorite granddaughter, so we have to find Angela immediately, and all we had was this post office number. Please help us, sir, or her grandmother will die and never be able to show peace before she gets to Heaven, the Lord help her!">

The postal clerk nodded energetically, his own eyes maybe even looking a little wet, and gave them an address.

"Forget using your law degree," Tony told her in the car. "You should have been an actress."

"That was so much fun!"

The address, however, did not appear on any map apps, so they were forced to ask around. A man selling pizza from an oven-equipped cart knew the way. About a mile up the road, past the stadium, he told them, keep turning and turning until you get to the pink house, the one with the big rooster sign, not the one with the big *coqui*, then turn left.

The mile turned into three miles until up ahead was the *cuchifrito* stand. They stopped to have lunch, and, just to double-check, asked the waitress if she knew Angela, and she said she did, but she said yes, it was a right turn on one of those roads ahead, and to look out for the dead mango tree that looked like it was bending over to pray.

As they ate at a table outside, Magaly said, "I know this is going sound paranoid."

"Yeah? I don't mind paranoid. It seems like the right way to be nowadays."

"Well, did you see a big SUV parking at the post office the same time we were parking?"

"No," Tony said, "I was too busy trying to remember how

to parallel park. Not that that matters in Cayey. But what about it?"

"Well, I know all big SUVs look the same, but that car parked down the street behind me looks like the same one that was parked at the post office. It's brown on top, tan on bottom. I noticed it when we sat down."

"All SUVs do look the same, it's part of the ongoing homogenization of our culture, and I will look surreptitiously over your shoulder. All right, I see it. Looks like a rental. Nobody's bothering us here. Let's see what happens as we proceed."

When they got back in the car, the SUV stayed put. But after a few turns, Tony looked back and it was behind them.

"I can't believe it," he said.

"I see it, too."

"I can't believe they'd follow us to PR either. What is up with these people?"

"Can't you drive faster?"

"Have you seen these roads and these drivers? If I drive any faster, we'll end up in the jungle or in someone's windshield."

Tony picked up speed. This was one article he'd never written or read: How to lose a car that's following you. The SUV sped up but didn't get closer.

"Of course," Tony said, "they're not trying to kill us. They want to find out where Jorge Marte is too, to close all the last links to Rosa. And then they'll kill us."

"Chino, I'm scared."

"Hold on," he said. "I'm going to try something stupid."

"What? No!"

"Um, you better look behind us. Don't look ahead."

Tony spotted a sedan coming toward them. There was barely enough room on the narrow road for both vehicles. Tony floored it, and as they passed the car he nudged the wheel slightly to the left, smacking the rental car into the back of the sedan.

"Chino!"

Their rental car spun and Tony fought to gain control. He drove into the turn. He breathed in and out and stayed calm. When the car stopped, he found himself facing the road ahead. He floored it again.

"That was not completely disastrous," Tony said to himself. Then he asked Magaly, "What's happening back there?" But she was mumbling something to herself.

"What are you doing?

"I'm chanting and praying. Hold on."

"The other car stopped. I think the driver is getting out. He looks pissed."

"But what about that SUV that was following us?"

"He's stuck on the other side."

"Yes!"

"You did it!" Magaly said. She turned back in her seat and kissed him on the cheek.

This made him lose concentration and wobble the wheel and almost run into a ditch.

CHAPTER FIFTY-THREE

It took an hour to come back to the road with the dead mango tree again, and another long while to spot the dead tree. Tony drove them onto a paved road that soon turned into a dirt road.

They drove up to a large wooden gate. From the car, Magaly could see things moving around in the front yard beyond the gate.

"Is that...what an emu looks like?" Magaly said.

"I've never seen one in real life before," Tony said, "but, yes, yes, that looks like an emu. And coming up on our left is a peacock. Definitely a peacock."

Through the slats of the gate, a colorful bird with its full plumage on display pranced by.

"The female of the species is called a 'peahen.'"

"You're joking," she said. "Why do you know this stuff?"

They got out of the car and approached the gate. There was no bell to ring and no chains on the gate, so Tony reached over and lifted the small metal latch holding the gate closed.

Inside was a concrete house painted gray with a flat roof painted salmon pink and a matching enclosure. The door and all the windows were covered in elaborate curling metalwork gates, which was common for Puerto Rico. Three BRs, two baths, with garage, laundry room, and storage area. Adjacent land cultivates bananas. Completely fenced in. Great potential. Property sold as-is.

At the end of the driveway, a large dog barked furiously. It was kept at bay by a very long and very strong-looking metal chain.

"Oh my god, Tony. A Doberman." Magaly crossed herself. "They're possessed by the devil, those dogs. I never liked them."

"Don't be ridiculous."

"No, she's right. That one is possessed. But he came with the house."

The woman who said this stood in the now-open doorway. She was in her fifties or early sixties and wore her hair in a bright purple scarf. She wore a bright red T-shirt, lime green Capri pants, and pink sandals. She was altogether colorful. She also had a shotgun in her hands, very large, and pointed right at them. Without turning her head, she told the dog to be quiet. It yelped and whined and curled itself into a ball.

"Come closer," she said. "I won't shoot you unless I have to."

Magaly and Tony looked at each other. Then they nodded.

"Okay," Tony said. "We're not here to cause trouble."

"You don't look like trouble. But I have to watch out. Be careful where you walk," the woman said. "We have tarantulas."

Magaly and Tony stopped where they stood.

"Don't worry. They don't kill, but they bite," the woman said.

Magaly scanned the ground. "Is that supposed to make us feel better?"

"Are you two lost?"

"Are you Angela Roman?" Magaly said.

"Do I know you people?" the woman said.

"We're looking for Jorge Marte. We hoped he would be here," Tony said.

"I know you," the woman said to Magaly. "You're from Brooklyn. From El Flamboyan."

"Yes, I work there. My name is Magaly Fernandez."

"You used to visit Rosa. When she had all that trouble." The woman told them to bring their car in, and she closed the gate.

Then she said, "What do you want with Jorge? He's very sick. As a matter of fact, he's dying."

"What is he dying of?" Tony asked.

"Suicide," she laughed, then laughed bitterly to herself. "Come in if you want to see him."

The room immediately inside was a combination kitchen/ dining room/living room. It was pristine except for a swirl of ants near the door. Angela put her shotgun down and offered them something to eat. They declined, and she led them down a hall to a small bedroom. "That's where he sleeps after I kicked him out of my room," she said.

The first thing Magaly noticed was the stink of alcohol. Not from open bottles but rather the metallic-musky smell it gets as it oozes out of the body. Her father used to smell that way.

Marte lay on a small bed, covered by a mosquito net, facing them as they came in the door. A giant poster of Derek Jeter was peeling off the wall above him. He wore pants but no shirt or socks, and when he turned, Magaly was amazed at the man's gut, which stuck out hard and round as a pumpkin. Marte's face was red and bloated, and his swollen eyelids were so low it was hard to tell if he was looking at them or looking at any- thing at all.

Angela called his name softly and told him there were people to see him. He grunted as an answer.

"Jorge's English is not too kosher," the woman said.

"That's okay. Neither is his Spanish," Magaly said.

"Your husband?"

"*Amigo.*"

"Ah hah."

They stood over Marte, who remained unmoving behind the gauze of the mosquito net.

<"Did you come here to kill me?">

<"No, we need your help,"> Magaly answered in Spanish. <"Jorge, we're trying to find out the truth about what happened to Rosa Irizarry.">

<"God help me.">

Tony took out an old tape recorder held together with duct

tape, not the one he used with Iris Campos. He pointed to it, to ask Jorge if it was okay. The bloated man nodded.

<"Mr. Marte. Please tell us: Did someone tell you to put in the roaches and the rats and to start the fire in her apartment?">

<"God forgive me. She was not always nice. One time she threw a can at me, and it was full. But they did not have to kill her.">

So, Rosa Irizzary was dead, as far as this man was saying. It was what Tony thought, but he was surprised that he was disappointed, that he actually thought maybe they would eventually find her alive.

"Ask him who," he said.

Marte must have understood that and said, "El Señor."

Which Magaly knew could mean "The Mister" or could mean "God." But he didn't think Jorge was getting metaphysical. He needed to be specific. "*Quién?*" she said.

<"The Jew and the giant.">

<"Jackie Tomasello and Litvinchouk?"> Tony said.

<"Them. They were always together, if you get what I mean.">

"Aha. Now: We need to be as clear as possible. Ask him what the Tomasellos told him to do, exactly."

Jorge sat up then and swung his legs over the side of the bed. He burped. "They say they gonna fire me, to throw me out," he said, in a thick accent. "I was es-scared. They wanted me first to put the rats and to shut off the water. Then they wanted me to help put the fire. *Pero yo no quería hacer eso.*"

"He didn't want to do it," Magaly translated.

<"They told the son—Junior—to come with me. He was there to make me do it. But he is the one who did it.">

"So, how do you know what happened to Rosa? Is she dead?" Magaly asked, but he didn't answer. She asked again in Spanish: "*Entonces, ¿cómo saben que Rosa está muerto?*"

"Ah," Jorge said. "When she disappear, I got es-scare."

<"But you don't know for sure if they did anything?">

<"It had to be them. It had to be them. I think.">

Angela, who had been standing in the doorway listening, spoke. "Hombre. Tell them what you told me."

<"I don't know, Angela,"> he said. "I don't got no proof."

<"Tell them, you stinking drunk. They have to know everything. They came all the way from New York.">

<"What? What is she talking about, Jorge?">

"I don't got no proof."

"*Ai*, I'll tell you," Angela said. "He told me one night that if it wasn't the super and the big lady, then it was probably the white guy and his girlfriend."

"What white guy?"

"Her neighbors, the ones who lived next door to her…"

Tony looked at Magaly wide-eyed and then back at Marte. "What? Does he mean Patrick and Kirsten? Patrick Stoller?"

"Tony, calm down," Magaly said.

"This changes everything," he said.

"Okay." Magaly looked at Jorge. <"Tell us.">

Jorge paused to breathe. Then he said, <"The Jew, he always told me he didn't want to hurt her. He said scare her, not hurt her. He just wanted her to move out. And then after she came back, after the fire, he came to me and he told me to forget it, that she was an old lady and she would probably die soon anyway. So he said to forget about it, to leave her alone.">

Tony said, "That's fine for Livtinchouk, but he can't control the Tomasellos. So who were these neighbors? Can he describe them?"

<"The white man with the red hair and his girlfriend, who looked like a frog…>

There was no mistaking it was Patrick and Kirsten.

< "…They used to visit with her a lot. But after Rosa came back, I could hear they all yelling at each other up there. They would slam doors,"> Jorge said.

<"I used to hear it, too,"> Angela said. <"I couldn't under-

stand what they were saying, but I asked her. She told me they used to be really nice to her, but then they turned mean, and she didn't know why...">

"What makes you think they killed her?" Tony asked.

Jorge burped loudly and stared up at the ceiling, as if he were looking back in the past. <"The night before Rosa disappeared, I remember. Those two left the building in the middle of the night. I was awake because I have trouble sleeping. They took a big suitcase to their little car. I thought they were going on vacation, you know, with that suitcase. But the next day they were still in the building. They were still upstairs. They didn't go on vacation. But Rosa was missing.">

Tony sank to the concrete floor.

"What's wrong, Chino?" Magaly said, putting her hand on his.

"This whole goddamn time I've been looking to blame Litvinchouk or Tomasello. I had never even considered that Patrick and Kirsten would have anything to do with Rosa's disappearance. They blinded me."

"Angela, did you see this, too?" Magaly said.

"No," she said. "He snores, so I wear earplugs. I didn't hear anything."

Jorge looked ready to pass out again. He didn't look good at all.

They left him and walked outside, back into the animal-filled yard. They stood by the car while the satanic Doberman continued to bark no matter what Angela told it.

Magaly asked Angela, <"But why didn't you go to the police?">

"Because he was involved in the harassment," Tony said. "He was afraid they would lock him up, and he was right."

Tony turned to Angela. "I have a question for you. When you two decided to run away, you needed money. To get out of New York and to get this place."

"I have savings," she said. But she was looking down at a

passing chicken.

"The thing is, though, Rosa Irizarry hit the number just before she disappeared. No one seems to know what happened to that money."

Angela placed her hands together, as if in prayer. Then she looked up and there were tears in her eyes. "Rosa, she was my good friend," she said. "When she got the money, she was afraid to keep it in her apartment. She was afraid they would break into her apartment and take it. She was going to move, you know. She wanted to. But she wanted to stay in the neighborhood. But there was nothing she could afford. The money would not have lasted her a year. Anyway, she gave me the money to hold."

"And then?"

"And when she disappeared—I kept it. I was just holding it for her, I swear on my life and to Jesus Christ. But then she didn't come back. And me and Jorge had to run. We knew we was in danger. And it was the only money I had. We got this place cheap."

Magaly looked at her. "But, Angela, how did you know she wasn't coming back to get her money? Was it what Jorge saw?"

"No. It was because, in my heart, I knew she was gone to—"

The sound of a revved engine split the air and a brown SUV busted through the gate.

CHAPTER FIFTY-FOUR

Two men got out of the car, with guns drawn. One of them was short, fat, and Tony recognized him right away, despite the unfamiliar context. The man wore a gray paisley polo shirt tucked into his pants and a giant gold watch.

"Hello." Frank Tomasello Jr. had on a Panama hat, the cheap kind sold to tourists. His legs were so pale they almost glowed under khaki shorts. It would have been easy for Tony to laugh at him if not for the gun Tomasello pointed at him.

The other man looked as overgrown as a football player, one long past his glory days. His head was uncovered and shaved, and he had an s-shaped scar running from the right side of his mouth and down his chin. It gave him an expression that was probably intimidating in most circumstances, but it was diminished by a bad sunburn all over his face. Still, the gun he carried gave him a serious air as well.

Magaly had her hands in the air. Tony did the same. He looked for Angela, but she was gone.

"Okay, where's Marte?" Frank Jr. said.

"He's gotta be inside," the other man said.

"Check it out."

"So nice to see you again," Tony said, in what he had to admit was a poor effort to delay death. Or give Angela time to do whatever she was doing. Which, he hoped, was not running away.

"Give me the flash drives," Frank Jr. said. An emu calmly

walked in front of him, and he had to step once, twice, three times to keep the gun aimed at them. "Holy fuck! What the fuck are these fucking things?"

"Emus," Tony said, remembering an article he had done once on raising exotic birds for meat. "They're the second-largest living bird by height, after ostriches."

"What the fuck? Guy, give up the flash drives."

"What flash drives?"

"Yeah, right. Like you don't know what I'm talking about."

"Fine," Tony said. "I already gave what I had to Litvinchouk."

"What's this? When?" Magaly said, but Tony wouldn't look at her.

"That lyin' kike Jew bastard," Frank Jr. said. "He thinks he's the big shit, but he's not."

"Wow," Tony said. "So I guess you don't like the fact that he's fooling around with your wife. But I guess he would use the word '*schtupping.*'"

Frank Jr. didn't look surprised, but he said, "No fucking way."

"You ever been in his station wagon? It reeks of coconut lotion, you know, the kind that Jackie wears. And I saw a big, bright bangle there, the kind that does not belong to Litvinchouk's devout Hasidic wife."

"You're pulling my chain."

"Ask her. Watch her face. It's hard to hide the look of love. Or lust. I'm guessing they use the back of the station wagon as a honeymoon suite. Lots of room back there for cultural exchange."

The faded footballer came out of the house, looking confused and neon red. "There's nobody here."

"The fuck!" Frank Jr. said. "Check around back."

The footballer turned around the corner at the same moment the Doberman leaped. The formerly chained dog got him by the wrist holding the gun. The gun dropped, and the footballer tried to knock it off but the dog's jaws were clamped tight. Blood sprayed.

Frank Jr. shot once, twice at the dog, and the footballer grunted, "Don't shoot me," and in that moment Angela hit Frank Jr. with the barrel shotgun, using it like a staff. He dropped to the ground, dropping his gun. She flipped the shotgun around and aimed at him.

Frank Jr. made it to his car in a stumbling dash around a peacock. The footballer had somehow gotten himself free and jumped into the car, holding his bloody hand. They went in reverse and sped away in a whirl of dust and exotic feathers.

The Doberman chased the car into the road.

"I told you that dog was possessed," Angela said.

The blood on the ground reminded Tony of Patrick's dead body. He looked away. As he did, he saw Magaly throwing up and at the same time gently pushing away a peacock who seemed very interested in what she was doing.

Tony asked her, "Why didn't you use the shotgun? Shoot up in the air or something?"

"I don't have no bullets."

Magaly wiped her mouth and said, "Thank you. You saved our lives."

Angela had a huge grin on her face. "I've been ready for them. It's been keeping me up for months. I'm glad it finally happened."

"They might come back," Tony said.

"That's okay. I'll call my cousins and they'll stay with me. I got fifteen cousins, and they got bullets."

"Hey, where was Jorge?" Tony asked.

Angela ran back into the house. "Under the bed. I pulled the sheets and he came down and then I stuffed him under."

Inside, Jorge was wedged under the bed pretty good. It took all three of them, using all their strength, to yank him out. But he looked in much worse shape than before. He barely seemed to be breathing, and his face was turning purple. They carried him to Angela's car, and she raced off to the hospital.

Tony and Magaly walked to their car.

"Your turn to drive," he said. "If you're up for it."

"I can do it. Let's just get out of here before the tarantulas attack."

CHAPTER FIFTY-FIVE

Magaly was shivering and still nauseous with adrenaline. But she was able to keep the car steady and straight on the road. The drive back to Tony's aunt's house was taking forever, and they were covered in blood and dirt and puke.

She looked at Tony. He still seemed to be in shock as well. "So you spoke to Litvinchouk about the drives?" she said. "You gave him yours?"

"Yeah. He broke into my apartment with a walking, talking golem. They took the drives from my bag. But I knew you had your copies."

"Good thing I like free things."

"Good thing," Tony said. "I'm sorry I didn't tell you. These last few days have been spectacularly unreal."

"I do wish you had told me. But hearing you apologize for something may be the high point of my day. And that was quite a day."

"Listen, my family will have a lot of questions when they see us," Tony said. "And I'd rather leave them out of this. Do you mind if we stop somewhere and get cleaned up?"

The sun was getting low in the sky, and the roads, which were not always well lit, were getting harder to navigate.

"No, you're right," Magaly said, and suddenly she felt a little nervous twitch, a different kind, not a nauseous kind, in her stomach. "That's a great idea."

Driving south, they found a cheap hotel in Guayama, by the

southern side of the island. It was nowhere near the more exclusive hotels on the beach, and the room had taped-up windows and broken screens. But the air conditioner worked lovingly.

She called room service and asked them to run out for a bottle of rum and some soda.

In the meantime, Tony wrote up everything that had happened into Magaly's laptop. Then he called his mother and aunt to make sure they were okay, although he said he didn't think Frank Jr. would try anything else till he was back on his own home turf.

The rum arrived and Magaly poured them two strong drinks.

She thought about what they had gone through and the only thing she could think of to say was "Holy shit."

"Holy shit," Tony agreed. He sat down on the bed and said, "There sure are a lot of mosquitoes in this room."

"I don't see any," Magaly said. "Ow. All right, maybe that one."

"We better wash our clothes. We can wear towels while we're here."

Magaly looked at Tony and remembered how they used to be so long ago, when they were young and lean and crazy for each other. He looked older, more vulnerable, sitting there pulling his shirt off. She thought of the first time she had seen him undress. She made a decision.

"We don't have to wear towels," she said, unbuttoning her blouse and coming closer to him. An innocent trip, an investigative trip. She pulled him up to her. "Not if we don't want to."

CHAPTER FIFTY-SIX

The day before they flew back to New York, Tony's mother asked him to take her for a drive.

"Why don't you ask Titi Delia?" he said.

"No, you go with me."

"Ma, I really don't want to put you at risk."

"He's better than he thinks he is," Magaly said.

"No, no," his mother said. "We take a little drive. Just me and you."

So Tony drove his aunt's little blue car very slowly, as his mother gave directions.

"Everyone is passing us," he said.

"Let them. They ridiculous."

She led him to the town of Bayamón, and once there to the Puerto Rican National Cemetery.

"Are we going to visit Abuela?" Tony asked.

"No, I saw her yesterday. Park over there, under the tree."

"Then why are we here? Tell me you're not showing me your burial plot. Because you've got a long life ahead of you."

"*Venga*," she said.

They walked for a long while in the cemetery. It was different from most cemeteries Tony had seen, not because of all the crosses, but because of all the palm trees waving their leaves above the tombstones. The ultimate Caribbean getaway.

"*Aqui*," his mother said, finally.

Tony squinted at the tombstone his mother pointed to.

"This is your father," she said. "You haven't been here since you were a baby."

The tombstone read "Juan Antonio Morán Ortiz."

"I was eight."

"You was still a baby."

"Jerry comes with you every year to see this?"

"Yes," she said. "But he stay in the car."

"That sounds just like Jerry."

"Your father was a good man. I met him at church," she said. "The same day he made love to me in his car."

"Ma!"

"He was a good man. He worked hard. Too hard."

"But he left you. He left the family."

"No, no, no," she said. "He came here. He thought he could find work. He got a job at a factory. He used to send money for food. And then he stopped. Then his brother called me and told me he pass away. Heart attack."

"I didn't know that. Why didn't I know that?"

"That's the past," she said, which Tony knew was her way of ending the subject. Before he could ask more, she said, "You know, that girl Magaly is very beautiful. She loves you."

"Ma, we're in a cemetery."

"I didn't say anything. You could make me some beautiful grandkids with her."

"Don't you already have enough?"

"Cranky. Always cranky. Marry that girl already. Show her what you got."

He couldn't help but smile at that.

"Ma. Do you want to go live with Jerry? Or do you want to stay in Brooklyn?"

"How? I can't afford nothing."

"Ma, I'm sorry. I wish I could find you a new place. I wish I had the money. I wish I wasn't such a useless ass."

"*Dios mio*," she said. "You are not a useless ass. I don't mind living with your brother. The neighborhood, it's changing.

It's changed. My stores are not there. All my friends are gone, God have them in heaven. It's time for me to go. You'll be all right."

"Okay, Ma. If you say so."

"But you better visit!"

His mother crossed herself and then began to pray silently, moving her lips. Tony nodded at the tombstone. They both stood there in the sun by the grave.

While waiting for their plane to take off, Tony's mother ate half a cheeseburger. Even though he had his own, he knew she would give him half of hers. He took it but didn't eat it.

Magaly, who had only had a yogurt, took the half-a-burger. "You seem grumpy again," she said. "You weren't grumpy for like a whole day or two there, and now you're grumpy again."

Tony slid his French fries over to her. "Now that we're going back, I'm angry, very angry. It's not just Litvinchouk and Tomasello and the harassment, it's the possibility that Patrick and Kirsten—"

"Were not the people you thought they were?"

"Yeah, and—"

"The fact that they may have murdered Rosa?"

"Yeah, of course that, but, well, I should have seen it. At least gave it a thought. I was an idiot."

"Your investigative skills are a little dull, that's all."

"Well, I don't have proof yet. And I need it. Listen," he said. "I have a pretty good idea where to start. But there's still something else that's bothering me. This video evidence is fine, for a start, but it's not the whole story. I want to go to the police with as much as I can—"

"You want to break the story? Pitch it to the *New York Times*?"

"First of all, it sounds ridiculous when you say it out loud, but something like that, yes. Second, I get that Patrick and Kirsten may have been blackmailing Litvinchouk and Tomasello, and that they may have had something to do with Rosa Irizarry's disappearance and death. But then Patrick goes and gets himself slashed to death. Which seems like an awful lot to happen to one guy. I mean, it's either cruel justice or a hell of a sucky coincidence."

"I thought you thought coincidences only mean something because we try to make them mean something."

Tony smirked. "Why do you remember everything I say?"

"I don't know. It's not like you say anything interesting." She winked at him and then said, "Is there anything else I can do?"

"You've done plenty," Tony said. "And I don't want you to get into more trouble."

"Please! I faced down guns and only threw up once. What's your next step?"

"I have to talk to Bobbert about something he said, something that's been bothering me."

"If you need me, will you let me know?" she said.

"Yes," he said, and then he kissed her.

From her seat, his mother clapped. "About time!"

The public announcement system announced a delay because of an incoming tropical storm. The takeoff was bumpy. The plane's rivets clattered. As it began to climb, Tony reached and held Magaly's hand.

CHAPTER FIFTY-SEVEN

Brandon Taylor's vape needed to be where he could see it, or where he could get to it easily. If he could have, he'd have it permanently attached to him somehow. But it wasn't like he was addicted or anything. He just *loved* vaping. After all, the desire to vape was miniscule compared to the cravings he used to feel for cigarettes. He used to think about smoking 24/7, and when the urge came, he never said no. But with vaping, no, with vaping, he didn't really get a strong urge to use it. Well, all right, he did, maybe, sure, but nowhere near the intensity of an analog.

And now that he was thinking about it, he had to have one, but because his stupid new roommates were in, he had to go out. Katrina didn't care, but Scott, Christa, and Stacey were adamant about what they called his "cloud coverage." So it was out on the sidewalk for him, like a steam-powered leper.

It was a lovely morning for a smoke. Not a cloud in the sky. Only the ones he made himself.

He didn't mind his new roommates, really. Well, he did. He really preferred his old roommates—they were all smokers—but he had recently had to vacate the loft he shared with them. Luxury apartments on South 1st, glass façade, glass-enclosed mini-balconies, floor-to-ceiling windows. $5,500/month. The developers were supposed to divvy up the loft into four bedrooms, but Brandon and his three roommates lived without walls for months. And then the building was suddenly condemned, and they were forced to leave the building ASAP and go scrambling for apartments. Brandon had landed this three-bedroomer, sleeping in a sleeping bag at the foot of someone else's bed.

But he had heard good things about Hoboken. Nice views, quick commute.

He was thinking about going to McCarren to see if those pé-tanque guys were around when out of the fog around his head he saw a man on a bicycle coming toward him, wearing a bala-clava. The bike looked familiar.

He saw the blade and instantly he thought: "SLASHER."

And then it was too late, the blade cutting through his brown skin and leaving him dead on the sidewalk, his vape still tightly clutched in his hand.

CHAPTER FIFTY-EIGHT

Bobbert Swiatowski sat in his office staring at the computer screen in front of him, at the few words he'd typed more than an hour ago. Light streamed in through a small window at the top of the outer wall. He wished he drank because it seemed to help other people when they got like this. But he didn't, and besides it was only nine o'clock in the morning.

There was a knock on the door frame.

It was Tony. He looked tan and healthy, thinner—but that was probably because of the roof thing. But he didn't look grumpy. No, instead, he looked angry. In that moment, Bobbert knew that Tony knew.

"I've been expecting this," Bobbert said.

Tony picked up a stack of copies of the *Sentinel* and saw down in the guest chair.

"I started thinking when you said a burglar came in through the bathroom window," Tony said. "You were probably just trying to say something but weren't thinking straight. You and I both happen to know that sadly, very sadly sometimes, we are not gifted with a window in our bathroom here. Now, you could have made a mistake and meant that tiny thing." Tony pointed to the small window in Bobbert's office. "Or even the window in the writers' office. But today they all look just as dusty and dirty and painted shut as they did a month ago, a year ago. No one broke in here. So you lied, and it was a bad lie. Unless it was a purposeful lie. Maybe you wanted me to know."

Bobbert had a hard time looking at Tony in the face. Instead, he focused on the calendar behind and above Tony's head. "I've thought about a lot since I saw you at the hospital. I've thought about a lot of things."

Tony said, "Whoever wanted the flash drives from Patrick's place tried to break in there. The Stollers told me. Their dog warned them. So figuring out that I had copies of the flash drives was no leap of logic for anyone watching Patrick's place, or who may have been following me.

"But only one person could have told Litvinchouk and Tomasello that Gabby had flash drives from Patrick as well. That was why she was attacked. But she was smart enough not to carry them with her all the time. She told me she had them in her apartment with her three other roommates, and at least two are unemployed at all times, so there's always someone home. Good security."

Bobbert's wedding anniversary was coming up. August 20. It was circled in red on the calendar. He had planned to get Joanne something nice.

"The only person who could have told them was you— because there's nothing private in this office. You can hear everything that goes on in the next room and vice versa."

"Good. That's very good," Bobbert said.

"Then your eyes lit up when Gabby said she had them with her at the hospital, and you *really* wanted to hold on to them for me."

"I knew I went too far with that. I was an idiot."

"I have to know," Tony said, "how involved are you?"

Bobbert finally looked at Tony. He hadn't gone home the night before, had stayed in the office and slept on the floor. He'd done it before, but he knew he must have looked horrible, unshaven. He didn't remember the last time he had eaten.

"It's complicated. It's...it's like this. We're a very small paper. We're always on the edge of closing. Remember when we spent all the money we put into our website, hoping to turn out a web version. And then no one went there."

"Yeah. Three or four years ago."

"Right. That was my own money. What little savings I had. We were living on borrowed time since then. And then Patrick came to me with a story idea. The woman next door to him was being harassed. Someone was sneaking in and putting in vermin. We could record it, Patrick said. We could put it on the website and expose them. Make the big time, you know?"

"Okay."

"I had another idea, what I thought was a better idea. It was a cinch the video would expose Litvinchouk and Tomasello for some wrongdoing. They owned the building, and they'd had a reputation for harassment in the past. But, here's the thing: they also happen to be one of our biggest advertisers. They advertise under their own names, and a couple of other real estate offices they own. Ninety percent of our classified ads, that's them. If we exposed them, we'd be dead. I would be dead."

Tony took out his notebook, then thought better of it and began to put it away.

"No, go ahead. Can't help yourself now, huh?" Bobbert said. "I thought you hated being a reporter. Or pretending to be a reporter."

Tony ignored him and kept on. "What did you decide to do?"

"Well, one night, Patrick and his girlfriend and I were here, and we were talking, had a few beers, you know. Well, they drank, not me. So really I had no excuse. But the idea came up that we could just go directly to Litvinchouk and Tomasello for the money. I don't think any of us used the word 'blackmail,' but that's what it was. That's what it was."

"This is incredible, Bobbert. Why the risk?"

"The money, Tony, the money. The messed up things is it worked. They did the legwork, and I got a little bit from Patrick each month. They got the bigger share, of course. That was only right. And he and Kirsten made sure to keep my name out of it.

Litvinchouk and Tomasello didn't know I was involved at all."

"Funny about Patrick and Kirsten. I never would have thought they were the type for crime. Certainly not you either."

"Hah. Types. They don't mean anything. Anyone can come to a point where they lie or steal or kill. Anyone."

Tony leaned closer to him. "Bobbert, I have to know: Did you have anything to do with Rosa Irizarry's disappearance?"

Bobbert leaned back. He shook his head. "No. Absolutely not. No. I have no idea what happened there. I swear to god."

"What about Patrick then? When he got slashed to death, do you think that Litvinchouk or the Tomasellos could somehow be responsible? Maybe they got tired of the blackmail."

"Wow, that's quite a theory. But I can see it maybe would explain, but no, that's not Litvinchouk's or the Tomasellos' style, I don't think. I mean, Jackie is a big mouth, and Frank Jr. is a brute, but slashing someone in the street, no, that was just 'Wrong street, wrong time.' Patrick's bad luck. Supremely bad luck."

"It would have to be." Tony got up. "I'm going to have to talk to Kirsten. I need to get her side of the story. What are you going to do?"

"I wish I could print the story you're going to write. You got your big story finally, the one that can get you back in, the one you couldn't even admit to yourself you wanted."

Bobbert watched Tony look down at his sneakers. Bobbert had never been so direct with him, but the time for subtlety was gone.

"You're probably right, that I wished for it, and I kept that to myself. To tell you the truth, at this moment, I don't know if that's what I want anymore."

"Are you going to write about me?"

"No." Then after a pause he amended that, like a typical reporter. "Not if I don't need to."

Bobbert played with his goatee. It was something his wife said he did when he was nervous. "You know what I'm thinking? I have my house, right? It was my father's. Did you know that? Yeah, I took over the property. But I got an over-large mortgage during the housing crisis. It's been killing me. I've been foreclosed. Everything's falling apart at once. That's what I'm thinking about. But more than that: What will happen to my family? Where will they go?"

"Tell Joanne I'm sorry."

"She knows. She knows."

After Tony left, the office went quiet. Bobbert went back to staring at the screen. He kept wondering what to write after "My sweetest Joanne..."

CHAPTER FIFTY-NINE

Tony walked up to Kirsten's apartment building just as someone was coming out. Tony held the door, then went in, hopping up the stairs. The stairwell smelled like a millennium's worth of meatloaf. He knocked. He heard a shower running. He knocked louder and the shower stopped. Footsteps and then the click of the peephole.

Long pause. The door was pulled open slowly.

"Tony! Hey!" Kirsten said. Her smile was all sunbeams and rainbows. "Nice to see you."

Her hair was in a towel. She wore an oversized terrycloth robe and, Tony quickly realized, nothing on underneath. He tried not to stare. Her sleeves were rolled up partially, showing her still-wet arms and her tattoos—on the right forearm Johnny Cash sticking up his middle finger, and on the left, the entire text of something. A poem. Tony could just make out the title. "Invictus." She walked away from the half-open door.

"I need to ask you some questions," Tony said, pushing the door completely open. The apartment smelled of stale cigarette smoke and mango shampoo. The walls were lined with photographs of one woman praying after another. On one side of the room were two racks holding a collection of flashy looking guitars. On the other side, a door was open, revealing an unoccupied, unmade bed.

"But I have to ask about those first," said Tony, pointing to the beards.

"Gunnar can't grow facial hair, so."

"Oh."

"So what do you really want to ask me about?" Kirsten said, hands crossed over her chest.

"I need to talk to you about your old neighbor, Rosa Irizarry," he said, taking out his old tape recorder. "I need to know what happened to her."

"Come into the kitchen," she said. "I don't like to smoke in the living room." His instinct told him not to go deeper into the apartment, but she was moving and he had to follow her.

"Maybe I should wait for you to get dressed, and we can meet outside," he said.

"Why do that, silly man? It's nice and quiet in here."

She went into a small, eat-in kitchen. A super-sized blender sat on the counter, as well as a juice machine that looked new and unused, as most juice machines do. She sat behind a kitchen table that almost filled up the kitchen. The table looked new, as did the four elegant, high-backed chairs squeezed into the space around it. She faced him, with the window behind her. Tony molded himself into the chair across from her. There wasn't much room between the chair and the wall behind him. He put his messenger bag on the floor—his spare set of pétanque balls in it clacked against the tile. He put his mini-cassette recorder on the table and switched it on.

"Oh c'mon, Tony, what is this?" she said. She had a coy, flirtatious smile on her face. "God, how old is that thing?"

"My other one got...broken. This is one I still had at home. Kirsten, listen, I've already talked to Bobbert."

She stopped smiling then. "I'm not talking into that," she said, lighting up a cigarette.

"Fine." Tony switched it off. He was trying to get a sense of what she was thinking. Her bulgy eyes gave away nothing.

"All right. I'll tell you from the start," she said, moving her gaze from his face to some area above his head. She inhaled deeply then exhaled. Then she waved the smoke away from Tony's face. "Sorry," she said. "From the start. So.

"*So*. We were all great neighbors with Rosa at first. I mean, she could be very snippy sometimes when we had a party and the music was too loud or because we left the garbage in the hallway. Things like that. Anyway. Patrick said she reminded him of his grandmother. Because they were both old and they were both women, I guess. I never met his grandmother. Anyway. We were all good friends on the third floor.

"Then she came to us one night, asking us if we cleaned our house."

"What do you mean?"

"What I said. If we cleaned our house. If we were clean. Well, this pissed me off to no end, and it looked like we were going to fight again, but then she started crying, saying there were roaches in her house and that she never had roaches. We consoled her, but she swore someone had put them there. And then there were the mice. Two or three little brown things. The super, by the way, was a drunk bastard. You couldn't ask him to unclog a toilet or fix a fucking lock. He did nothing. So she asked Patrick to kill the mice, but he was a chicken.

"But I grew up in a house in PA that was practically a barn. So I was used to taking care of them and I knew what to do. I hooked up a bucket of water and some peanut butter, a tin can, and some rope. You thread the rope through the can, like a telephone, right? Then little Mickey comes running up for his snack, his weight makes the can jingle, which knocks the mouse off the rope and into the pool. Next morning, you have mice tea."

Tony winced, but Kirsten looked very proud of her technique. "And then the next day she got three *more* mice. So we knew something was up. Patrick and I thought this definitely looked suspicious. So he went to Bobbert with the story idea for your paper. He was into it, so with a little cash we got some mini-webcams and set them up in her apartment and, you know, we saw what we saw." She blew smoke out of the side of her mouth.

"Tell me."

"Well, we had the super doing dirty work, and we had that setting the fire with one of the Tomasellos, the chubby one—"

"Frank Jr."

"Yeah. That's him. I don't know who suggested it first, but one of us said no one would care about a story in the shitty little *Sentinel*, but we could threaten to take the recordings to someone, and with that threat, maybe it could work out in a good way for all of us: me, Patrick, and Bobbert. Tell me, Tony, what are you going to do with this information? So, we got a little money from the real estate bastards, so what. These people make millions. We weren't asking for much."

"To be honest, I don't care about the blackmail. Developers deserve whatever they get," Tony said. "I know the stuff you wanted from Patrick's apartment was the flash drives. Maybe you wanted them all for yourself, so you could go on blackmailing them. Like I said, I don't care. What I want to know is what happened to Rosa. I think you know. Tell me what happened. Tell me how she disappeared."

Kirsten reached for another cigarette. Her phone dinged and she quickly tapped it off. "Yeah, sure. I guess it's full confession time, right? 'Forgive me, Father, for I have sinned?'"

She laughed, a low, throaty laugh. Tony nodded. Instead of looking over his head, Kirsten kept her eyes right on him.

"It was late August and hot as hell, I remember. Our AC wasn't working and we were practically naked in the apartment, getting on each other's nerves with the heat. We hear this knock on the door, and it's Rosa, complaining that her AC wasn't working right, and this wasn't harassment, the old lady just didn't know how to use her AC right. We were tired and cranky, and in no mood to go over to her place, it still stank like smoke and was even hotter than ours, so we started arguing on the landing like we did sometimes. And I guess—I guess Patrick snapped..."

"Patrick? What did he do?"

"Oh, Tony, it was horrible."

"What did he do?"

"He went and hit her, right in the face. Not a punch, more like a slap, I guess."

"And she didn't do anything to provoke this?"

"What? No."

"Did she do anything after?"

"No, he hit her and she was right near the stairs at that point, and she fell down and—that was it, her neck was broken. I was horrified."

"And then what did you do?"

"Well, she had toppled down to the bottom of the stairs," she said. "We were lucky no one came out. Downstairs there was a classical musician who was in his own world, and next to her was some Spanish lady I never saw much of."

"What did you do then—with Rosa?"

She said, "Sorry. This is ugly." But when she said it she didn't seem disgusted. She could have been talking about wallpaper. "We took her to my car and then drove to the little area of water above Greenpoint, you know, between Greenpoint and Queens."

"Newtown Creek."

"Is that what it's called? Yeah, there. We dropped her in."

"But how did you carry her outside without anyone seeing?"

"Oh. Well, we waited until really late at night. And we had her in Patrick's suitcase."

"Suitcase?"

"Yeah, a gift from his parents. Was supposed to be an early honeymoon present. Like that was going to happen."

"Kirsten. Why not just tell the cops it was an accident?"

"We didn't think, I guess. You know, this is why we broke up. I was scared of him after that. I knew what he was capable of. I couldn't love him anymore. So I had to ditch. He kept calling me and coming around my new place and posting stuff on Facebook. Finally, I blocked him. And I—I hooked up with

Gunnar because I was afraid. I needed protection."

"You know, Patrick was writing a story—or at least he said he was. He was asking about Rosa last month."

"That's guilt. Straight-up guilt. He never got over it. I suppose he could have been trying to see if the police knew anything, but I think he just wanted to seem like he was doing something—for himself, you know, to pretend he was a good person."

"But you had these videos and you did what you did and you still were blackmailing the Tomasellos?"

"Oh yeah, we had them by the balls. You know, we also bugged the super's apartment. It was easy to get in there because he was drunk all the time on the stoop or in the cellar and he left his door open. We heard him talking about the fire with that big, super-tanned lady."

"Jackie Tomasello."

"Yeah, her. That was the real clincher."

"I've seen the videos but I haven't heard the audio recording."

"I have it. That was the deal when Patrick and I broke up. Insurance. He kept some parts and I kept the others. It was something we were always going to share between us, like a bond." She crushed out a cigarette and instantly took out and lit another one. "Hey, listen, did you want a beer? It's happy hour somewhere in the world."

"No, thanks."

"I think I'm going to have one, if you don't mind?"

When she got up, Tony could see the sun blazing off the windows of the buildings across the street. Kirsten went to the fridge, got a beer, popped it open, and sat back down.

"This happened on Saturday night," Tony said. "The next day Rosa got some phone calls."

"Yeah. A few. Patrick had her phone. He texted back. We got rid of the phone, too."

They sat there in silence as she drank. It was cool in the apartment, and the hum of the AC covered the silence between them.

Finally, Kirsten said, "So, are you going to tell the cops what I told you?"

"I have to. They have to search for Rosa."

"Oh, her body's long gone." Her pale face was flushed. Her voice was getting louder for some reason. "Out into the Atlantic. And I mean, what's done is done. And Patrick—well, in a way he's paid for what he did. Somebody did him in. It's karma, don't you think?"

"I wanted to ask about that, too," Tony said. Kirsten was looking behind him. He turned—and a huge machete was headed straight for his head.

CHAPTER SIXTY

It was Gunnar, the bouncing boyfriend. He must have been in the shower, too. He was naked from the waist up, still wet. And his face was as smooth as a baby's.

Tony would have kicked himself in the ass, but he was too busy folding himself forward and to the left. The big knife narrowly missed his head, although the meaty fist holding it cuffed him in the ear. With his legs, he shifted his chair back and pushed the table forward—both screeched on the kitchen tiles. He rolled to the floor.

"Get him!" Kirsten was saying. "Get that fucker."

When Tony had pushed the table forward, he'd squeezed Kirsten against the window in the tight space.

Gunnar tried to reach him but caught himself on the high chair back. He swung but with his reach the machete caught in the fine new kitchen table and got stuck. Tony had an opening. He grabbed his bag and pushed past Gunnar. The bouncer tried to grab his shirt, but only succeeded in ripping a sleeve.

In the living room, Tony grabbed one of the flashy guitars and, spinning, tried to whack Gunnar. And failed. Gunnar ducked back—but slipped to the floor. Wet feet. Tony wound up again and aimed for the beard mannequins, knocking them all off the shelves and onto the floor. Trying to get up, Gunnar yelled in pain, and not from his second stumble, "Noooo!"

Running down the stairs, Tony thought of how much of an idiot he was. *Machete!* Of course, Patrick's death hadn't been random. Of course, Kirsten would have gotten greedy. Of course, she had her big bodyguard take him out. How stupid of him to just walk into her house with no plan.

Now if he could just survive long enough to fully appreciate the depths of his own stupidity.

He opened the door to the street and, stepping out, he halted. In front of him flowed a bloated sea of people on Bedford Avenue. Of course. It was close to lunchtime on a nice day on the most crowded street in Williamsburg, a hundred feet from the Bedford Avenue train station, Ground Zero for hipness. The hipsters, the yuppies, the deliverymen, the waiters, the busboys, the workers, the tourists, the tourists, the tourists, they moved past Tony like a never-ending, achingly slow-flowing mass of molasses.

He had no choice. He dove in.

The crowd was so thick he was forced to shuffle, squeezing here and there but unable to move much faster than the pace of the mass. He had froggered himself this way ten feet down the block, waiting for a phalanx of people staring at their phones to move just a little bit over to the right, when he looked back to see Gunnar glaring at him from the doorway. Dressed now but with the ginger beard, a bit askew on his face.

"Somebody call the cops!" Tony yelled and then realized how ridiculous he sounded. No one even looked up.

He ducked and spun and elbowed, got some rude looks, but for the most part the people of the mass were trapped in their bubbles. He looked back and saw Gunnar trying to navigate through the mass as well. At least he wasn't trying to slash his way through. At least not yet.

Tony and Gunnar made their way slowly across North 9th Street.

Tony figured Gunnar was about half a block behind him.

It was the world's slowest foot chase.

Tony worked his new cell phone out of his pants. Maybe he could quickly dial 9-1-1. But he turned again to look behind him, and an immensely fat man dressed head to toe in black leather bumped into him, and the cell phone flew out of his hands. He heard but did not see it crack on the pavement. "Crap."

He turned. Gunnar had lost his patience and was elbowing people aside. He held the machete in his hand.

Seriously, Tony thought. *Does no one see that? Does no one care?*

Out of desperation, Tony ran onto Bedford Avenue, onto the blacktop, the weight of his messenger bag banging against his back. Gunnar got the same idea. The cars were lined up, practically parked on Bedford Avenue. Gunnar was close. Tony jumped and slid over the hood of a car. Someone gave him a long honk.

He ran down a side street—there would be fewer people to run around, less of the mass, but that went for Gunnar, too. He'd have an easier time catching up.

A bell jingled. A woman was just coming out of a shop on his right. Tony ducked past her into the open shop door.

It was a narrow, cramped jewelry shop. Black walls and black floors. Headless torsos and necks with expensive necklaces, disembodied hands with rings and bracelets. Glass cases filled with shiny objects.

"Well," Tony said. Sweat covered his face. His shirt was stuck to him. He breathed as heavy as a pervert. He realized he was probably making a poor impression.

Two women ogling a case did not look at him, but a sour-looking, cyan-haired salesperson behind the counter noticed him and smiled. She seemed about to ask him how she could help him, when, with a jingle, Gunnar walked in. And stood there.

"Shopping for earrings, too?" Tony said. He stepped behind a horizontal display case.

Gunnar looked around. He held the machete down, tapping it against his thigh. The two women continued to look at the jewelry. The saleswoman looked confused, as if she suspected something, but she still kept her smile on. "Is there something I can help you with today? Our nose rings are on sale at thirty percent off."

Gunnar nodded and smiled at her. Then he held up the machete.

"Holy shit!" the salesperson said.

Gunnar stepped toward Tony and slashed. Tony moved to the side and bumped against a display case. The machete caught him on the left arm and cut just above his elbow. A long cut but not deep. He put his right hand on it to apply pressure.

The oglers were screaming now, too, along with the sour salesperson. Gunnar stood between them and the door.

"Get out of here!" the salesperson yelled. "Get out of my store!"

"Call the cops," Tony said. "It's the slasher!"

"My phone needs juice!" one of them yelled.

Gunnar took another step forward. His beard was just holding on by a few whiskers now. Tony looked for something, anything as a defense. He grabbed a neck mannequin with his bloody right hand and tossed it. The silk scarf around it flowed in the air. Gunnar tried to slap the mannequin away but the machete got caught in the flowing scarf, and he had to chop in the air a few times to dislodge it, finally getting through and cracking into the glass of the horizontal display case.

Tony swung his messenger bag off his back and put it in front of him as a shield. Gunnar swung again, cutting open the messenger bag. The pétanque balls clunked to the floor.

"Give it up. The cops will be here any minute," Tony said. "Tell me somebody is calling the cops!"

"What's their number?"

Gunnar came forward. Tony went back behind the broken display. Gunnar stepped to the right, Tony went left. Gunnar stepped left, and Tony went right.

"Why did you kill Patrick?" said Tony. "Did she make you do it?"

Something rolled at his feet. A pétanque ball. Tony picked it up and hurled it right at Gunnar's head. He tried to swat it away with the machete, but missed. It connected with a crack. *A different kind of carreau.*

Gunnar slashed wildly in the air, knocking the display case over. Glass and bracelets and charms flew. More screaming.

Tony heard someone behind him, the salesperson.

"These two guys are having a fight. One of them has a big knife. I think they're on drugs. One of them is Mexican, I think. No, not the one with the knife."

Tony smirked. Then he said, "You hear that, Gunnar? The cops."

Gunnar's eyes went wild. He was a trapped animal.

"Put the machete down. Maybe—"

Gunnar kicked the display case. It came forward with a force that knocked Tony back. He fell on to the two customers, who had been crouching behind him.

Tony looked up. Gunnar put a foot on the toppled display case and raised the machete. Tony felt something in his right hand. Must be jewelry. He didn't think about how it hurt his hand to hold it. As Gunnar began to slash, he threw whatever it was in Gunnar's face.

Gunnar screamed at the same time Tony winced. Glass. It was glass.

Gunnar grabbed at his face. Blood seeped through his fingers. The beard was completely off now, stuck to Gunnar's pants. One muffled word came through the fingers. "Bastard." Then he turned and ran out of the door.

Tony slowly picked himself up off the two customers. "Sorry about that."

He looked down to see his right hand was bleeding—a lot. Blood flowed down his left arm as well. He wouldn't be donating at any blood drives soon.

The salesperson pointed her phone at him. "Get out! Please! Please leave my store!"

Tony ran outside the store. Nothing. He ran to the corner.

Into the molasses-slow mass of people. From horizon to horizon. Molasses. Slow. And no sign of Gunnar.

Tony walked back into the store.

"Did you call the cops?" he said to the salesperson.

"Oh my god. You're back."

CHAPTER SIXTY-ONE

"Pretty bad, huh?" Tony said to the nurse as she stitched up his hand. There was blood all over his jeans. "At least the scar will make me look more macho."

"O-M-G," Gabby said. "That is the stupidest thing you could say."

The nurse snorted. "I seen three fingers hanging off just an hour ago. That little girl is macho."

"Thanks," Tony said. He turned to Gabby. "And thank you. I owe you."

"Somebody has to help you pay the bills. Why didn't you call your girlfriend?"

"She's not my...I tried to reach her, but no answer. I'll pay you back."

"You have to. Sucks to have no insurance. Sucks worse to have no savings. What do you do with your money?"

"I've been going to a lot of hospitals lately. It's great fun, but it adds up."

"Sorry, right. Listen, do I even have a job anymore? Bobbert left me a weird message. He said not to come in today or anymore. Totes cryptic."

"I'm not sure myself what's going to happen, Gabby. But you should be looking for another job."

"Me? I'm always looking for another job. What about you?"

"I honestly have no idea."

"Patrick always used to say you could be a great reporter.

288

He said you had the stubbornness you needed."

"Maybe I—"

"Hey, you think I could get a job at *Vogue*?"

Just then, Detective Petrosino walked in. "You okay to talk now?"

Petrosino held out a hand to be shaken, but Tony held up his bandaged right hand.

"Right-o. Looks bad."

"They tell me it's no more than a mosquito bite around here."

Tony asked Gabby to wait for him outside, and then he said, "Hey, did you get the package I left for you this morning?"

"Yes, very interesting video there," Petrosino said. "And the rest. Did you read it all?"

"I didn't have to. I finally had a chance to look through the drives when I was in Puerto Rico. I got curious—well, I was bored—and I finally took a look at the other documents on the drives. And then I saw one was Patrick's novel."

"A novel that was all about the gangs of Williamsburg."

"Yep. Which was why he wanted to talk to Eladio Cortés, not for an exposé."

"I talked to Cortés. He says he never heard of Patrick Stoller, and I believe him."

"I expected as much. But Patrick thought he was in touch with him. I think that's how he was lured out to that spot by the waterfront."

"By his ex?" Petrosino said.

"Yeah, that's what I think. Kirsten Waters, the person who knew most about Patrick's literary ambitions. She exploited that to get rid of him. Contacted Patrick with a burner phone pretending to be Cortés."

"Because of this blackmail scheme you mentioned."

"Right. She wanted all the money for herself. But I think she didn't trust Patrick not to snitch on her about the blackmail and the disappearance and murder of Rosa Irizzary. She says Patrick did it by accident, pushed Rosa down the stairs, but from the way she told the story I'm not sure Kirsten didn't do it herself and on purpose."

"Jeepers. She sounds like an angel."

"She said they dumped her body in Newtown Creek."

"Oh christ," Petrosino said. "I'll talk to the harbor patrol guys. They'll have to drag the creek. Fact is, they find a body in there about every other day, so they may have discovered her previously. We'll look to see if a Jane Doe answering her description turns up. Now, you think it's possible this boyfriend of hers, this Gunnar Neumann, did all the slashings?"

"I mean, it could be. But it's a hell of a lot of trouble to slash all those people just to get to Patrick. No, I think it's more likely she took advantage of the situation. She saw all these slashings happening and figured, what's one more? The police'll never catch the slasher or slashers anyway—sorry, no offense—"

"None taken."

"—and extrapolating from that, I think Gunnar had to kill that Erin Cole woman, the one who was pregnant. The papers say she and her husband witnessed Patrick's murder. I'd bet Kirsten sent Gunnar after her, to keep her quiet."

"Could be, and that would be pretty sad and pretty nasty. I'm looking forward to talking to Ms. Waters and Mr. Neumann. We're on the lookout for both now. We'll get 'em."

Tony looked for a pen and paper but saw none. "Listen, if you don't mind, I'd love to get some of this written down, and maybe get an exclusive interview with you, but my recorder is still back at Kirsten's house. Can I call you in a little?"

"We'll try to get that recorder back to you. I'll give you some quotes, but, um, an exclusive is a no-go. I already talked to three news types on the way over here."

"Just my luck."

"Well, you did survive an attack by a man wielding a machete. That's pretty lucky."

"There is that," said Tony. "Oh, one more thing for you. I have a source that tells me the slasher rides a funky-looking red bike, one that looks like it was made of different parts. I don't suppose you found Gunnar's bike."

"No, but we're looking. We've heard so many different things about the look of the bike, but thanks anyway for the tip."

Petrosino went to shake Tony's hand, but Tony waved his bandaged hand again, so Petrosino gave him a friendly smack on his other arm.

"Take care," the detective said. "Stay out of trouble."

CHAPTER SIXTY-TWO

A week later Petrosino was enjoying a cigarette in peaceful solitude. It was one of those surprisingly balmy late August days in New York City where a person could actually enjoy being outside. He paced back and forth and inhaled and exhaled with pleasure. He was considering lighting up a second one when his phone rang. It was Hadid.

"How's it going?" Petrosino said.

"They got me on desk duty at Police Plaza. Better than sitting in my own stink."

"Right-o. I heard."

"But that's not why I'm calling. Remember you wanted me to keep an eye on that phrase 'hipster death rattle' online."

"Yeah?"

"Well, the Twitter page with that name blew up about a week ago. Just about the time the news was breaking on the story of that 'Hipster Slasher' Gunnar you guys have been looking for."

"Blew up how?" Petrosino inhaled as he listened.

"Whoever it is started posting. Remember it had just sixty-something followers. Now he's got more than a thousand. And, get this, apparently there's a T-shirt going around with the phrase on it. Can you believe it? Capitalism never sleeps. Zamorano is going to try to find one, so I can trace the manufacturer."

"I believe it, jeez. So, what was posted? Anything useful?"

"I think so. I'll start at the oldest, dated August 12, 10 a.m.: 'hello, world!' 10:02: 'nice to meet you.' Following that is a retweet of the *Daily News* piece on the slasher, then a retweet of the *Post* article, then a retweet of the *Gothamist.*"

"Get to the good stuff."

"Just wait. Then at 11 a.m. same day: 'it's time you met the real me.' 11:02: 'the more the merrier was fine for a while, but it's time to take credit.' Then he posts a YouTube video on how to make a homemade machete."

"Jeez Louise. Anything else?"

"Well, it looks like he 'Liked' just about every other post about the slasher, and there were a few thousand. And then people starting retweeting him. Just this past hour, the hashtag started trending."

"What does that mean?"

"That means it's popular. But his last three posts are from yesterday: 'it ain't over til it's over,' 'as always, die hipster-yuppie scum die,' and, get this, 'bye bye brandon boy.'"

"As in Brandon Taylor, our last vic. Dammit. Is there any way to trace—"

"Through the IP address, yes. We're working on it now."

"Good," Petrosino said. "Let me know. I'll be back at my desk in a minute."

"No rush. It'll take a while. Enjoy your cigarette."

CHAPTER SIXTY-THREE

Yogi Johnson breathed out and eased himself into a flying crow position on his mat.

His hands were planted in front of him, holding his entire weight. His right leg was tucked under his torso and lay loosely on his triceps, while his right leg was thrust straight toward the ceiling. His graying dreadlocks hung in his face, and sweat soaked his headband and rolled like worms down his forehead, down his arms, beaded on his hands. He did not believe in air conditioning, and he couldn't afford it anyway, so he kept window fans going at both ends of his railroad apartment. He considered it his cheap bikram.

His arms began to tremble but he held the pose, counting to 1,010...1,011...1,012. He was glad to be able to hold the pose for so long, especially as he was nearing fifty-six years on the planet. He knew he should just be enjoying the pose but he couldn't help challenging himself.

He exhaled with a grunt and gently moved himself out of the pose. He should have moved into less stressful positions from there, but instead he stood up and wiped the sweat off with a towel. Usually, an hour of yoga would exhaust him in the right way, calm his nerves. But it wasn't working anymore.

He went into the kitchen to get some water from the tap.

His homemade machete lay there on the table.

He paused, for the thousandth time that day, to admire it. It was a work of art.

The steel was almost thirty inches long, two and a half inches wide, and just under an eighth of an inch thick. He'd found the steel piece in an abandoned lot in Greenpoint, one of the last abandoned lots in the neighborhood. Sitting right there on a pile of bricks and debris. It had stood out like a sign, something he had looked for his whole life.

The blade made perfect sense, a perfect analogy. The hipsters in the neighborhood had proliferated like wild, turning the once-peaceful neighborhood into a noisy, overgrown, fetid jungle. They needed to be weeded, and a machete was the perfect tool for the job.

Following an instructional YouTube video, he had outlined the shape he wanted in pencil and then in marker, so he could see it better in the dim basement light of his building. He had used a metal cutting disk to create the shape he wanted. Sparks flew, lighting up the basement, illuminating thick layers of dust on the workbench, the rusty tools, the old laundry machines. The blade did not have to be perfect, but he did want the rounded nose to look right.

A half hour of wire brushing had made the junk steel gleam.

When he was done, he took it out of the vise and tested its balance. It was a little heavier at the end, just where the weight should be.

He took a step back and made a few practice swings, although there wasn't much room there under the staircase. He made sounds: "Whoosh," "Shoooom," "Slice! Slice!"

"Hello?"

He stopped in mid-swing and put the blade down as quietly as he could on the lower shelf of the old workbench.

Light spread into the basement from the hallway door upstairs. "I heard some noise down here." It was Mr. McShane at the top of the staircase, directly above him.

"I'm working," he said. "I'm making a new part for my bicycle."

"Please don't start a mess down there because it takes me a long time to clean the basement."

"All right, Mr. McShane, all right," Yogi said.

"I'm going to come down and do my laundry in a little while. Both my socks!"

It was the same joke the old man always told. "Fine," Yogi said.

Quickly, neatly, Yogi cleaned up the work area and packed away the new grinder. He put the blade inside some old T-shirts and went upstairs to his railroad apartment.

Mr. McShane never strayed very far from the building. He was tethered to it, like an astronaut to a spaceship. But every once in a while he went to the C-Town supermarket on Graham Avenue. Yogi knew when he heard the distinctive sound of the old man's stepping his rickety shopping cart down the front steps that it was one of those days. Yogi ran to the window and saw the geezer wheeling his wobbly red cart down the block. Even though the supermarket was just three blocks away, Mr. McShane would be gone at least two hours.

Yogi flew downstairs, two steps at a time, back to the basement and put the blade in the vise. To avoid burrs, he kept the grinder moving along the blade, evenly sharpening, always moving, never stopping in one spot. He turned it over and did the other side.

The blade now had a rough sharpness, and it would have been nice to temper it in a forge. But Yogi didn't think Mr. McShane would let him get away with building a forge in the basement.

He ground the edges to razor sharpness. He used sandpaper to remove any burrs.

He was halfway through making the handle when Mr. McShane returned.

"Is that you down there?" he said from the top of the stairs.

"Yes."

"Are you gonna be a long time?"

"No, no, no," Yogi said. "I was finished for the day."

He went upstairs imagining what he could do to Mr. McShane if he didn't stop annoying him. He was so thin. It would be like chopping weeds.

Two days later, Yogi had epoxied two pieces of decking spindle onto the tang of the blade to make a handle. With a rasp, he beveled its edges to make a better grip, and he added pop rivets to make it look professional. He found that he had become proud of it, and now he wanted to make it look pretty.

He drilled a hole through the handle and added a new leather lanyard that would hang around his wrist.

He had sewn a special pocket into his long shorts to function like a hidden scabbard. He slid it into the pocket and quickly whipped it out. "*En garde!*"

Maybe it was all just part of some midlife crisis, his red sports car, his hot blonde teenage girlfriend. If it was supposed to make him feel good, it was doing a great job.

The blade was to be anointed with blood, of course, like any atavistic weapon of sacrifice. So he took it for a test spin. He bicycled it around the neighborhood, unsheathing it at potential sacrifices. Some people laughed and took pictures. So he decided to be stealthier, more menacing, so he wore a balaclava. And then one guy just threw his knapsack at him and ran. He realized then that he needed to be more self-empowered.

He meditated. He chanted. He prayed. And then he found her, the first actual victim. She was a young woman. Maxine was her name, he found out later, and he still felt bad about what he'd done. Women had always been victimized, so it just didn't seem fair and he didn't want to contribute to that victimization, at least not for the first one. But she was just the perfect target. It had been late, maybe two in the morning, and he had been riding around and riding around, and he was getting tired.

He had passed her on the corner of Wythe Avenue and Broadway. There was no one else around for a block or two. She had just gotten out of a taxi and was just standing there, hypnotized by her cell phone, headphones on, oblivious to the world. She was a white, young, pretty hipstress. He became nervous, his heart beating hard. He thought he might chicken out. But her bland, distracted face made the difference, made it easier to finally do what he had been dreaming about.

He had turned around, went up a block and came back down again, picking up speed. He unsheathed the new machete and held it out. He breathed deeply, channeling his life force into the blade. He felt it getting warmer, glowing with his *qi*. She was still completely concentrated on that cell phone, her fingers stabbing into it, probably asking her boyfriend where the hell he was or asking her bff where the club they were supposed to meet at was.

He cut right across her at full speed. In hindsight, he realized he had been going too fast to get good aim and accuracy. He heard her scream—a yelp really—but he didn't look back. He biked faster, turned the corner near the river and booked out of there.

He had anointed his blade, and so he peddled to an open bar and had a beer and a whiskey shot to celebrate. And then another. And another. He lost count. Oh, what a headache he'd had the next day.

For the third time that day, the old man went into a coughing jag, coughing long, hard, bottom-of-the-chest coughs that seemed about to turn him inside out.

"Hold on, Mr. McShane. The nurse is going to be here soon."

The old man whispered something that kind of sounded like "cocksucker."

"It must be horrible to suffer so," Yogi said.

When the visiting nurse arrived, the two put the old man into bed.

"He'll sleep for a while. It's cold in here," the nurse said. "You shouldn't keep it so cold."

"The old man likes it that way, the air conditioner turned all the way up. What's wrong with him now? I thought he was getting better."

"I don't know what it is. It's not the gall bladder. It's the rest of him. His blood pressure is through the roof. He's pale. He's listless. In my professional opinion, he looks like shit."

"What should I do?"

"Listen, I'm recommending you take him in to the hospital doctor sooner rather than later. Have you contacted his next of kin?"

"'Old age comes on suddenly, and not gradually as is thought,'" Yogi said.

"Uh huh."

"He won't give me their numbers, and I can't find it in all this crap he's got around."

"And they haven't called all of the time you've been here?"

"Nope." Yogi saddened at the thought of careless family members.

"Eesh, another one of these. Hey, I done my job. You want, I can call the ambulance for him. They can take care of him at the hospital."

"I don't mind."

"It would take him off your hands."

"That's all right. What else have I got to do?"

After the nurse left, Yogi sat and watched the old man breathe. Every breath seemed like a struggle. It wasn't peaceful. It wasn't beautiful. What a horrible thing to live so long and die without any meaning.

Thinking about it made Yogi hungry, so he decided to go to the local bodega and get some beer and cold cuts for dinner. But first, he needed cash. He bent down and reached into the space under the old man's mattress.

The old man's gnarled hand grabbed his shoulder. Yogi looked up and saw Mr. McShane was giving him the darkest stinkeye of all.

"Cocksucker."

CHAPTER SIXTY-FOUR

She had been looking at his armadillo when she first had the idea.

Patrick was on top of her, pumping away, and Kirsten had been looking around, and her eyes rested on his stupid, pleather albino armadillo and she said, "We have too much stuff."

"Really? You think so?" Behind her, he was breathing hard. Patrick had always worked hard at everything.

"Yeah," she said, getting off her knees and turning to scoot up against the headboard. "It would be so great if we could get a bigger place but not have to pay so much. *Ugh.*"

"How much space do you think we need? I mean, it's a little cluttered here, but I think we fit fine."

"No, no, we can't have anybody over. There's just so much junk."

"We could get rid of stuff."

"That's not the point," she said, tugging casually at her own nipples. "You know, Rosa next door is paying less than four hundred dollars a month. It's rent-controlled. That's gold. That's better than gold."

"Yeah, so?"

"Imagine what we could do with that space." She got giddy with the idea. She imagined having the whole floor, hosting parties, art salons, exhibitions.

"Is she moving?"

"No, but she's old. She might die any day. Slow *down.*"

"That's not nice to say," Patrick said, pure sap that he was.

"Yeah, but they would renovate her place and rent it for market value, like they did for the violinist. He's paying fifteen hundred. That is too slow. I can't even feel that."

"How do you know these things?"

"I ask," she said. "*Better, yes.* The thing would be to get her to put us on her lease. I wonder how possible that would be. Keep going. Just like that. *Just like that.*"

That was how the idea began.

After Tony had come by and she told him *a version* of the truth, and after Gunnar went out after him and didn't come back, Kirsten knew she had to skedaddle. She checked the news and saw what had happened with Tony at that boutique. Gunnar wasn't coming back. Not even for his precious guitar collection. Didn't matter. She took her best camera, and she wanted to take all her gorgeously framed photographs, but there was no way. She had them in digital format anyway. She would just have to frame them all again one day, wherever she was going. She packed her clothes and rolled up her gorgeous leather yoga mat then realized, dammit, she couldn't take her gorgeous leather yoga mat. And then she made sure to take all the digital video and audio files, and she left.

She went straight for SubBar. Happy hour was just starting so Black Martin was there. Of course. She asked him if she could stay in his apartment. He looked at her and what was he going to say? At his place, she asked him to go out and get her some hair dye, and he brought it back and watched as she blackened her hair.

He also got two six packs and some tequila, so she stayed there while he got progressively drunker as he talked and talked and fell asleep. She was glad she wouldn't have to have sex with him.

Her plan was to take his car early in the morning, but in the middle of the night he got up to piss and had his phone with him and he checked the news. He started freaking out at her. *Ugh!* So she left.

Bobbert's phone was disconnected, and the *Sentinel* office was closed. Litvinchouk wouldn't pick up when she called, and she didn't know where he lived. Jackie Tomasello told her: "I don't want to get involved in this slasher shit. Stay away from me. I got problems of my own."

When they had first moved in, Kirsten instantly disliked the old lady. She didn't like old people, period, but Rosa especially— she reminded Kirsten very much of her own grandmother. Her parents made her go live with GrandMeemer for entire summers, and you never knew what you were going to get with the old bat: the belt, the iron cord, a spatula across your back. That Rosa, she looked and smelled like GrandMeemer. It creeped Kirsten out that this woman lived next door.

Then one day, after Kirsten and Patrick had had their chat, the old lady came to them with a story about how someone had broken in and put roaches in her place. *Ugh.* Kirsten rolled her eyes. The lady was probably senile. But Patrick, good-hearted soul Patrick, he loved a lost cause. It was his idea to put cameras in the old lady's apartment—always looking for the big exposé, that Patrick. But after he caught the super on video, it was Kirsten who suggested they bug the super's apartment for more dirt.

Then she had the idea to blackmail the owners. Patrick was aghast, but she could see desperation in Bobbert's eyes. They pressured Patrick into it.

After she left Black Martin's place, she slept in Prospect Park. But she was humiliated to find a homeless man masturbating near her. She had to get out of town that day.

She took the G train to the 7 train to Port Authority. She figured if she showed off her new hair color and acted calm, she'd get past the cops. She bought a bus ticket for Philadelphia. From there, she would make her way to Texas. She had always wanted to go to Austin. There was a thriving artistic community there. She could show her photographs.

The lower terminal was a long hallway with doors every fifteen feet leading out to where the buses parked. In the terminal, there were very few seats, so most of the people just stood there like dumb sheep, and many of them slid down to the dirty floor to wait.

Kirsten waited outside her gate. She was too exhausted to stand, and slid down to the floor next to a family of fat out-of-towners. A fat dad, a fat mom, a chunky son, and a daughter who obviously was deceiving herself about her correct jean size.

Ugh. These were the kind of people she had been running away from her whole life.

It was a happy year of extra cash for photography equipment and rent and food and booze—and the promise that if the old lady moved out, she'd get the apartment, at a rent control price.

But then Rosa had moved back in. And that made everything suck.

Kirsten was furious. She didn't say "Hello" on the landing, ignored the old lady's requests to not store their garbage in the hallway.

One day, the lady knocked on her door and told her to take away the garbage because it was bringing flies. Kirsten told her to "Fuck off." Rosa called her a "bitch," which just sounded stupid with her accent.

That was it. She punched the old lady in the face. But Rosa was tough. She ran to her apartment, and Kirsten went after her. The old lady threw shit at her, a ladle, a glass, coffee grounds.

Kirsten punched the old lady to the floor and then bent

down to put her hands around her throat.

Patrick came home late that night. He was always coming home late, working at that stupid newspaper for pennies.

She made him help her. She made him fold the body into the suitcase his parents gave them. She made him take it downstairs and put it in the trunk and drive it to the water. That car stank after that. Stank like old lady. Kirsten had sprayed and scrubbed and bleached but she couldn't get the stink out. She loved that car, but she had no choice but to sell it. The new owner didn't seem to have noticed the smell, so that was fine and money in her pocket.

Things were not the same between them after that. She had thought it might bring them closer together. But he kept crying about seeing Rosa's face. *Ugh. Cry. Cry. Cry.* So she moved out.

But she didn't like that he had the video copies. It was something he could hold over her for the rest of her life. So she bided her time, waiting till Patrick felt complacent. And, once she heard about the couple of slashings that had happened, she had another idea—a masterstroke, you could say, when she was in the kitchen looking at the stupid machete Gunnar had brought back with him from some drug-crazed trip to Belize. So she had Gunnar call Patrick. She knew how much he was fascinated by gangs, how desperate he was to tell what he called "an authentic story." So Gunnar pretended to be a gang member looking to have his story told.

Poor Patrick. He had never questioned why a gang member had contacted him out of the blue. What a sucker.

The bus was late, very late, and Kirsten needed to go to the bathroom. She asked Fat Mom to hold her place. "Sure thing," Fat Mom told her.

Kirsten went to the ladies' room, which was full of flies, and got into a stall, made a nest of toilet paper, and pulled down her pants. *Ugh.*

Then she heard a lady say to someone, "You sure you in the right place, honey?" And then the lady, in a half-whisper, "Okay, okay."

Kirsten heard people scurrying. She quickly finished her business and exited the stall. There was no one in the bathroom. Very unusual. Outside the door she heard voices, lots of voices, and different from the usual hum on the Port Authority. She looked behind her. She looked all around the bathroom.

There was no place to run.

She was so close to getting away. She would have gone to Philly first. She had a few college friends there. They would have helped her, sure. And from there she could have gone anywhere in the country, or out of the country. She could have.

She opened the door of the bathroom, and a tall man with white hair and a mustache that was both white and yellow pointed a gun at her and said, "Kirsten Waters, you are under arrest."

CHAPTER SIXTY-FIVE

Magaly hadn't seen Luis since she came back from PR. He hadn't called and he hadn't come in to the El Flamboyan office for days. But she got in one morning (early this time, a new thing she had decided to start working on), and there he was in his office, making a lot of noise.

She did a quick chant under her breath, *Nam-myoho-renge-kyo*, in hopes that he wasn't having another tantrum, and walked toward his open door. Surrounded by boxes and open drawers, he was creating a jenga stack of file folders.

"Luis! What's going on?"

"Good morning!" he said. "I have resigned!"

"Oh my god."

"My last day is Friday. I'll have to make sure someone arranges a cake."

Magaly smirked. That "someone" meant her, and it meant he wanted her to arrange his going-away party, which took a lot of nerve, but that was typical Luis.

"I have a higher purpose now," he said, leaving the leaning pile of folders to turn to his now nearly empty bookshelf. "I decided I'm going to run for Congress."

"What? But how?" She wondered if this was about them and their abrupt breakup. Was this some melodramatic way to try to prove she would miss him? She knew that, on the one hand, it was self-absorbed of her to think so. But on the other hand, it was completely in Luis's wheelhouse.

"Last week," he said, "I went after campaign pledges like a lion, and I got them, from several places, including a very substantial one from O'Connell Construction."

"Oh my god, Luis! They're one of the worst developers."

"I know. I know. But they're local, and they believe in helping the people as much as I do."

She shook her head and was going to argue, but she could see that it was no use. He was serious about this. He hadn't made a disrespectful comment or tried to get her behind closed doors in two minutes, a record for him. "And what about El Flamboyan? You're going to leave us in a lurch..."

"I'm not. They'll probably appoint you interim director, and you'll do great. They might even give you the job."

"That'll be the day." Magaly thought it was unlikely, given the fact that no female had ever headed the organization in its forty-plus years of existence, and the board of directors was all male. But she found herself welcoming the chance to sit in the director's chair, something she had never thought about before.

He stopped packing and looked at her with that super-serious look that he must have practiced. It didn't affect her. She had seem him do it too often in his underwear. "Listen," he said, "I know you probably think this is about us. But it's not. I understand that that's over now. I was heartbroken, but we must move on with our lives. I'm going to be a public servant, and I have a moral standard to uphold..."

Luis had obviously no idea what public servants were like.

"...and you'll want to get married before it's too late."

Son of a bitch.

He kept talking. "I've already formed my campaign team. I'm sorry, as much as I would like to, I cannot ask you to be on it. Seeing us together, well, you know how people talk, how they make assumptions. Please understand."

"Oh, I understand, Luis. I get it!"

"Where are you going? I want to tell you about my platform."

"I have to go order you a cake. A big goodbye cake!"

* * *

Instead of calling the bakery, Magaly found herself leaving work and walking back to South 3rd Street. It was time to do something she had been putting off.

When she got there, Iris Campos seemed smaller, older. At the kitchen table, Iris seemed to understand the news that Magaly brought her, that her sister Rosa Irizzary's neighbors had at first seemed to be helping her. Then they killed her and got rid of her body in the river. But Iris said nothing. Magaly had expected tears or anger.

But what Iris did was walk over to a kitchen drawer and get out a rosary and begin to pray. Magaly hung her head and prayed/chanted silently with her.

After a time, Iris said, <"Do you want something to eat?">

Magaly was not hungry but she said she would eat. In five minutes, Iris fixed her a full breakfast of eggs, bacon, and *platanos*.

They talked about Iris's son Danny, who was currently awaiting trial for public disturbance and aggravated assault. With his prior record, he was looking at a long stay in prison.

There was a good chance Iris would not be around when he came out, and until then she'd be living alone. Magaly asked her if she was going to stay or, like so many Puerto Ricans her age, move back to the island or, the closest thing to it, Florida.

"*No 'stamos yendo a ningún lado,*" she said, shaking her head. She sipped some coffee, then she said, "Like Danny say to me, '*Quedamos en los Sures hasta que los tiren o morimos.*'"

We stay in the Southside until they kick us out or we die.

CHAPTER SIXTY-SIX

Things were certainly getting back to normal. Freelance work was complete (a how-to on low-histamine dieting, a how-to on buying co-ops, and two resumes), and Tony's hand was healing nicely. Nicely enough for him hold a pétanque ball.

It was a warm late August afternoon. McCarren Park was not packed end-to-end with people. There was room to move. There was even a slight breeze.

A perfect day to play.

Yogi was there by himself when Tony walked up. There was a thick haze of marijuana surrounding him like a skunk fog.

"Hey, there, Yogi."

"Dude," Yogi said. "Good to see you. Ready for a little one on one?"

Tony saw that Yogi's eyes were slightly glazed and red-rimmed. Yogi had been very indulgent, and it wasn't even tea time.

"Absolutely," Tony said.

Tony set down his messenger bag, now repaired with duct tape, right next to Yogi's bike. He looked at it for the first time. He had seen the bike before, sure, but he had never really noticed that, had he, all the duct tape on it? The body was made of what looked like electrical pipes, and the handlebar was a flat piece of metal that had been bent smoothly into shape. Duct tape was wrapped around many of the parts, and it and the parts had been painted over in red, which may have made the bike menacing except for the banana seat with Goofy on it. He was almost obscured by more duct tape.

Tony felt a flutter in his stomach.

It was a funky-looking bike, all right.

"Oh man, you got cut pretty bad?" Yogi said, looking at his bandaged hand.

"Uh, paper cut. But I can still toss a pétanque ball," Tony said.

"Did you get that catching this—what do they call him—the 'Hipster Slasher?'" Yogi made air quotes.

"I didn't exactly catch him."

Yogi tossed the cochonnet to start a game. It landed outside the court. "Tell me something, do you know why this guy was doing it?" he said, walking to retrieve his ball. "Why this so-called 'Hipster Slasher,' according to the news, was slashing people?"

They flipped a coin to see who would start. Tony called heads and won.

"Yeah. I think I know why he did it." Tony tossed a ball. It landed miles from the cochonnet. "For this guy, this guy that cut me, it was part of a scheme to blackmail some real estate guys."

"Well, you have to admire that," Yogi said and he giggled. "Anything to stick it to the fat cats." When his turn came, he breathed out a long "Ommmmmm" and then tossed his boule, landing inches from the cochonnet. "So, the police think the case is solved? It's all over and done?"

"Isn't it, though? Why do you ask?" Tony took his turn and tossed. His ball knocked Yogi's ball and rolled closer to the cochonnet.

Yogi smiled widely, and then giggled to himself for a while, almost convulsing into a ball. Then he stood up and his face got serious. "Ahhhhhh," he said forcefully as he tossed. His ball went far, bouncing off the court. "Maybe there was more than one slasher. You ever think of that, Tony?"

"Yeah, as a matter of fact, I have. Police told everyone it was the gangs, but that was a lie. And for Kirsten and Gunnar to go around slashing so many people, that doesn't make sense to me. Why would they continue to do it, three or four other people after Patrick. One of them was someone you and I had beers with, Brandon. Remember him? With the ear things?"

"Yeah, Brandon, black hipster, ear things, yeah, him…"

"From what I understand," Tony said, "the slasher likes to find people late at night or in lonely places. Not out in the open, not like a show-off. More like an artist at work."

Yogi giggled. Then he made a visible effort to get serious. Tony stood perpendicular to him, a few feet away.

"You know, Tony, I have been wanting to talk to you." Yogi took out a dirty chamois and began polishing a pétanque ball in his hand.

"Uh huh," he said. "I remember. From that time at Tim Riley's."

"Yeah, yeah. About how this neighborhood got fake and could be saved. *Has* to be saved. If someone had the nerve to do something to preserve it. To keep it as it is."

The hair on Tony's arms stood up. "Oh yeah."

"Someone had to do something. This slasher, he has the right idea. To make sure the neighborhood doesn't change."

"But, Yogi, it's already changed. It's way too late." Tony looked around. There were people all around. He was in no danger.

"Fuck, man, no!" Yogi's dreadlocks danced as his head shook. "Not to make it go all the way back. That's retarded. But to stop it from changing *more*. From changing into fucking Park Slope. Into fucking suburbia. Into fucking Disneyland."

"That would be goddamn tragic, but it seems pretty inevitable," Tony said.

"It's not. It's not inevitable! Someone can make a difference. They can make this neighborhood seem like anathema to the yuppies and rich cats."

Tony decided to take a chance. "So you chose to be that someone."

Yogi smiled again. It was a big bright smile on a sweaty face. He nodded, his chin beard vibrating with it. "Yeah. Yeah, I did."

Tony reached into his pocket, where his new, old-model smartphone was, and wondered if he could punch in 9-1-1 without looking.

And then he saw Magaly. Walking toward them, with her huge purse over her shoulder.

"Hey, Chino!" she said. "I knew I'd find you here. You told me to come see you play and—"

Tony shook his head at her and waved at her, trying to direct her to go back.

Yogi moved quickly. He got behind her and at the same time—to the sound of Velcro ripping open—he unsheathed his machete. Those long shorts had a side pocket that had been oddly stitched. He grabbed Magaly from behind and put the machete to her throat.

"Fuck! Fuck you! What's going on?" she screamed, but she turned smoothly and elbowed Yogi in the chest, hard. Yogi seemed surprised but he stopped the kick she was aiming for his crotch and cut her quickly across her shoulder.

"Bastard!" she yelled.

"Magaly!"

Yogi locked an arm around her neck and held her tightly. He lay the machete across his arm pointed straight at her throat.

Tony ran closer. But Yogi said, "Stop! Stop, stop, stop. No more fooling around, Tony. No more fooling around."

"Okay, okay," Tony said.

Magaly looked more pissed than frightened. Tony hoped she didn't try some judo she had learned. He hoped she didn't try to move. He wouldn't be able to take what might happen if she moved.

Yogi held up her body in front of him like a shield. "I'm sorry,

Ms. Magaly. Is that your name? I hate using women as victims. It's totally against what I stand for."

"Let her go, Yogi. This is not what your...your crusade is about."

"Hey! 'Crusade.' 'Crusade' is a good word for it. That's the right word." Yogi started walking backward with Magaly in front. "Don't follow me."

Tony tried to stay calm. *No pain. No pain.* He said, "You're going to go where, Yogi? Walking backwards with her the whole time? I can tell you this: She's feisty. Trust me. Let her go. We can talk about it. I can do a story, tell your side. If you let me go into my pocket, I'll get my phone to record it. Then I write your story and tell the world."

Tony reached into his pocket and slid out his brand new phone, bought on credit. He tapped on a recording app. "See? Whenever you're ready, I'm ready."

Yogi smiled and nodded. "Okay. Okay." But he kept the blade side of the machete right under Magaly's chin.

"Please be careful, Yogi." Tony held out. "Go ahead. This is your best chance to tell your story. I'm listening."

Yogi cleared his throat, smiled like a cartoon, nodded, and then he began.

"I was just passing through, you know. I was going to see the world. I didn't mean to make a home here. I just couldn't stay where I was. It was so small there, so dead. Dead inside, you know what I mean?"

"Where'd you come from? Midwest? Seattle?"

"New Jersey."

"Oh, okay."

"I lucked into a loft, and we were all artists, man. We were all in love with each other. It was creative heaven, man."

Yogi was silent, staring at some area in front of him. Time traveling in his mind, Tony figured. Then Tony said, "What happened, Yogi? What happened to those good times?"

"It happened slowly, you know? Then people starting moving

in who looked and dressed like artists but weren't artists. It was confusing. First, it was just a few, and then they started coming in waves, and then it wasn't about art anymore, it was about bars and restaurants, and then everything started costing so much more. And then came the yuppies, lowest, least intellectual being you could be. But that's what these hipsters really were, they were proto-yuppies in disguise..."

Tony saw that people walking by the court had begun to notice what was going on. Some just looked and kept walking. Sure, a man holding a machete to a woman's throat. Happens every day. But then one person stopped and looked on. Then someone stood next to that person.

"...So I figured, something had to make the neighborhood unpalatable to them, so they wouldn't want to come here. Then I got it. Only one thing could keep them away: crime. Violent crime. I would be a one-man crime wave. It would get in the papers, on the Internet, and they'd all say, 'Fuck Williamsburg. That's a crazy town. A Dodge City. I'd rather stay in Duluth or Dubuque.' It was a great plan, a brilliant plan. It was like a fucking piece of art. Do you know—"

The sound of sirens made Yogi stop.

Tony saw one car pull up over the curb on Bayard Street, behind Yogi. Two officers came out. Another car pulled up on Union.

"Did you do this?" Yogi said.

"No. But look around. You have an audience."

A group of people had formed on the part of the track where the breakdancer practiced. Some aimed their phones at them.

"Isn't that what you wanted?" Tony said.

CHAPTER SIXTY-SEVEN

"You really charge that much for a cup of coffee?" Petrosino said. He looked up at the chalkboard menu above the barista station. Six bucks for a regular coffee. Juan Valdez must be grinding the beans in the back himself.

The cafe manager, a short young woman with old lady glasses, said, "Well, yeah, it's what the market can bear, so..."

Tabby Estate Coffee was a big cafe, big for a place that only served coffee and a small variety of baked goods. Petrosino guessed the Wi-Fi was the draw. Every single customer was bent over a laptop. Some had piles of paperwork, and there was clearly a job interview going on at another table.

The Twitter account user for "hipster death rattle" had been traced to the IP address at this cafe. The store manager, Caroline, was a young woman who appeared to be wearing a blouse made of grass. She was unable to single out any one weird customer who might be using the Wi-Fi to send dangerous tweets. She didn't think any of them were capable of anything criminal, and she couldn't tell him anything about who rode what bike. But she agreed to let them place a couple of undercover officers there who would keep an eye on the customers while keeping an eye the Twitter account.

"So you'll have two steady customers all day, I can tell you that, with the way cops drink coffee," Petrosino said. Not that the place needed help. There was a line almost to the door. "And there'll be an undercover unit outside."

"I'm happy to help, detective."

"Listen, uh, while I'm here can I get one of those latte things to go? I'd sure like to see what a nine dollar cup of coffee tastes like."

He was thinking about getting something sweet to go with it. He looked over at the baked goods case. A chocolate cream cheese muffin caught his eye. But then he saw a display case above the baked goods. In it were several T-shirts: "I heart coffee," "Espresso Yourself," and "hipster death rattle."

His body tensed, for the first time in a while, a cigarette was the last thing on his mind.

"Miss?" he said to the manager. "Where did you get those— that one on the end?"

"Those are on consignment. Handmade. They're very popular right now. I can see if we have any left in large, or extra-large, if you want one."

"No, no. Who makes them? Do you know?"

"Um, yeah, that's Yogi," she said. "Older hippie dude, very cool. He silkscreens those."

"You don't happen to have his address?"

"Uhhh, yeah. He must have filled out a consignment contract. Let me see."

She found the contract quickly and put it on the counter with the latte. Petrosino picked it up and thanked her and rushed out in a hurry. Getting into his car, his hand hit the door and he dropped the pricey latte on the sidewalk.

CHAPTER SIXTY-EIGHT

Steve Pak sat on the couch and stared at nothing. His dog Deeogee sat on the parquet floor, looking at him, wagging its tail, waiting. The TV was on. His phone was on. There was an iPad open on his lap.

He hadn't been sleeping or eating very well for weeks. He spent most of his time on the couch. He slept there every night.

He could not go into the bedroom. He could not go into the nursery. His mother was taking care of the baby, for now. He had only seen it once, at the hospital.

On the coffee table in front of him was his wife's purse. He had taken it home from the hospital, and he hadn't noticed how heavy it was, not even when he got it home and put it down with a clunk. He had remembered the clunk. He hadn't wondered about the clunk or the weight until, as he got home that day and stepped past the dog and sat down, he looked at the purse and carefully picked it up.

It was so heavy. How had she walked around with this? His curiosity fought with the knowledge that opening the purse would just bring him more misery, more memories of his dead wife. His curiosity won. He opened the purse.

He stared.

He was looking at what he found in his wife's purse when he heard the TV reporter above the music from the radio and the whimper of the dog.

"...a tense scene here in Brooklyn's McCarren Park. Inside

that crowd you see behind me are three people. One is an uni-
dentified male, the other is a young Hispanic woman, and she is
apparently being held hostage by a man who may be *another*
Williamsburg Slasher, similar to the one who has been terroriz-
ing this trendy neighborhood for several weeks. We'll have
more details as…"

Steve looked at what he had found in his wife's purse.
Deeogee whimpered. It needed to go out for a walk.

Instead of taking the elevator, he took the stairs that led out
to the exit onto the new riverside park, so the policeman sitting
in the patrol car in front of the building would not see him,
would not stop him.

CHAPTER SIXTY-NINE

Magaly stood where she was, not moving. She was frightened but also amazed that the whole thing was happening. What kind of life was she leading to have it threatened twice in one summer? She chanted under her breath and kept her eyes focused ahead on Tony. Sure, there was a giant machete at her throat, but altogether she thought she was handling herself pretty well. She didn't tremble. She stood her ground. At the same time, she could feel the cylinder of her pepper spray right near the top of her purse.

If only she could get her bag open.

There were police cars around the edges of the park, but that didn't seem to bother the big hippie who held her. But then helicopters suddenly appeared in the sky. She could smell sweat and marijuana—lots and lots of skunky marijuana—on the old hippie with the knife at her throat.

"You think there are snipers?" he said.

Tony said, "Probably the local news, Yogi. Nothing to worry about."

She could tell Tony was lying. A man in a pinstriped suit stepped forward and, speaking into a megaphone, he said, "My name is Lieutenant Esteban Tuchman, and I am taking command of the scene."

He looked more like a salesman than a hostage negotiator. What were they doing? They totally needed a real hostage negotiator, not some overly handsome slickster with a tie clip. The hippie yelled at this Lieutenant Esteban, telling him to shut up, telling him he was in the middle of a conversation. *Okay, hippie, don't get your whiteboy dreads in a bunch.*

"Hey, you know that T-shirt you saw me wearing?" the hippie said to Tony.

"'hipster death rattle?'" Tony said. "Yeah."

"I actually silkscreened that myself. In my workshop in the basement."

"Oh, really. They look great. I'd like to get one for myself."

Good, Tony, good. Keep him talking. But try to sound a little more interested!

Magaly's purse was hugged to her chest, and the clasp was just under her left elbow. If she could just move her right hand a couple of inches she could get it open.

"Don't patronize me, Tony."

"Yogi, all I wear are T-shirts. I'm always looking for new ones."

"Yeah, well," this Yogi guy said. "I'll see if I have your size. Anyway, I went back to all the places and marked all the—well, the ones I was a part of anyway—with spray paint. I wanted people to know which one was which. I wanted history to know. I worked really hard on the design, and it came out so good I realized I could sell them on Bedford Avenue for ten dollars each."

"Did you make a lot of money?"

"Three hundred dollars the first day.

"Wow," Magaly said, breaking from her chant. "That's actually impressive."

And when Yogi said, "It paid my rent for June and July," she slipped her right hand on top of the clasp and opened. That was the tough part.

Now all she had to do was dig in past her lip balm, lipstick, stain-removing stick, deodorant, house keys, and Metrocard, and latch on to the pepper spray. And then take it out, uncap it, and aim it at this skunky bastard's face.

Easy, right?

"There sure are a lot of people watching," the hippie said.

He was right. They were surrounded by a ring of people that the cops were barely holding back. All of them had their cell phones out, pointed at them. Hipsters and yuppies and Polish and Italian and Latino and African-American and white and Asian. Magaly felt they were staring, gawking, waiting to see if some crazy bastard would slash a woman's throat, her throat, live. Talk about—what was the word?—*schadenfreude*. Schadenfreude was only fun when you weren't the *schaden* being *freuded*.

"I bet there's a lot of people watching this on the Internet."

"You bet," Tony said. "The is probably live-streaming all over social media."

"Really? Spectacular."

"You know what I thought was very clever of you," Tony said. "I noticed that you selected people from a wide variety of backgrounds. Congratulations on being inclusive. I'm guessing you wanted to make everyone afraid, not just one group."

The hippie chuckled. *Who doesn't love a compliment?* His movement gave Magaly a chance to slip two fingers past the clasp and into the purse. She reached down. *Ew, what was that? Was that gum?* Lipstick was the first thing she touched. Which made sense since she just touched up before walking into the park, hoping to look her best for Tony. He did like to look at her lips a lot, and so. And then there was the stain stick, which made sense because she had just spilled iced coffee on her white blouse walking over here, and she had had to wipe it out.

"Exactly! Yes! I'm glad someone caught that. I'm very proud of that. I thought a lot about who should be...you know. I didn't want any group to think they were being targeted more than any other group. I wanted everyone to be afraid. The Indian guy I got might have been gay, too. Do you happen to know if he was?"

She had to reach deeper. She had to take a risk.

"No," Tony said. "I didn't read that."

"Honestly, it's hard to include everyone. I did try a woman once, but then I stayed away from them. It didn't seem fair. I thought young white men getting killed would be more attention, right? But I didn't want anybody else to feel left—"

Magaly faked a cough and reached deep into her purse.

"Stay still, lady," the hippie said, tightening his grip. "Please. I really don't want to hurt you.

Her fingers found the little nozzle of the pepper spray. She grabbed the fat bottle and pulled it out. Now was her chance. But she could feel the hippie tensing up, the knife cutting into her skin.

And then there was a sound like a firecracker but that, as she felt herself fall back, she knew was not a firecracker.

CHAPTER SEVENTY

As soon as he got to the park with Deeogee, Steven Pak spotted the crowd, a mass of them by the southern exit. He squeezed past the outliers and saw that the police were keeping them all back. But there were too many people and not enough cops. With the happy dog leading the way, Pak walked easily through the crowd and right past two cops. No one saw him. No one had ever seen him besides Erin.

He stood near some people holding up their phones, on the inner edge of the circle.

And there in front of him was the man who had killed his wife, the mother of his child.

No one saw him slide the 9mm out of his jacket. He knew how to use it. Erin had shown him a couple times, taken him target shooting on one of their vacations. But he was no marksman. And there was a woman in the way, which would make it harder. The woman looked scared. But that didn't matter.

Pak couldn't let the killer get away. "Too many people get away with things in this country." That's what Erin used to say all the time.

He had to do it and he had to do it right. He wouldn't get another shot, maybe not even a second shot. He aimed for the woman's chest. If he did it right, the bullet would go through her and kill the man who killed his wife.

When he raised the gun up, someone screamed. He knew

they would try to take the gun away, so he aimed quickly, a shot that could not miss, a shot that would stop the man. Aiming straight at the woman's chest—he fired.

CHAPTER SEVENTY-ONE

A fresh piece of chewing gum in his mouth, Petrosino knocked on Tuchman's door. The lieutenant sat at his desk, talking loudly on his cell phone.

"I don't know what to tell you, Jimmy," Tuchman said. "No...This guy came out of nowhere...There's nothing more I can tell you...You'll know as soon as I know."

It sounded like Tuchman was talking to some lugnut up the ladder. Petrosino sat down and waited for him to finish.

"Come on in. Sit down. Well, you're already sitting." Tuchman stood up, took his expensive-looking plaid jacket off the back of his chair and put it on.

"Some good news. Your partner's been cleared of any wrongdoing," Tuchman said.

"Lucky guy."

"Yeah, you bet. The slasher thing came along and wiped him out of the headlines. He still could face a criminal negligence suit, but personally I think it's unlikely to get far."

Petrosino picked up the Batman figure on the desk. "Our Mr. Pak turned out to be quite a marksman. Or a lucky shot."

"Right into our perp's mouth, I know. It was beautiful and absurd at the same time."

"It is a goddamn shame," Petrosino said. "It is, in fact, what they might call 'irony.'"

"I hate irony, detective."

"You said it."

Tuchman slumped back into his chair, rumpling his pin-striped suit. It was the first time Petrosino had ever seen Tuchman close to unkempt.

"That was the PR people from Police Plaza on the phone," Tuchman said. "They're shitting paperweights over there. We tell the press we know who the slasher is, we send out an All Points on this Gunnar Neumann and people are happy. They have someone to blame. And now suddenly there's a slasher number two, this yogi guy."

"Brian Henry Johnson, who went by the name of 'Yogi,' for some reason."

"Yeah, who turns around and gets popped by a grieving husband in a public park."

"All this after we blamed it on the gangs," Petrosino said. He put the Batman down and Tuchman picked it up immediately.

Tuchman shrugged. "*Caca pasa*. But that's the way I thought the wind was blowing at the time. It's on me. I'll handle PR."

Petrosino made to leave, then remembered something. "Oh, jeez, listen, they found what might be another victim at the residence of Slasher Number Two. Or Number One. Whichever. I can't keep track. I guess he expanded his demographic to the elderly. A Michael J. McShane, eighty-four, lived on the first floor. Throat slashed in bed."

"This gets better and better."

"I'm going over, but right now that grieving husband is waiting downstairs. You want me to talk to him?"

"Let's both do it. Like in the old days, partner."

Steven Pak sat in the interrogation room. He looked small and thin but also very calm.

"Can we get you anything?" Tuchman said.

"No, they gave me some water. I'm okay."

"Right-o," Petrosino said. "Mr. Pak. You understand why

you're here, don't you?"

"I killed the man who killed my wife."

"Murder is against the law," said Tuchman. He looked at Pak intently, with not a little sympathy. "Revenge is no justification."

"I got justice. I got justice for my Erin."

"Mr. Pak, it's not easy to tell you this," Tuchman said. "But we're fairly sure the man you shot today—who was dead immediately at the scene—that man was not the man who killed your wife."

Pak looked up, the placid face fading. "I don't understand."

"The man who slash—the man who murdered your wife, the man you shot today, he was a different slasher. He did slash people, but not your wife."

"I don't understand."

"Mr. Pak, I'm not exactly sure I understand it all myself."

CHAPTER SEVENTY-TWO

"Thirty dollars? For this?"

"Thirty dollars. Yes," said the very tired-looking cashier in the gift center.

Tony thought it would be hilarious to get Magaly some flowers because she'd never expect it from him. Also, he just wanted to get her flowers, what the hell.

"How much is this one?"

"Twenty dollars."

"Sold," said Tony, hoping the tiny bunch looked impressive enough.

When Tony walked into the room with the tiny bouquet of flowers, Magaly tried to think of something to say before he noticed the giant bouquet of roses sent from Luis. They were signed "El Flamboyan," but she knew they were from Luis, who had somehow learned discretion. Mr. Politician probably had a campaign manager giving him advice now. And he'd probably charged the roses to El Flamboyan. But she knew what Tony would think, seeing them there.

"Those are beautiful," she said. "The best flowers I've ever gotten."

"Sure," Tony said. "That's all they had left, so. I hope you like them."

She was sitting up in bed when he walked in. He noticed she looked tired. A headband struggled in vain to keep her hair back. A large bandage covered part of her chest. On the way over, he had thought about kissing her, smelling her hair, holding her. He had thought about what happened in Puerto Rico, not their making love in that hotel—well, that, but not just that—but their working together like a team. He had liked the idea of that very much. But then he saw the bushel of roses and he knew exactly who they were from. *No pain, no pain*, he thought.

"The roses are from my co-workers are El Flamboyan," she said.

"Yeah?"

"Yeah."

"So, how are you feeling?"

"High as a kite on painkillers," she said. "It's the best thing about being in a hospital. Oh hey, I heard we were in the paper."

"Yeah. All of them. But I'd always hoped I'd be writing about the news, not be a part of it. At least most of them quoted me right."

"Sorry, Chino."

"I hadn't started planning my Pulitzer acceptance speech or anything. Well, maybe just a few lines. There's been nothing in the paper about Kirsten. Maybe it'll come out tomorrow. Petrosino told me that she's under observation. I think she'll probably end up getting her own special episode of *Dateline*."

Magaly could see he was nervous, could see he wanted to come closer. She wanted to reach and touch his hand and bring him closer.

Instead, she said, "What about Litvinchouk and the Tomasellos? Did he tell you what would be happening with them?"

"Whereabouts unknown."

"*Ai*, at least now that they've caught that crazy psycho Kirsten—I hate even saying her name. Iris and Danny will have some peace now. You helped that happen, Chino."

"I guess," Tony said.

He worried he was overstaying his welcome. But at the same time, he didn't want to leave. Tony realized he was still holding the cheap but no-longer-impressive bouquet he had bought in the gift shop. He handed it to her, and she cradled it to the side of her chest that wasn't bandaged.

"I see your, uh, that De Moscoso is running for Congress," he said.

"Yeah, he thinks it's the best way for him to save the neighborhood."

"He just wants to turn back time. That was Yogi Johnson's plan. See how that worked out."

"That's not fair, Chino. He's not going to be going around slashing people."

He was going to say something cruel, something mean. Instead he said, "Well, good luck to him. He'll need it. What about Flamboyan?"

"I'm interim director starting next week, and my first job will be to hire Gabby."

"Really?"

"Yes, I called her this morning. She's into it."

"That's great, good for her. Just don't ask her to proofread anything for you."

"She'll learn. Hey, how is your mom?"

"Oh, she's all moved into my brother's house. She says her room is very nice and they gave her a poodle."

"That's nice. I love your mom," she said. "Hey, are you going to the anniversary ceremony for Rosa next week?"

"I'll be there."

"Will you be covering it for any paper? There are other papers."

"No, I don't think so. I really am just a hack right now, with the *Sentinel* closed. I'll have to find more of a lot more freelance work. A lot more. Pay the rent somehow."

"Yeah, I know what you mean."

"And I was thinking about moving out. It's getting way too pricey around here, and it just seems to put me a bad mood."

"Oh, is that what causes it?" She laughed, then she said, "I would miss you."

"I'd miss you, too. I think it's my turn to change the real estate values in someone else's neighborhood."

Magaly laughed at again, and he smiled. He looked good
when he smiled, which wasn't often enough. She looked at him
closely. She thought about how much fun the last few weeks
had been, and how crazy. She thought about having just finally,
finally cutting ties from Luis. Despite the flowers, she knew he
was going to keep his distance from her. She made a decision.

"Chino. Listen. What happened between us in PR, I don't
regret that."

"Me either, no, I—"

"Chino, it's just that you and me, we've been there already."

"Yeah. Been there, done that."

"*Ai,* don't say it that way. But, Chino, we know how that
turns out."

"Are you sure?" was what Tony was going to say, but he
figured she was trying to make things easy for him. They had
had fun, she was trying to say, so it was time to move on.

"What? What were you going to say?" she said.

"I was going to say something in Latin, but then I thought
better of it."

"Enough with the pretentious maxims, thank you."

"I'll just say, 'Good luck to both of us then.' *Buena suerte.*"

"That I like," she said.

Tony kissed her on the cheek, awkwardly.

"Are you smelling my hair?"

"No, why would I smell your hair?"

He left soon after. A late summer heat wave had started,
burning up the pavement, shimmering off the sidewalk. He
thought it was too bad people weren't allowed to walk around
naked, it was that hot. Still, it wasn't too hot to play pétanque.

CHAPTER SEVENTY-THREE

Out in front of Our Lady of Mt. Carmel, a brightly printed placard on an easel read:

Doo Wop Extravaganza!!
Starring The Excellents,
The Accords + The Jackson Avenue Five & Jimmy
and the Brooklyneers
$15 Proceeds Benefit
OLMC Youth Programs and Activities
No outside food or drinks allowed—Lower Stage

"Whaddya know," Hadid said to himself. He could hear the music already. He walked in and down marble steps that reminded him of junior high school.

He paid his fifteen dollars and got a ticket for the buffet. He could see through an open door to the stage, and there was Petrosino in his green tux, standing next to three middle-aged guys wearing matching getups, white shirts, red bowties.

Only the first three rows of folding chairs were occupied and just barely. The other ten rows were all empty. Children ran around, a group of priests chatted on the side, and flocks of elderly people milled and nodded like pigeons.

Hadid didn't recognize the song but he liked the tune. Petrosino and his boys moved pretty good for old guys. At the buffet, he got himself a big plate of lasagna and macaroni salad and potato salad. He took a seat in the empty back row.

On stage, Petrosino cleared his throat and said, "That was 'A Place in My Heart' by Joey Columbo and The Del-Chords, 1962, Taurus Records. The label only says Joey's name, but he did it with the Del-Chords. All these guys were from Brooklyn, and Joey didn't live too far from me. He used to run a lot of the sock hops we went to as kids. Some of you may remember him. Okay, this next song is for my beautiful granddaughter, Brittany." Petrosino pointed to a young girl in a pink dress, running around and oblivious to what was happening on stage. "It was originally done by the Camelots, 1963, '64. I hope you like it."

The men began picking their legs up one at a time as if stomping and then, all with their right hands, tapped their mouths and sang, "Way-whoa, way-nan-nee, way-whoa, way-nan-nee, way-whoa."

To his surprise, Hadid found himself tapping his feet along to the music.

After the song, Petrosino said to his granddaughter, "That was for you, honey. I know how you love Pocahontas." But the little girl had her head down on one of the seats.

Hadid heard the little girl sob, saying, "No. Princess Elsa."

After the set, Petrosino came right over to Hadid and shook his hand. "Thanks for stopping by."

"Nice tux," Hadid said. "But you were great. Great job."

"You should have heard me back when I could still do a decent falsetto." Petrosino swung down to catch his granddaughter in a hug, but she wiggled away. He stood up. "Kids."

"I didn't know people still listened to this music." Hadid was going to add something about hearing aids but dropped it.

"Doo-wop is forever, my friend. Good music is timeless."

"I'm into more modern classics: Madonna, U2, stuff like that."

"That stuff's okay. I guess. Hey, how's the Bronx?"

"Home sweet home. Thanks for the tip on that security job. I got an interview next week."

"Oh yeah. Glad to hear it. You're a good man."

"Thanks, Petr…"

"Jimmy," said Petrosino.

"Thanks, Jimmy."

"And how's things with the wife?"

"One thing at a time."

"Right-o. C'mon, I'll buy you a beer."

"Is your wife here? I'd like to meet her."

"Yeah, sure. Just look for the Buick in the blue dress."

CHAPTER SEVENTY-FOUR

Litvinchouk shut off his station wagon. They were parked at the extreme end of the parking lot at the Sloatsburg rest stop in upstate New York. They were on their way to one of his friends in Albany. They would lay low there for a little while and assess their futures. They had spent the past week in hotels in Long Island, avoiding the police and Frank Jr., who had somehow found out about them. Litvinchouk was sure it was his former pupil's inquiring and mischievous ways that brought Frank Jr.'s wrath down upon them. He considering calling Noah to take care of Moran, but what was done was done. What would be the point of revenge? This was the life he really wanted, wasn't it? With his giant *shiksa* with her amazing mouth.

Still, he missed his kids an awful lot.

"C'mon, I don't like dawdling like this. We have to get a move on," said Jackie Tomasello, pulling her hair back into a ponytail. "And you sometimes take a long time is alls I'm saying."

"*Exegi monumentum aere perennius,*" said Litvinchouk, who opened his zipper. A cool breeze came through the open car windows. What a pleasure this was going to be!

"I'm all yours," he said.

"I cannot resist this thing," she said. But before she made another move—the station wagon was slammed in the back. Its rear wheels reared up.

"Jesus Christ!" Jackie said.

"*Merda*!" Litvinchouk had blood on his forehead from hitting the steering wheel.

"What is it?" she said. But she saw what he was looking at through the rearview mirror. It was Frank Jr. Her husband and his favorite goon, the one with the scar on his face.

Frank Jr. came up to the side of the car. "So, where do you lovebirds think you're going?"

Litvinchouk surrendered to the inevitable. *Quod differtur, non aufertur.*

CHAPTER SEVENTY-FIVE

All he ever wanted to do was be in a band, didn't matter if it was good or not.

Gunnar Neumann biked fast as he could, jumping curbs, cutting off cars, working up a good sweat on a mid-August night. He had been staying with Lizbeth, an old bandmate from his old band the Plaintive Gunsuckers, occupying her couch in Bushwick, sometimes occupying her bed, like old times. But that afternoon, when she was out at her job at Sephora, she texted him saying she'd just "FCKIN SAW YR FACE" on the cover of that day's *Metro* and that he should "YR FOR REALZ FACE. GT THE FCK OU NW."

Gunnar had planned to stay another week or two or more. But Lizbeth was the serious type, so before she got back and kicked him in the balls, which she had done in the past, several times, he got his things and, at twilight, headed out.

He put on his hoodie and wrapped a bandanna over the bandages on the lower part of his face like a bandit. His lovingly curated beard collection was far behind him now.

He had emigrated to Brooklyn from Bernau bei Berlin, to live in the city where some of his all-time favorite musicians use to work and love and dream. *Iggy Pop! The Ramones! Patti Smith! Blondie!*

Now he was headed for Harlem, where three people he knew from his other old band, 7 Pods of Pepper, lived. They were cramped into a studio in a recently renovated brownstone and could barely make the rent. So maybe they'd be open to making room for one more body. He just had to cross the Willy B Bridge to get to Manhattan. The cops would be watching the trains, he figured, watching for cars. But there couldn't be enough cops to watch the bike path, right?

To get to the bridge, he took back streets as much as he could. Still, he felt like he was being watched.

On Metropolitan Avenue, he stopped and looked back. Far behind him, there was some Mexican delivery boy on a bicycle. A nobody.

Gunnar crossed into Continental Army Plaza to approach the bridge. In the plaza was a statue of George Washington on a horse facing the bridge and pointing his back and the horse's ass toward Brooklyn. The plaza was empty except for beer cans and garbage and two delivery boys hanging out by their bikes. No cops anywhere.

He sped up and onto the pedestrian walkway on the northern side of the bridge, standing up and pumping the pedals to take the steep uphill. The on-ramp was caged on all sides with metal barriers painted a dyspeptic pink. He didn't see anyone, not even a Hasidim, who were always walking back and forth on the bridge.

At the top of the on-ramp, he looked back. Another guy on a bike, standing up, pumping his pedals, way behind him.

Wait. Was that the same delivery boy he spotted back on Metropolitan?

Couldn't be. They just all looked the same.

There was a right-angle turn to the left and then immediately another to the right. As Gunnar rode through, he passed three guys standing by their bikes. More Spanish kids. They were all in hooded sweatshirts. Local kids, getting high probably.

Most of the walkway sat above the bridge's car traffic and next to the tracks for the elevated M and J trains. They rattled by every few minutes, in a cloud of ground metal that got into your lungs and into your snot. The sun had set over the city, and underneath the canopy of the brick towers and the suspension cables of the bridge, the walkway was dark. The best light was from the electric skyline of Manhattan ahead. *The city that never sleeps*, Gunnar thought. The city where he had come to fulfill all his dreams.

Just as Gunnar passed the Brooklyn side of the bridge—the water looming underneath where he was, the abandoned factory with the gigantic "Domino Sugar" logo way over on his right—he came upon a group of teenagers, lined up on either side of the path.

He recognized it for what it was. A gauntlet.

He spun the bike around. They were there, too. They moved closer together, blocking the way.

There must have been twenty of them, maybe thirty. All Spanish. All gangbangers in the same clothes, same colors. Their uniform.

Before he could react, one of them came from the side and knocked him and his bike down. Another kicked him, with metal-tipped boots. He reached for the machete, inched the handle toward him by his fingertips. But just as he grasped it, someone stepped on his hand, pried it out, took it away.

They were saying things to each other, yelling, in Spanish. He didn't understand a word. They didn't even try to take his money. They continued to kick him, pulled him away from his bike. He tried to crawl out, to make it back down the bridge, even if it had to be on his knees.

He felt ribs break. And his cheekbone. Teeth.

And then he was being lifted. They raised him up and above themselves, and he was in the air like a crowd surfer at a rave.

Then one hand after another moved him forward.

He realized he had been screaming, telling them to leave him alone, pleading for his life. His voice was hoarse from it.

He felt a breeze. He wasn't over the walkway anymore. He was being held right at its edge.

And then, first one voice said, and then another, shouting,

chanting: "For Beyoncé!"

Gunnar thought it was a weird thing for them to say, since he didn't read the U.S. newspapers, so he didn't know that Beyoncé was the name of the girlfriend of Eladio Cortés, head of the Southside Quistadoreys, the girlfriend who was accidentally shot and killed by a police officer, as part of an investigation into the local slasher killings. He had no idea that they blamed him for her death, in a roundabout way.

And with a final chant, they flung him far over the side, out over the protective railing and out over the shiny darkness of the East River.

There was nothing underneath him, like the end of a billion nightmares. Falling, spinning, he smelled the chemical smell of the river, wondered how long it would take to hit its surface. He wondered if he would survive and be able to swim to shore. He wondered what diseases he would catch in the dirty water. An East River ferry to India Street was passing right at that moment, and before Gunnar collided with its prow—at almost a hundred miles per hour, the impact like a gigantic bullet hitting his entire body all at once—he looked again and saw the electric lights of the skyline of Manhattan. The City of Dreams. The City that Never Sleeps.

ACKNOWLEDGMENTS

I owe numerous pints of thanks to beta readers Stoney Emshwiller, Andrew Nette, Julia Pomeroy, Ernesto Santos, Alex Segura, and Erich Wood, with special perfect Manhattans of gratitude to Ralph Westerhoff and Christine Debany, for their guidance, their glazed ham, and their friendship. Thanks to forensics experts Barbara Butcher and Jonathan Hayes. Thanks to the super-supportive members of the Mystery Writers of America, New York Chapter, but especially to Bernie Whalen, for his police insights, and to Gerald M. Levine and Sheila J. Levine, who said, "We might be able to recommend an agent." Thanks to Diane Stockwell, for being the kind agent kindly recommended by Gerald and Sheila. Mille grazie to the incomparable Annamaria Alfieri, for believing in me more than I did. Thanks to Ellen Finnegan, my Creative Writing teacher at Brooklyn Tech High School, in whose lively and encouraging class I wrote my first crime fiction story. Saludades to my friends and family from the Southside—there are way too many to name, but they know who they are, and this, I hope, won't be the last time I thank them — and to the bricks, the blacktop, the smell of the Southside itself for inspiring me. Thanks to my Brooklyn brother Reed Farrel Coleman, the mensch of mystery writers, and thanks to and a fawning fan crush for Sara Paretsky, who was generous enough to read this work. Thanks to Stacey Emenecker, for insight into PA, to Leen Al-Bassam and Charles Salzberg for needed and heeded advice, and to Scott Emmons, for looking over my mediocre Latin. Thanks to Eric Campbell and Lance Wright of Down & Out Books for liking my words enough to publish them. And super special, lifetime of Malibu Bay Breezes thanks to my lovely wife, Denise, for putting up with a writer in the house.

Born and raised in Williamsburg, Brooklyn, **Richie Narvaez** is the author of *Roachkiller and Other Stories*, which received the 2013 Spinetingler Award for Best Anthology/Short Story Collection. His work has appeared in *Latin@ Rising: An Anthology of Science Fiction and Fantasy, Long Island Noir, Mississippi Review, Murdaland, Pilgrimage, Shotgun Honey,* and *Tiny Crimes: Very Short Tales of Mystery and Murder*. He teaches writing at Fashion Institute of Technology in Manhattan. He lives with his wife in the Bronx. *Hipster Death Rattle* is his first novel.

BOOKS

On the following pages are a few
more great titles from the
Down & Out Books publishing family.

For a complete list of books and to
sign up for our newsletter,
go to DownAndOutBooks.com.

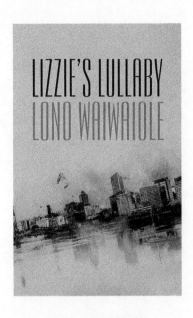

Lizzie's Lullaby
Lono Waiwaiole

Down & Out Books
February 2019
978-1-948235-74-7

Say you're a wicked woman who calls herself Satin because she thinks she's smoother than silk. You're a talent scout for a perverted prince looking for the perfect little girl to be his next "daughter"—a very special girl he can train to fulfill his every twisted fantasy until she grows too old for his taste.

So when you stumble on a runaway seven-year-old in a Portland shopping mall that you know from painful personal experience is a perfect fit, you snatch the kid and cash in, right?

The snatch goes without a hitch, but the process of cashing in reveals that this girl is actually the worst choice possible...

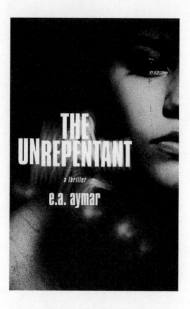

The Unrepentant
E.A. Aymar

Down & Out Books
March 2019
978-1-948235-58-7

Eighteen-year old Charlotte Reyes ran away from an abusive home only to end up tricked, kidnapped, and taken across the country by criminals. Charlotte manages to escape with the help of a reluctant former soldier named Mace Peterson, but she can't seem to shake the gang.

With nowhere to run and nowhere to hide, Charlotte realizes she only has one option.

She has to fight.

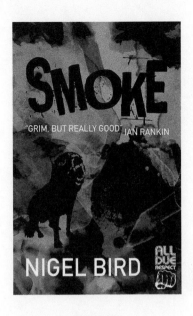

Smoke
Nigel Bird

All Due Respect, an imprint of
Down & Out Books
978-1-64396-007-4

The Ramsay brothers are keen to move up in the world. They gather all their hopes in one basket and set up the Scottish Open dog-fighting tournament. In Leo they have the animal to win it.

Carlo Salvino returns home missing an arm and a leg. He's keen to win back the affections of his girlfriend and mother of his child. If he can take his revenge on the Ramsays, so much the better.

The Hooks, well they're just a maladjusted family caught up in the middle of it all.

Smoke: a tale of justice, injustice and misunderstanding.

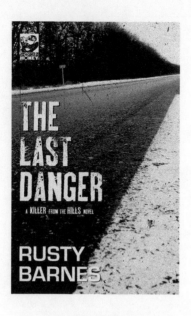

The Last Danger
A Killer from the Hills Novel
Rusty Barnes

Shotgun Honey, an imprint of
Down & Out Books
978-1-64396-001-2

Three months after a shootout with the renegade Pittman family robbed him of his brother, Matt Rider is trying to put his life back together. His wounds are many, his sworn enemy Soldier Pittman may wake up and begin to tell what he knows, his wife is on the knife edge of sanity, and his teen daughter has gone missing with the son of his sworn enemy.

In a whirlwind series of killings, thefts and rash decisions, Rider ends up muling drugs across the Canadian border in order to save his daughter and wife from an even worse fate...

CPSIA information can be obtained
at www.ICGtesting.com
Printed in the USA
LVHW090629050319
609387LV00007BA/584/P